LOYALTIES IN CONFLICT

Ukrainians in Canada
During the Great War

Edited by
Frances Swyripa
and
John Herd Thompson

Canadian Institute of Ukrainian Studies
University of Alberta
Edmonton 1983

THE ALBERTA LIBRARY IN UKRAINIAN CANADIAN STUDIES

A series of original works and reprints relating to Ukrainians in Canada, issued under the editorial supervision of the Canadian Institute of Ukrainian Studies, University of Alberta, Edmonton.

Copyright © 1983   Canadian Institute of Ukrainian Studies
                    University of Alberta
                    Edmonton, Alberta, Canada

Canadian Cataloguing in Publication Data
        Loyalties in conflict
        (The Alberta library in Ukrainian Canadian studies)
        Essays from a symposium held at the University of Alberta in 1980.
        ISBN 0-920862-22-5

1. Ukrainians—Canada—Congresses. 2. Ukrainian Canadians—Congresses.* 3. World War, 1914–1918—Canada—History—Congresses. I. Swyripa, Frances, 1951– II. Thompson, John Herd, 1946– III. Canadian Institute of Ukrainian Studies. IV. Series.
FC106.U5L6 *1983* 971'.00491791   C82-091407–X
F1035.U5L6

48,485

Cover design: Alexander Korenfeld

Printed in Canada by Printing Services, University of Alberta
Distributed by the   University of Toronto Press
                      5201 Dufferin St.
                      Downsview, Ontario
                      Canada M3H 5T8

Contents

Introduction

On the eve of the First World War approximately four-fifths of Ukrainian lands lay within the Russian empire; the remainder belonged to Austria-Hungary of the Central Powers. Although oppressed in both empires, the Ukrainian peasants loyally supported their respective monarchs when war erupted. The next few years, however, helped to crystallize an awakening national consciousness, culminating in a bid for statehood that united all Ukrainian territories. These events in Europe were followed eagerly by Ukrainians in North America, who had left to find the "better life" but remained emotionally attached to the homeland.

Had the Russian empire, as Canada's ally, been a more significant source of Ukrainian immigration to Canada, a painful chapter in the Dominion's history would have been written differently. As it was, most of the 170,000 Ukrainians in Canada before 1914 came from the western portion of Ukraine under Austrian rule, from the provinces of Galicia and Bukovyna. Discriminated against and disliked by many segments of Anglo-Canadian society, Ukrainians formed the largest minority from the Habsburg empire in Canada, and the war years brought bitter frustration. Half-way in the emotional journey between the Old World and the New, they watched as their former homeland was convulsed by war and revolution. In Canada they desired acceptance as loyal sons and daughters who appreciated and identified with the aspirations of their adopted country. Instead, they were labelled "enemy aliens" and subjected to harsh treatment by an Anglo-Canadian majority which harrassed, interned, threatened and finally disfranchised them. This repression, coupled with independence struggles in Ukraine, heightened the Ukrainian identity of the immigrants in Canada and nurtured a national consciousness that outlasted the war.

The wartime experience of the Ukrainian community in Canada embittered Ukrainian Canadians, who considered the subject best forgotten.

Canadian historians, too, recognizing that Canada has twice failed the test in its treatment of minorities in wartime, have found the subject sensitive. With a new generation of professionally trained students of Ukrainian Canadian history more willing to probe painful periods in the group's past, and with the acceptance by mainstream historians of ethnic tensions as a fact of Canadian life, it is now possible to explore such issues in greater depth. In their original form, the essays in *Loyalties in Conflict* were among the papers presented to the symposium, "World War One and Its Aftermath: The Ukrainians in Canada," sponsored by the Canadian Institute of Ukrainian Studies at the University of Alberta in October 1980. The symposium marked an important stage in the writing of Ukrainian Canadian history and its integration into Canadian historiography.

The papers by Peter Melnycky and John Herd Thompson examine the two most invidious government measures to touch Ukrainians in Canada during the Great War—internment and disfranchisement. Melnycky's study taps Ukrainian-language sources and augments previous studies by exploring the attitudes and actions of the internees as well as the Ukrainian immigrant community outside the internment camps. Thompson demonstrates that the disfranchisement of naturalized "enemy aliens" in 1917 was marginal to the confrontation between English and French Canada over conscription. Frances Swyripa contends that Ukrainian loyalty was never a serious popular issue among Anglo-Canadians and suggests that its sporadic appearance was often manipulated by political factions within the Ukrainian community. Ukrainian grassroots support for the Canadian war effort is evident in the patriotic fund raising and enlistment. Andrij Makuch challenges the claim that Ukrainian workers and farmers were guilty of war profiteering and argues that the war merely accelerated socio-economic changes among the Ukrainian Canadian population. Donald H. Avery examines ethnic and class tensions in postwar Canada when unemployment, veteran hostility and political radicalism affected relations between Anglo-Canadians and the alien worker. By emphasizing the persistence of nativism before, during and after the war, the five articles demonstrate that Anglo-Canadian treatment of Ukrainians during the war had less to do with their status as enemy aliens and more with pre-existing prejudices fed by wartime patriotism. David Saunders looks at the imperial dimension of the aliens question, in particular Britain's treatment of its own aliens; the Ukrainians form a case study. Finally, the essays by Nadia O. M. Kazymyra and Oleh W. Gerus examine the relationship between Ukrainians in Canada and Ukrainian independence struggles overseas. Kazymyra focuses on Ukrainian Canadian efforts to influence decision-making at the Paris Peace Conference by sending two representatives to assist the cause of the Ukrainian National Republic. Gerus illustrates the opposite—the campaign by Galician Ukrainian political leaders in exile in western Europe to garner financial and public support from their compatriots in Canada. The appendices to the volume contain both public addresses by Ukrainian spokesmen about wartime loyalties and selected government documents that provide an official record of the regulations controlling and monitoring enemy aliens in Canada.

The Canadian Institute of Ukrainian Studies wishes to acknowledge the financial assistance to the symposium of the Secretary of State, Multiculturalism Directorate, and the Social Sciences and Humanities Research Council. The co-operation of the Department of History, University of Alberta, in organizing the conference is also gratefully acknowledged. The editors wish to thank John Sokolowski for his translation of Bishop Budka's two pastoral letters, which appear in Appendix I.

Frances Swyripa
John Herd Thompson

Chapter 1

The Internment of Ukrainians in Canada*

Peter Melnycky

Canada's entry into the First World War precipitated government restrictions that included registration and possible internment of Ukrainians as enemy aliens. During the war approximately 80,000 enemy aliens were registered, and 8,579 were actually interned. Ukrainians formed the largest ethnic element in the camps, constituting the majority of the nearly 6,000 interned as Austro-Hungarian nationals. This essay examines Canadian internment policies during the war, the events which transformed unnaturalized immigrants from the countries of the Central Powers into enemy aliens and the process of internment. Its main purpose, however, is to explore the Ukrainian reaction to internment in Canada through government records, first-person accounts and Ukrainian-language sources.

I

In May 1914, with the passage of the British Nationality, Naturalization and Aliens Act, Ottawa had begun to re-evaluate the naturalization of immigrants of non-British or non-French origin. Formerly, naturalization required only the submission of an affidavit to a commissioner, establishing that an immigrant had lived in Canada for three years, but the new act required five years' residence, an adequate knowledge of English or French, and an application to a superior court judge. The secretary of state was also given absolute discretionary powers to withhold naturalization from persons not deemed conducive to the "public good."[1] With the outbreak of war, a series of proclamations and orders in council directed against immigrants

*The author wishes to acknowledge the J. S. Ewart Memorial Fund for assisting his research at the Public Archives of Canada in Ottawa.

from enemy countries made the status of certain groups even more precarious.

On 15 August 1914 all subjects of enemy countries were declared liable to arrest and detention, especially if they attempted to leave Canada. Those pursuing their normal occupations quietly would continue to enjoy the law's protection, and the respect and consideration due to peaceful, law-abiding citizens. Any persons suspected of or participating in proscribed activities, however, could be apprehended. If considered trustworthy, they would be released upon agreeing to report periodically; if the authorities were not satisfied, if the detainees refused to report, or if parolees failed to abide by the terms of their parole, then those apprehended were to be interned under guard of the Canadian militia (see Appendix II: 5).

Within a week of this declaration, the War Measures Act gave the federal government sweeping emergency powers that enabled the cabinet to administer the war effort without accountability to Parliament or existing laws. Covered under the act were powers of media censorship; arrest, detention and deportation; and the appropriation, control and disposal of property. No person held for deportation under the act, or arrested or detained either as an enemy alien or to prevent departure from Canada, was to be released on bail, discharged or tried without the consent of the Ministry of Justice.[2]

By late October, growing unemployment and destitution among enemy aliens, coupled with the government's increasing fear of alien intrigue, precipitated an order in council that not only allowed those not considered a security threat to apply for a permit to leave the country in search of work, but also authorized the appointment of civilian registrars across Canada. Responsible to the chief commissioner of Dominion Police, the latter were to register all enemy aliens according to age, nationality, place of residence, occupation, desire or intention to leave Canada, intention of military service and next of kin. All aliens within twenty miles of a registrar's office were to report within one month of its opening. Those who did not wish or were not allowed to leave Canada could remain at large, but had to report monthly and carry special internal travel documents and identification cards. Aliens considered dangerous or indigent, along with those who failed to register, were to be interned as prisoners of war (see Appendix II: 7).

To deal with those enemy aliens slated for internment, an Internment Operations Branch was created within the Department of Justice, with sixty-nine-year-old William D. Otter as its head. A distinguished retired major-general, Otter was authorized to take any military action necessary to carry out the provisions of his mandate. His duties included the physical care of interned enemy aliens, as well as the direction of the work prescribed for them. The Department of Militia and Defence was to make military forces available as required, while the Royal North West Mounted Police

(RNWMP) and Dominion Police were to provide police and secret service aid when needed.[3]

Thus, the power to intern enemy aliens lay entirely with the Department of Justice, through the Dominion Police and its appointed registrars across Canada, while the task of guarding the internees fell to men of the Department of Militia, under Otter's command. During the six years that Otter headed the Internment Operations, twenty-four receiving stations and permanent internment camps were established across Canada. Facilities ranged from tents, railway cars and bunkhouses to armouries, barracks, forts, exhibition buildings and rented industrial factories. Some stations operated for a matter of months while the camps at Vernon, British Columbia, and Kapuskasing, Ontario, lasted for over five years.[4]

By Otter's own calculation not more than 3,138 of the 8,579 who passed through the camps could be classified as prisoners of war—"captured 'in arms' or belonging to enemy 'reserves.'" Of this number, 817 had no prior connection with Canada, being German sailors and merchant seamen transferred for internment from Newfoundland and British colonies in the West Indies. Only 1,192 Germans from within Canada were actually interned as opposed to 5,954 Austro-Hungarians, and only 2,321 of the 7,762 internees from within Canada were bona fide prisoners of war.[5] The rest were civilians who, under discretionary powers vested in the Canadian government, could be interned if the latter considered them to be either "agents" or of potential service to enemy powers.

II

The government's possession of broad discretionary power is particularly evident in the large number of Ukrainians placed in the internment camps. Anglo-Canadian prejudices, which had developed against the Ukrainians at the turn of the century, intensified during the war years. Anglo-Canadians doubted the Ukrainians' innermost loyalties and made little effort to ascertain their true sentiments. Consequently, although they had been a subject and oppressed people within Austria-Hungary, the Ukrainians were considered a dangerous element, capable of hostile acts against Canada and Britain on behalf of the Central Powers.

The main reason behind the internment of Ukrainians, however, was economic misfortune. Often homesteading on marginal land and accustomed to seeking outside work, Ukrainians had already suffered from the depression that enveloped Canada in 1913 after nearly a decade of continuous expansion. In the early stages of the war the economy slumped further, with "aliens" in particular being laid off as industry slackened. Ukrainians and other immigrants prominent in certain vital resource industries also faced nativistic reaction as Anglo-Canadian workers began to covet their jobs and employers displayed patriotic preference for "Canadian labour."[6] Unemployment among Ukrainians in western Canada reached crisis proportions, and the federal internment camps became centres for those who faced destitution. At the end of the winter of 1914–15, Otter was in control of 4,000 indigent internees, three-quarters of whom were "Austrians."[7]

According to first-person accounts, most former Ukrainian camp inmates were interned as a result of trying to enter the United States in search of work, as was common at harvest time, without the required documents.[8] During the summer and fall of 1915 the English-language press in Winnipeg carried almost daily accounts of "Austrians" being apprehended at the border and subsequently transferred to Brandon.[9] In Manitoba and Ontario a number of "Austrian" aliens were charged with high treason for attempting to enter the United States or aiding others to do so. In Toronto Paul Mazur, who had helped registered aliens leave Canada, was acquitted of treason but nevertheless interned.[10] In some instances, as with Filip Kapustiak at Lethbridge, simply stating one's "intention to go to the U.S. without permission" was sufficient for internment.[11]

The records of the Internment Operations contain a series of letters pertaining to John and Philip Marchuk of Bienfait, Saskatchewan. The brothers' internment, for alleged repeated crossings of the American border, had followed their complaint against a RNWMP constable, M. Watson. They charged that Watson had approached Philip for money and livestock as security for the brothers' good behaviour. The two men were initially kept in custody to appear as witnesses at the Estevan assizes at which Watson was convicted and sentenced for accepting bribes. At the time of his arrest in May 1916, Philip Marchuk had left his pregnant wife, Maria, and two children on a newly settled homestead that offered little shelter or support. In spite of his wife's impassioned letters to General Otter and various camp commanders, it was not until April 1919, almost three years after his arrest, that Philip was paroled as a farm labourer. In the meantime, letters and statements of recommendation from Anglo-Canadians in his home district had stressed the injustice of his internment, testified to his loyalty and confirmed that he had been offered employment by a mining company in Bienfait.[12] This case is particularly interesting as an example of the official corruption and inertia that had crept into the control and internment of "enemy aliens." It also sheds light on the plight of dependants deprived of support and companionship for several years, with no recourse through the courts.

The support of Maria Marchuk and others like her fell to the government, which issued monthly cheques for some forty women and eighty-one children whose breadwinners were interned. Other dependants were permitted to follow their men into the camps. Accommodation, which was available only at the Spirit Lake and Vernon camps, provided support for eighty-one women and 156 children.[13] Many women, however, received no help. Left without family, friends or means of support after her husband's internment, Catherine Boychuk was sentenced to a month in prison for committing minor theft and her eight-month-old daughter was placed in an orphanage, where she died eight days later of "natural causes."[14] While Mrs. Boychuk's case may be extreme, it suggests that the 348 women and children for whom the government provided some assistance represented but a fraction of those who desperately needed it.

With the outbreak of war, communication with relatives in Europe became complicated. In Glace Bay, Nova Scotia, Wasyl Ciuga was threatened with internment after he sent six dollars to his wife in Austria in response to a bank advertisement in *Ameryka*, a Ukrainian Catholic newspaper in the United States. The officer in charge of Ciuga's case reported to his superior:

> I explained to him through our interpreter that he could be interned for even attempting to send money to Enemy Countries, he pleaded ignorance of the matter, stating that he was anxious about his people at home and thought this was a good chance.[15]

On the argument that he had come from Bukovyna, three miles from the Russian border, and thus ultimately sympathized with the Russians, Ciuga was acquitted and allowed to continue working.

In the case of the thirty-seven-year-old Austrian, Maftey Rotari, the reason for internment was quite practical. Rotari was by occupation a carpenter's helper and his skills were needed in the initial construction of the camps. His record of internment makes this clear: under "cause of arrest" appeared "Requests for Carpenters to build huts at Spirit Lake Camp." On completing his duties at Spirit Lake, Rotari was transferred to Kapuskasing and subsequently to a railway crew from which he escaped for a period of fifteen days.[16]

Ukrainians were also interned for attempting to enlist in the Canadian Expeditionary Force. Ukrainian immigrants from the Russian empire were obligated to serve in Europe whether naturalized or not, and approximately two thousand fought with the Canadian Expeditionary Force overseas.[17] Unnaturalized Austrian Ukrainians, however, were not permitted to serve in any capacity, although thousands registered as Russians, Poles and Bohemians or anglicized their names in order to enlist. In a number of cases, Ukrainians who had successfully enlisted were subsequently discharged as enemy aliens and interned. Such was the experience of five prisoners at Lethbridge, who had been discharged from the 214th Battalion, and of Kapuskasing internee, Nick Derryck, who had been a private in the First Canadian Contingent.[18]

The files of the Internment Operations contain numerous additional reasons for Ukrainian internment. Among them were contraventions of the wartime regulations: refusing or failing to register, breaking parole, destroying registration cards, travelling without permission, registering under a false name, writing to relatives in Austria and status as a reservist. Other reasons were less concrete, illustrating the extent of the power of the law: acting in a "very suspicious manner" or showing "a general tendency toward sedition," using "seditious" or "intemperate" language, being found hiding and destitute in a freight car, or being generally "unreliable," "of shiftless character" and "undesirable."[19]

It is also evident that occasionally the threat of internment was levelled at Ukrainians—in some instances Canadian citizens—over purely domestic matters. In Manitoba, where the right to education in one's native language was guaranteed to all linguistic groups by the Laurier-Greenway agreement of 1896, bilingual schools became an increasingly controversial political issue. In 1915, following the defeat of Sir Rodmond Roblin's discredited government, the Liberals under T. C. Norris entered office on a platform of civil and political reform. Among their concerns was the allegedly "un-Canadian" nature of the province's non-British residents, including the Ukrainians. After an initial period of silence on the question, the Liberals launched a final campaign against bilingual education.

The campaign was launched despite assurances by some Liberal MLA's during the election that language rights of non-English-speaking Manitobans would be respected. The metamorphosis of Liberal D. A. Ross (St. Clements) is particularly revealing about the connections made between bilingual education and enemy-alien status and internment of Ukrainians in Canada. Prior to the Liberal victory, Ross had assured his "Brother Poles and Ruthenians" that he would protect their rights and stand by the Laurier-Greenway agreement.[20] After the election he denounced delegations supporting bilingualism as "Austrians" who had "no right to talk on this question" in wartime. "If you don't stop this agitation," he warned, "I'll run you all to Brandon [internment camp]."[21] Ross was undoubtedly the "unidentified Liberal MLA" whom the *Winnipeg Telegram* reported as favouring the "intern[ment of] all Ukrainians" and who supposedly responded to an invitation to a pro-bilingual meeting with the threat that "if you Ukrainians don't stop this, I'll have you all rounded up and interned at Brandon."[22] Asked to comment, Premier Norris dismissed the threat of internment "in connection with the Ukrainian people," but added that "any man speaking against the British institutions or saying anything openly against the best interests of the country should be rounded up."[23]

Although there is no evidence of Ukrainians being interned specifically for defending bilingual educational rights in western Canada, their identification with the issue was sufficient ground for scrutiny, which might lead to internment. In 1915 Fred B. Livesay, press censor for the west, informed Major E. J. Chambers, the chief press censor, that editorial material in *Ukrainskyi holos* (Ukrainian Voice) was unacceptable; "This does not," he said, "seem a very appropriate time to push claims for nationalities or bilingual schools."[24] Chambers' initial response was that his department had no say in such matters. Six months later, however, he sent materials on Orest Zerebko, co-editor of *Ukrainskyi holos* and a vocal advocate of bilingual schools, to General Otter and the Dominion Police, hoping that "this Zarebko [sic] will find himself attacked from two sides at once."[25] The registrar of alien enemies in Winnipeg also appealed to the Dominion Police, suggesting action against Zerebko for his editorials on bilingualism.[26] The chief commissioner pointed out that Otter had no control over aliens until they were actually transferred to him for internment, and that Zerebko, as a Canadian citizen, was not considered an enemy alien and thus was of no concern to the Dominion Police.[27] Nevertheless, Chambers informed Zerebko (along with other editors of the non-English press) that continued agitation in favour of bilingual schools would jeopardize national security and lead to suppression of their newspapers by Dominion censorship authorities.[28]

III

In the camps prisoners were segregated into two classes according to occupation, previous military service and nationality. Generally better educated and treated as an officer class, German internees as a group received preferred accommodation and rations, confinement in urban settings and exemption from work that might encroach on their comfort, health and cleanliness. Amherst (Nova Scotia), Vernon (British Columbia) and Fort Henry (Kingston, Ontario) became the main holding points for German internees.[29]

In contrast, Austrian Ukrainian internees were assigned "second-class" status. Primarily unemployed workers, they were interned as far as possible from major population centres, in primitive work camps or large internment camps isolated on the northern frontiers of settlement. Unlike the privileged "officer" class, Austrians were compelled to work for the Canadian government—building roads, erecting and repairing buildings, and clearing and draining land. Internees received twenty-five cents a day, the equivalent of the supplement paid to Canadian soldiers for work outside their routine military duties. The internment camps at Lethbridge and Brandon were predominantly "Austrian"—Ukrainian—in population, and acted as main assembly points for internees in the Prairie provinces. The life span of these two camps was relatively short, with little of the pioneering type of labour to which Ukrainians had been relegated nearby. Within two years they were closed and their inmates transferred to alternate worksites and internment camps across the country. The "Austrian" or Ukrainian component was particularly large at Spirit Lake, Quebec; Petawawa and Kapuskasing, Ontario; and in Banff, Jasper and the interior of British Columbia.[30] Where both first- and second-class internees were confined within the same facilities (as was often the case), accommodation, food and job differentiation was enforced.[31]

At the peak of its holding capacity in late 1915, the internment camp at Brandon held between 800 and 1,000 Ukrainian internees along with smaller numbers of aliens of other nationalities.[32] The internment facility was located in the Brandon Winter Fair Arena, a one-and-a-half-storey frame building occupying the area of a city block. The physical layout of the camp included parallel exercise, dining, recreational, lavatory, sleeping and hospital areas for prisoners and guards. Fourteen German prisoners were assigned to a special section containing spacious living quarters with adjoining dining and reading rooms. Four-inch cotton and wool mattresses on iron cots with springs were provided instead of the standard issue of wooden cots with straw-filled mattresses. These special occupants enjoyed free access to any part of the camp.[33]

As the Brandon camp was located in an urban centre, there was no opportunity for employment for the majority of the internees. The only prisoners to receive the twenty-five-cent daily government wages were those employed within the camp as barbers, shoemakers, tailors, cooks, carpenters, hospital orderlies and firemen. All mail was censored, and outgoing mail was limited to eight letters a month per prisoner. Friends and relatives could visit once a month, but the camp had no facilities for housing wives and dependants. Camp routine consisted mainly of a series of roll calls and inspections, as well as two daily exercise marches of one hour's duration.[34] The ratio of guards to prisoners at Brandon was one to ten.[35]

"To a prisoner who conducts himself properly and obeys camp orders," reported the American consul general at Winnipeg after an inspection, "life in this camp is not a hard one."[36] Despite this reassuring assessment, during the first year of operations Ukrainian internees at Brandon showed considerable resistance to their enforced confinement. In early 1915 there were numerous escape attempts, some more successful than others. In the spring of that year, three Ukrainians broke out and it was not until February 1916 that one of them, twenty-two-year-old Metro Mahomnuk, was discovered hiding among the Ukrainian community of Stuartburn in southeastern Manitoba. Although prior to his internment Mahomnuk had offered to fight for Canada, he was put on trial for his escape.[37] In May 1915 Dmytro Kowalchuk leapt from a second-floor window of the Winter Fair Arena and managed to hobble on a broken ankle to within nine miles of the American border before being apprehended. That same month internee Harry Hajduk was subjected to disciplinary action for threatening to get even with internment officers after his release.[38] At the end of May, Martin Borozchuk and Peter Dulce, both twenty-one-year-olds from Winnipeg, fled the camp, again via the window.[39]

Early in June the camp witnessed a mass escape attempt by seventeen Ukrainians, which resulted in the fatal shooting of eighteen-year-old Andrew Grapko as he scrambled through a stable window. The unsuccessful bid for freedom entailed cutting a hole in the arena floor and squeezing through a basement boiler room into a stable. The local Brandon paper briefly mentioned Grapko's shooting and the "pitchforking" of other prisoners, then elaborated on the fact that soldiers had soiled their uniforms pulling an escapee out of an inactive boiler. A week later the *Brandon Sun Weekly* ran an article announcing that local "Firemen Offer to Fight, Not Guard the Interned Aliens."[40]

In the wake of Grapko's death, the incidence of escape and insubordination at Brandon declined sharply, as Ukrainian internees accepted their daily routine without great opposition. Card-playing and handicrafts became major preoccupations. Some interned craftsmen carved intricate picture frames, violins and even an altar, using scrap wood from old boxes. Ukrainian-reading and English-study classes were established, as was a reading association called "V poslidnim iarmi" (literally, "In our last captivity"). It appealed regularly to the Ukrainian community for books. The society's social highlights included lively Sunday dances and mock Ukrainian weddings with internees dressed as women and as Austrian and Canadian soldiers.[41]

Ukrainian internees organized strikes in a number of camps. In Sydney, Nova Scotia, a group of young Ukrainians sent from Ontario as paroled labourers for local mines and steel mills refused to eat or work, demanding to be returned to Ontario or sent back to Austria.[42] In 1916 a full-scale riot between 1,200 Austrian internees and 300 guards at Kapuskasing was sparked by the arrival of several prisoners from Petawawa, where they had refused to work after having been forced to labour during religious holidays. At Kapuskasing they not only maintained their stand but won the support of the local internees. The unrest culminated in a serious confrontation that lasted several hours, with camp guards firing on the prisoners and using their bayonets freely. Although initial accounts of the clash reported the death and fatal wounding of several prisoners, the actual toll appears to have been less—the hospitalization of less than a dozen seriously wounded internees, with no casualties among the guards.[43]

Although civilians, Ukrainian internees were subject to the laws and regulations of the Canadian military. They could be fired upon when attempting to escape and were subject to a variety of punishments for crimes, misdemeanours and insubordination. Reduced rations, solitary confinement in cold isolation cells and hard labour were common punishments. Prisoners with bad conduct records were refused parole to work on projects outside the camps.[44]

IV

Internment destroyed the illusions of many Ukrainian immigrants that Canada was a country of freedom and democracy. A contributor to *Kanadyiskyi rusyn* (Canadian Ruthenian) noted that Canada had all the characteristics of Russian despotism—the denial of human and democratic rights, summary arrest, unemployment, discrimination and chauvinism:

> It can no longer be this way. We cannot look on passively as a small group of deranged howlers attempts to terrorize everyone and endeavours with all its strength to take us loyal citizens of this Dominion under its feet and completely without cause cast upon us the veil of disloyalty and the like.[45]

An interned Ukrainian worker writing to the socialist *Robochyi narod* (Working People) was equally bitter:

> Who levelled the mountains from sea to sea?... Who built the railroads and cultivated this wasteland where formerly only the wind howled? We, the victims who today are being tortured in a manner reminiscent of the Christian captives held by the Turks 500 years ago. [We] make our case known so that all Ukrainians and all the nations of the world might see how the blind, "civilized" English chauvinists and their Canadian hangers-on treat foreigners.[46]

The plight of the interned did not go unnoticed by the Ukrainian community outside the camps. The Ukrainian Catholic clergy, for example, made regular visits; in eastern Canada the Reverend A. Redkevych toured the camps in June 1915,[47] while the Reverend Ivan Perepelytsia of Montreal visited internees at Spirit Lake regularly, instructing them to construct a chapel for the celebration of mass.[48] At Brandon the spiritual needs of Ukrainian internees were served by the local parish priest, Father Kaluzniatsky. Bishop Nykyta Budka himself visited the camp in October 1915, addressing the internees, hearing their confessions, promising to send books for their library and to arrange English-language classes, and pledging to help them in any way possible. A high mass planned for the morning of 27 October had to be cancelled, however, when the camp guards refused Budka entry on the grounds that they had received no prior notice of his visit.[49]

The approach of January 1916 meant that thousands of Ukrainians would be spending the Christmas period in internment camps, and the festive season became the focus of a community-wide effort to ease the trauma for the internees. The Volodymyr Vynnychenko Amateur Theatre Group of Winnipeg, for example, donated one-half of the proceeds from a play to the internees at Brandon. "The least we should do is help our brothers during the holiday period," read the playbill. "This is why we feel that it is the holy obligation of every Ukrainian to attend this performance, and in this way demonstrate his aid for our prisoners of war at Brandon."[50]

Ukrainskyi holos co-ordinated an effort among its readers to send Christmas parcels to Ukrainians in the camps, "where fate cast them through no fault of their own, but because the times commanded it."[51] Efforts to share Christmas with internees were also made by Ukrainian communities in Alberta, Ontario and Quebec; Christmas presents were transmitted to the camps at Spirit Lake, Kapuskasing and Petawawa, for example, with internees at Kapuskasing receiving presents from as far away as Chicago.[52]

The most ambitious scheme of Christmas relief came from the Ukrainian Catholic community. *Kanadyiskyi rusyn* urged its readers not to forget those unfortunates who would be singing carols within the camps while everyone else gathered around family tables for Holy Eve supper. It proposed a collection so that every Ukrainian internee could receive a Christmas gift of fruit and tobacco; the committee formed for the purpose by women of SS. Vladimir and Olga parish in Winnipeg raised almost two hundred dollars.[53] On Christmas Eve (6 January 1916) the Ukrainian internees at Brandon were visited twice by the Reverend Kaluzniatsky. In the morning he said mass and participated in singing religious and Christmas songs; in the evening, accompanied by a local committee, he brought the barrels of gifts purchased with the money raised in Winnipeg. That night the standard camp diet was replaced by traditional Ukrainian dishes, prepared by Ukrainian women in Brandon. After supper, carols echoed through the internment building until curfew. On the second day of Christmas, students of the Ruthenian Training School in Brandon and members of the local Ukrainian reading association visited the camp, presenting two plays for the internees. A prisoners' choir also performed, with special dedications to camp officers for contributing space and materials for a makeshift stage. The following day, the prisoners performed a play of their own. The Ukrainian internees in Brandon were greatly moved by these efforts on their behalf; writing to *Kanadyiskyi rusyn*, a spokesman expressed "special thanks" to those who "remembered us here in captivity" by providing a "true Christmas Eve."[54]

Although the campaign of Christmas 1916 tried to bring solace to Ukrainian internees, a more serious movement in the community sought their release altogether. Somewhat paradoxically, the initial catalyst was Fred Livesay, the western press censor, whose wife, the writer Florence Randal Livesay, was keenly interested in Ukraine. The Livesays made their home a regular meeting place for the discussion of Ukrainian literature and history. With misguided yet sympathetic ideas about the Ukrainians, Fred Livesay favoured the release of the thousands interned because they were "ignorant and illiterate" with "an almost superstitious terror of a uniform" that had made them afraid to register. While convinced that there were many "pro-Austrians" and "noisy agitators" who deserved to be locked up, he told his superior, E. J. Chambers, that he wished "something could be devised for separating the sheep from the goats—the well-satisfied and right-intentioned Canadian peasant farmer from the Teutons."[55] The "sheep" could be allowed to leave the camps.

With this in mind, Livesay organized a meeting with several prominent Ukrainians in Winnipeg in early January 1916, hoping to secure their co-operation in clarifying to the government the position of interned Ukrainians. The group included Bishop Budka; Manitoba MLA, Taras Ferley; A. Malofie; Frank Dojacek and O. H. Hykawy, publisher and editor respectively of *Kanadyiskyi farmer* (Canadian Farmer); Wasyl Kudryk, editor of *Ukrainskyi holos*; the Reverend M. Glowa, editor of *Ranok* (Dawn); and Paul Crath (Pavlo Krat), editor of *Kadylo* (Sprinkler).[56] In another letter to Chambers, Livesay summarized the main points discussed:

> The Committee is of the opinion that certainly not more than fifty of the thousand to fifteen hundred Ukranians [*sic*] interned are in any way undesirable or dangerous. Mostly they are ignorant people, and many did not know enough to register; and are harmless inoffensive people. Some of them have been a number of years in Canada. Had they been released these people might have been engaged in harvest work last summer instead of being a charge to the State.... Many friends of these men are willing to enter into bond for their good behaviour—even if some of them were disaffected, they already have had a sharp lesson.[57]

The language barrier was a major problem in determining the sentiments of interned Ukrainians:

> It is said that the form of question now being put to these people is half English and half in their own language; that in their own language the word "pro" [*proty*—against] has an exactly contrary sense to what it has in English; that therefore some of these people, asked if they are "pro-German," have

answered, Yes, meaning they are anti-German. Careful interpretation is an essential in dealing with these men.[58]

The meeting had passed a resolution urging the federal government to co-operate in the release of interned Ukrainians. Chambers replied that Otter was quite prepared to consider the matter, but that

> the difficulty would seem to be to have individual cases properly described and set out for the information of Sir William Otter and the Officers acting under him.... I would suggest that you explain the favourable attitude of mind to the leaders of the Ruthenians in the West, and suggest that they take definite steps to bring as many clear cases as possible to the attention of Sir William Otter.[59]

Livesay's crusade to secure the release of innocent Ukrainian internees was short-lived, however. The escalating controversy over bilingual education in Manitoba dampened his enthusiasm. As he explained to Chambers: "Now that the situation is so embroiled by the bilingual school question I [would] rather wash my hands of it."[60]

Representative Ukrainian organizations and institutions in Winnipeg, however, continued to seek the release of the internees, and designated Ivan Petrushevich, Taras Ferley, Dr. J. K. Pazdriy and Theodore Stefanyk to petition the minister of the interior, Robert Rogers, during his visit to Winnipeg in the summer of 1916. The delegation presented Rogers with a lengthy memorandum explaining why many Ukrainians were unnecessarily interned, and asked that he make representations on their behalf to the government. Although Rogers reportedly received the delegation favourably, promising to intervene personally to help innocent internees, no releases seem to have followed.[61]

In response to the various wartime legal and social indignities inflicted upon the community, the Ukrainians formed various committees to lobby for just and equitable treatment. Both the Ukrainian Canadian Citizens' Committee (formed 1918) and its Catholic counterpart, the Ukrainian National Council (formed 1919) sent several delegations to Prime Minister Borden to discuss the suppression of Ukrainian Canadian publications, and the disfranchisement and internment of Ukrainians.[62] The Ukrainian Social Democratic Party also petitioned the Canadian government, protesting the classification of Ukrainians as enemy aliens, criticizing naturalization restrictions and calling for the establishment of employment bureaus.[63] As late as 1918, the Borden cabinet assured a delegation that those Ukrainians held in internment camps solely because of their Austrian origin would be released.[64]

V

Ultimately, it was the economic situation in Canada that led to the release of the majority of those in the camps. By the summer of 1916 the task of caring for large numbers of internees was becoming burdensome, and physically fit, "non-dangerous" Austrians were sent to paroled employment outside the camps. At the same time the massive flow of Canadian manpower into the armed forces, creating a serious labour shortage in industry and agriculture, forced the government to reassess its "policy of keeping thousands of harmless Austrians" forcibly idle or occupied "with deliberately non-essential work."[65] Increasingly, large corporations and farmers turned to the internment camps to solve their needs, and by the spring of 1917 virtually all of the nearly 6,000 "Austrian" internees were released on parole.[66] Parolees could not leave Canada without proper authorization while the war lasted, and were to report as directed by the police. Their certificates of release functioned as internal passports, to be used when travelling.

Not all prisoners wanted to be paroled as contract labourers to the railways, other corporations or farmers. Austrian reservists were reluctant to sign a release, fearing punishment if they returned to Austria after the war.[67] Others were prepared to leave the camps only if they were not restricted to a given job or locality.[68] Major D. W. Coleman, the officer in charge of the Brandon camp, complained: "At present I can hardly get a man who will accept parole to farmers without almost begging each one to go."[69] Otter advised Coleman to tell medically-fit prisoners reluctant to work for the Hudson's Bay Railway that "they must either accept employment offered or be turned out of camp, as non-dangerous prisoners who refuse their liberty and employment cannot be permitted to remain a public charge."[70] In similar instructions to the commandant of the Vernon camp, Otter indicated that all "non-dangerous Austrian prisoners fit for outside employment who refuse to accept same should be sent out of camp, but no compulsion must be used." The commandant was simply to "advise such that no further subsistence will be given them in camp" and provide "transportation and subsistence to point of original arrest."[71] Tom Boby, a twenty-four-year-old Austrian (Ukrainian) interned at Morrissey, British Columbia, was one of those affected. His release certificate read: "Released because refused to accept employment offered on two occasions and it is not considered desirable to subsist him at the expense of the country after refusing such offers of work."[72]

Acceptance of restrictive paroled labour was often detrimental to the internees. Many of those paroled for railway labour, for example, were sent to sites in northern Ontario and forbidden to leave without special authorization. The hard work, extreme isolation and primitive conditions made these camps equally as oppressive as the internment camps. Otter received numerous letters from Ukrainians on railway crews, such as this request in broken English from Haliburton, Ontario:

> So we beg you Sir again let us know who is now to give them [parole cards granting permission to rejoin their families] for us because we are working here 6 months in the bush and we cannot stand any longer to stay in the bush we are sick from haard work; we have ours friends and famielies at Oshawa and we can work with them in the same factories so good as as ours friends and rapport to the police ewery Month at Oshawa, Ontario.
>
> We beg send us our parole cards or tell us who keept them for us.
>
> We think that our employer Frank Austin have them only he not want to return them to us.[73]

A number of Ukrainians paroled to work on the railway at Sturgeon Falls, Ontario, wanted their status clarified. Requesting Otter's permission to visit relatives in Montreal, one of them wrote:

> Here the police authorities do not permit to leave, they say that if I leave without a registry card I will be sentenced to six months.
>
> I am not looking for anything like that, I want to abide by the law of the land. If you Sir General gave me freedom I do not see why I should be punished when I wish to go without a registry card, I request you Sir General this favour.[74]

In another case, thirty-two internees paroled from Kapuskasing to work for the Canadian Pacific Railway in northern Ontario went on strike to protest dangerous and unsanitary working conditions. For breaking their employment contract, all members of the crew (almost exclusively Ukrainian in composition) received six-month sentences at Burwash industrial prison farm.[75] It was not uncommon for Ukrainians paroled as railway labourers to make good their escape in short order.[76]

Although the Armistice ending the war was signed on 11 November 1918, it was not until 24 February 1920 that the last of Canada's internment camps was shut down, and not until 20 June of that year that the Internment Operations office officially closed.[77] By December 1918, 2,222 aliens were still interned, 489 of them Austrians.[78] In the postwar period the camps held the remnants of the wartime enemy aliens as well as a new influx of "radical aliens."

By 1918 the social and political climate of Canada had changed significantly as increasing numbers of demobilized soldiers returned from Europe. Strikes led to stubborn conflicts between labour and capital. The non-British were blamed for economic unrest and political radicalism, and consequently, legislation was passed to cover the investigation, incarceration and possible deportation of hostile or undesirable aliens.[79] For Ukrainians who remained interned in the postwar period and for the newly interned who were filling up the camp at Kapuskasing, the threat of deportation became very real. A number of Ukrainians arrested during the Winnipeg General Strike were transferred to Kapuskasing and quickly spirited out of the country under the new legislation.[80]

Of 1,964 enemy aliens deported from Canada, 302 were Austrians.[81] Initially questions of mental and physical health were prominent factors in the selection of internees to be sent out of the country. Some had incurable diseases like tuberculosis; others were slated for deportation as incapacitated invalids for such ailments as chronic inflammation of the bowels and inoperable hernia—all conditions which might well have developed as a result of life in the camps. Anthony Pozlucki, aged fifty-four, was listed as deportation material for suffering from a "persistent headache."[82] Many of those interned contracted some form of mental illness during their confinement. In Otter's words:

> Insanity was by no means uncommon among the prisoners, many being interned it was suspected to relieve municipalities of their care, while in others the disease possibly developed from a nervous condition brought about by the confinement and restrictions entailed.[83]

A total of 106 internees were confined to mental institutions by Internment Operations, sixty-one of them Austrians; all but three were ultimately deported.[84] Watson Kirkconnell, who had been on staff at the Kapuskasing camp, contended that those placed in asylums were but a small part of a much greater problem:

> These, too, were only the severe cases, and among the camp population there were few on whom the long years of captivity had not left their mark . . . confinement in a strange land, inactivity and hopeless waiting were in themselves enough to shatter the nerves and undermine the health.[85]

Kirkconnell's assessment of the incidence of mental breakdown is corroborated by other accounts:

> My wife's brother went nuts in one of their camps. He was taken away and when he finally got back he was never the same man again. They had broken his spirit up there in northern Ontario. He could never get over the injustice of his treatment, the falseness of his hope in this new world.[86]

Altogether, 107 internees died in the camps, sixty-nine of them Austrians. The majority succumbed to tuberculosis, pneumonia and heart disease, with a handful dying during escape attempts and from suicide.[87] Otter's official list of death statistics did not reflect the less serious casualties alluded to by Kirkconnell:

> Throughout the winter the thermometer sported daily between 40 degrees and 60 degrees below zero. Snow lay six feet deep on the level. The wilderness of spruce stood everywhere, infinite and obdurate. The hospital records showed a tragic list of heads bruised by falling trees and of hands and feet chopped and frozen.[88]

In contrast to the early deportation lists that focused on mental and physical disabilities, later ones paid more attention to political and social deficiencies. In November 1918 Otter asked his camp commanders to identify prisoners who had been "very troublesome" or who had shown "decided antagonism to British or Canadian rule."[89] The list submitted by Major Nash, the commander at Vernon, included those who were "well behaved and not antagonistic," "well behaved but strongly pro-German or Austrian," "bitter against Canada and Great Britain," "bitter and troublesome and agitators and insubordinate," "trouble-makers and reported as being I[ndustrial] W[orkers of the] W[orld]," "aged and feeble and not likely to secure a living" and nine who were simply "decidedly eccentric."[90] The list from Kapuskasing was similar. Austrians made up the dominant contingent in several categories and reflected the emphasis of postwar internment operations on radicalism; internees marked for deportation were described as "agitators amongst workmen" and "strike fomentors" who "congregate[d] at secret meetings."[91] A subsequent list of one hundred recommended deportees from Kapuskasing characterized the predominantly Austrian group as

> men that are more or less of a nuisance to us, I.W.W.'s, agitators, also the type of man found around city pool rooms, making an easy living. They are a loafing, good for nothing lot, and the sooner the country is rid of them the better.[92]

The rights of enemy aliens before Canadian courts during the First World War was a disputed issue, even on the matter of naturalization.[93] What was certain, however, was that interned aliens were deprived of legal rights from the time they were interned to the time of their possible deportation.[94] In spite of this it is clear that the Department of Justice did entertain representations on behalf of persons in the camps. Ivan Tymchuk, for example, was released in early 1916 after eight months internment at

Brandon due to the efforts of lawyer J. T. Beaubien; the Tymchuk family publicly thanked Beaubien and the government in *Kanadyiskyi rusyn* where Beaubien's regular advertisement stressed that a Ukrainian law student was articling with him.[95]

Without legal rights, however, there was little the internees could do either to obtain their release or to counter the corruption and brutality to which they were occasionally subjected. Several thousand dollars in cash and valuables confiscated from internees at the Toronto internment centre, for example, vanished without trace and without anyone's being charged with theft. At Sault Ste. Marie enemy alien Peter Kramerinck permitted a local militia colonel to take his bank book and later to extort a mortgage from him in an effort to forestall his internment; later Kramerinck "was ordered to shave his mustache to make him look less like a German and threatened with death if he made trouble."[96] At Spirit Lake a former commandant used internees to clear timber and open roads on colonization lots he had obtained adjacent to the camp.[97] Complaints from internees of deliberate mistreatment by guards were not infrequent. After visiting the camp at Banff, Otter was inclined to believe charges of bad and inadequate amounts of food and cruel punishments like being suspended by the wrists.[98]

In April 1918 thirty-one internees at Vernon appealed to Beni R. Iseli, the Swiss consul general in Montreal. They complained of guards who compelled them to do degrading work and threatened them with corporal punishment; of being beaten and kicked and placed in close confinement for refusing to do work not in their exclusive interest; and of not being allowed to lie down during the day, without a permit from the medical sergeant, even if ill, tired or hungry.[99] In a letter to Otter, Commander Date of Kapuskasing described how he had handled troublesome prisoners during a roll call. After posting armed sentries to cover other bunkhouses, Date entered the rebellious unit and ordered the men forward: "A few hesitated, but an automatic six shooter pointed in their faces made them step lively. They stood up like sheep and answered their names."[100]

Although they faced bayonet and bullet, the prisoners, to their credit, tried to fight back. Passive resistance was the only realistic weapon. Describing the work habits of internees at Kapuskasing, Kirkconnell commented:

> Ignorant, sullen, inert, the mass of these internees were the very incarnation of passive resistance. They worked because they were compelled, and they exerted themselves as little as possible, though by dawdling steadily they accomplished much through sheer force of numbers. Early each morning they would be told off into gangs of a score each and would march off languidly to the bush in Indian file, with one armed sentry in rear and a drowsy Slav in front setting the pace in a slow, lurching shuffle.[101]

According to one Ukrainian internee at Kapuskasing, "we worked pretty poorly, goofing off most of the time. We'd pretend to be working while really we were relaxing in shifts."[102] Another internee described his first day on the job, digging ditches:

"This is a fine story," I thought to myself, "to exploit us in some kind of forced labor camp." I worked so-so until noon, but after lunch, which was as tasty as pepper to a dog, my whole being rebelled. "Did I come to Canada to do statute labor? Why is this being done to me? Have I murdered or robbed someone? Am I responsible for the fact that the country in which I was born is at war with the Allies, and in turn England? No, I will not work at the point of a bayonet for a spoon of plum preserves!" I stood there and turned that shovel aimlessly, as if I was churning butter with it.[103]

VI

The internment of Ukrainians in Canada during the First World War was prompted less by concern for national security than by a combination of existing prejudice fed by wartime patriotism and economic factors. Restrictions and inconvenience in time of war are unavoidable, but it is debatable whether the encroachment on liberty, ill-treatment and indignity that internment inflicted on such a large civilian population was justified or necessary. Many questions remain concerning Canada's incarceration of enemy aliens and its treatment of civilian internees during the Great War. Already, however, the passing away of many of the original actors, particularly those who personally experienced internment, has made the prisoners' story and interpretation of events difficult to obtain. At the same time, the destruction of government records[104] has decreased the official source material available to historians.

Notes

1. Canada, *Statutes*, 4–5 Geo. 5, chap. 44.
2. Canada, *Statutes*, 5 Geo. 5, chap. 2.
3. W. D. Otter, *Internment Operations, 1914–1920* (Ottawa, 1921), 3.
4. *Ibid.*, 4–5.
5. *Ibid.*, 6; and D. Morton, *The Canadian General: Sir William Otter* (Toronto, 1974), 338.

6. R. H. Coats, "The Alien Enemy in Canada: Internment Operations," in *Canada in the Great World War*, 6 vols. (Toronto, 1917–21), 2: 148–9.

7. Morton, *The Canadian General*, 337–8.

8. See, for example, P. Iasnovsky, *Pid ridnym i pid chuzhym nebom* (Buenos Aires, 1961), 216–17; the memoirs of Dmytro Kruchak in *Ukrainske slovo*, 30 May 1951; and L. Luciuk, "Internal Security and an Ethnic Minority: The Ukrainians and Internment Operations in Canada, 1914–1920," *Signum* 4, no. 2 (February 1980): 56.

9. See, for example, *Manitoba Free Press*, 1 July and 2, 3, 5 and 11 August 1915.

10. *Canadian Annual Review* (1915): 355–6; *Toronto Telegram*, 10 February 1916; and *Winnipeg Tribune*, 2 February 1916.

11. Date to MacPherson, 11 July 1916, Internment Operations Files, file 3326 (1), Secretary of State Papers, Public Archives of Canada (hereafter PAC), Ottawa, Ontario.

12. Internment Operations Files, file 3565, PAC.

13. Otter, *Internment Operations*, 7.

14. *Ukrainskyi holos*, 13 June 1917. The fate of another destitute wife, Paraska Holik of Coleman, Alberta, and her child is described in H. Potrebenko, *No Streets of Gold: A Social History of Ukrainians in Alberta* (Vancouver, 1977), 135–6.

15. Noble to Tait, 5 November 1915, Chief Press Censor Files, file 144(1), Secretary of State Papers, PAC.

16. Internment Operations Files, file 3466(2), PAC. Rotari's nationality was not specified.

17. M. H. Marunchak, *Studii do istorii ukraintsiv Kanady*, 4 vols. (Winnipeg, 1964–72), 4: 188–9.

18. Internment Operations Files, files 3326(4) and 3466(2), PAC.

19. Internment Operations Files, files 3194(1), 3326(1,5), 3466(2) and 4680, PAC.

20. *Winnipeg Tribune*, 8 February 1916; and *Manitoba Free Press*, 5 February 1916.

21. *Winnipeg Tribune*, 8 February 1916; see *ibid.*, 11 February 1916, for Ross' denial of the charges.

22. *Winnipeg Telegram*, 3 February 1916.

23. *Ibid.*

24. Livesay to Chambers, 24 November 1915, Chief Press Censor Files, file 144(1), PAC.

25. Chambers to Livesay, 27 November 1915 and 3 July 1916, Chief Press Censor Files, file 144(1), PAC.

26. Davidson to Sherwood, 21 June 1916, Chief Press Censor Files, file 144(c), PAC.

27. Sherwood to Chambers, 5 July 1916, Chief Press Censor Files, file 144(c), PAC.

28. D. H. Avery, "The Radical Alien and the Winnipeg General Strike of 1919," in *The West and the Nation: Essays in Honour of W. L. Morton*, ed. C. Berger and R. Cook (Toronto, 1976), 214, 227.

29. Otter, *Internment Operations*, 6; and Morton, *The Canadian General*, 333, 336–9.

30. Otter, *Internment Operations*, 6, 9; and Morton, *The Canadian General*, 333, 336–9, and "Sir William Otter and Internment Operations in Canada during the First World War," *Canadian Historical Review* 55, no. 1 (March 1974): 45–6.

31. Morton, *The Canadian General*, 337; and F. M. Ryder, "Official Inspection of the Internment Station at Brandon, Manitoba" (Winnipeg, 1916), 2–3. A photocopy of the latter is in the possession of the author.

32. *Kanadyiskyi rusyn*, 15 December 1915.

33. Ryder, "Internment Station at Brandon," 1–5.

34. *Kanadyiskyi rusyn*, 15 December 1915; and Ryder, "Internment Station at Brandon," 9–11.

35. Otter to Adjutant General, Department of Militia and Defence, 1 November 1915, Internment Operations Files, file 3473, PAC.

36. Ryder, "Internment Station at Brandon," 9–10.

37. *Manitoba Free Press*, 11 February 1916.

38. *Brandon Sun Weekly*, 6 and 27 May 1915.

39. *Manitoba Free Press*, 31 May 1915.

40. *Brandon Sun Weekly*, 3 and 10 June 1915.

41. *Kanadyiskyi rusyn*, 3 and 10 November 1915; and "Voienni plinniky v Brendoni," in *Ukrainska rodyna. Narodnyi iliustrovanyi kaliendar na perestupnyi rik 1916* (Winnipeg, 1916), 106–8. Iasnovsky, *Pid ridnym i pid chuzhym nebom*, 229–31, describes similar activities at Kapuskasing.

42. I. Beskyd, ed., *Almanakh Torontonskoi eparkhii. U Khrystovim vynohradnyku* (Toronto, 1964).

43. Iasnovsky, *Pid ridnym i pid chuzhym nebom*, 232–8; *Toronto Globe and Mail*, 16 and 19 May 1916; *Toronto Telegram*, 16 May 1916; and *Kanadyiskyi rusyn*, 31 May 1916.

44. Rodden to Otter, 13 June 1916, Internment Operations Files, file 3360(1), PAC.

45. *Kanadysikyi rusyn*, 9 June 1915.

46. Cited in O. Martynowych, "The Ukrainian Socialist and Working Class Movement in Manitoba" (unpublished paper, 1973, in the Provincial Archives of Manitoba), 25.

47. *Kanadyiskyi rusyn*, 23 June 1915.

48. *Ibid.*, 12 May 1915; and K. I. Mervitsky, "Spohady pionera," in *Propamiatna knyha z nahody zolotoho iuvileiu khramu sv. Arhystratyha Mykhaila v Montreali*, ed. A. Hladylovych et al. (Toronto, 1966), 21.

49. *Kanadyiskyi rusyn*, 3 November 1915.

50. Flyer, Ukrainian Cultural and Educational Centre, Winnipeg, Manitoba.

51. *Ukrainskyi holos*, 6 December 1915.

52. *Kanadyiskyi rusyn*, 22 December 1915 and 26 January 1916.

53. *Ibid.*, 15 and 27 December 1915, and 5 and 19 January, 22 March 1916.

54. *Ibid.*, 19 January 1916.

55. Livesay to Chambers, 27 December 1915, Chief Press Censor Files, file 144(c), PAC.

56. Livesay to Chambers, 29 December 1915, Chief Press Censor Files, file 144(c), PAC.

57. Livesay to Chambers, 6 January 1916, Chief Press Censor Files, file 144(c), PAC.

58. *Ibid.*

59. Chambers to Livesay,14 January 1916, Chief Press Censor Files, file 144(c), PAC.

60. Livesay to Chambers, 10 February 1916, Chief Press Censor Files, file 144(c), PAC.

61. *Ukrainskyi holos*, 5 July 1916. Outside the Ukrainian community, voices opposed to internment were few and far between. In 1916 Liberal MP Frank Oliver was one of the few to speak against it, complaining that although the internees had committed no crimes they were subjected to compulsory labour at twenty-five cents a day. See Canada, *Parliamentary Debates* (Commons), 122, 1(1916): 849–50.

62. Se T. Iastremsky, *Kanadiianizatsiia. Politychnyi rozvytok kanadiiskykh ukraintsiv za poslidnykh 46 rokiv* (Winnipeg, 1946), 113–15; and M. H. Marunchak, *The Ukrainian Canadians: A History* (Winnipeg, 1970), 331–7.

63. J. A. Boudreau, "The Enemy Alien Problem in Canada, 1914–1921" (Ph.D. thesis, University of California, Los Angeles, 1965), 173.

64. *Ukrainskyi holos*, 6 March 1918.

65. Morton, *The Canadian General*, 341.

66. Otter, *Internment Operations*, 13.

67. Coleman to Otter, 29 June 1916, Internment Operations Files, file 3326(1), PAC.

68. Date to MacPherson, 6 August 1917, Internment Operations Files, file 3466, PAC.

69. Coleman to Otter, 17 June 1916, Internment Operations Files, file 3326(1), PAC.

70. Otter to Coleman, 23 June 1916, Internment Operations Files, file 3326(1), PAC.

71. Otter to commandant at Vernon, 13 July 1916, Internment Operations Files, file 3326(1), PAC.

72. Internment Operations Files, vol. 772, PAC.

73. Steve Zwarun and Ignacy Klimink to Internment Operations, 28 February 1917, Internment Operations Files, file 3203, PAC.

74. Bodnar to Otter, 16 April 1917, Internment Operations Files, file 3326(3), PAC.

75. MacPherson to Bell, 14 May 1917, and Mactier to MacPherson, 23 April 1917, Internment Operations Files, file 3326(3), PAC; and D. H. Avery, *"Dangerous Foreigners": European Immigrant Workers and Labour Radicalism in Canada, 1896–1932* (Toronto, 1979), 70.

76. See, for example, ? to MacPherson, 13 February 1917, Internment Operations Files, file 3326(2), PAC.

77. Morton, *The Canadian General*, 362, and "Otter and Internment Operations," 58.

78. Canada, *Parliamentary Debates* (Commons), 134, 1(1919): 757.

79. Morton, "Otter and Internment Operations," 56–8.

80. Avery, *"Dangerous Foreigners"*, 86.

81. Otter, *Internment Operations*, 14.

82. Internment Operations Files, file 4680, PAC.

83. Otter, *Internment Operations*, 8.

84. *Ibid.*

85. W. Kirkconnell, "Kapuskasing—An Historical Sketch," *Queen's Quarterly* 28, no. 3 (January 1921): 274.

86. Quoted in Luciuk, "Internal Security and an Ethnic Minority," 41.

87. Otter, *Internment Operations*, 13.

88. Kirkconnell, "Kapuskasing," 267.

89. Otter to Camp Commanders, 18 November 1918, Internment Operations Files, file 6712(1), PAC.

90. Nash to Otter, 28 November 1918, Internment Operations Files, file 6712, PAC.

91. Internment Operations Files, file 6712(1), PAC.

92. Date to Otter, 12 May 1919, Internment Operations Files, file 6712(2), PAC.

93. Morton, "Otter and Internment Operations," 41; and *Canadian Annual Review* (1914): 283–4, and (1915): 356.

94. Morton, "Otter and Internment Operations," 41.

95. *Kanadyiskyi rusyn*, 26 January 1916.

96. Morton, *The Canadian General*, 335, and "Otter and Internment Operations," 43.

97. Morton, "Otter and Internment Operations," 50.

98. Morton, *The Canadian General*, 339, 344.

99. Letter to Beni R. Iseli, 2 April 1918, Internment Operations Files, file 4738, 251–2, PAC.

100. Date to Otter, 1 October 1917, Internment Operations Files, file 5330, PAC.

101. Kirkconnell, "Kapuskasing," 268.

102. Quoted in Luciuk, "Internal Security and an Ethnic Minority," 57.

103. Iasnovsky, *Pid ridnym i pid chuzhym nebom*, 225–6.

104. Internees' personal files in the Internment Operations Files at the Public Archives of Canada have been weeded, leaving the certificate of release as the only significant document. It would appear from the few documents which

were transferred to the main body of internment files that the destroyed material would have contained valuable information on the cause and location of initial detention, the inter-camp movement of internees, the origins and vital statistics of the prisoners and their conduct and treatment during confinement. See M. Swift, "Arrangement of Archival Units," in *Papers Prepared for the 1974 Archives Course* (Ottawa, 1974), 10–14. Original finding aids and documents lists for the Internment Operations Files would also suggest that a number of controversial files (with such titles as "Brandon escapees," "Complaints at Castle and Spirit Lake" and "POWs' charges of ill-treatment"), particularly relevant to the Ukrainians, are missing. Most of the surviving files pertain to mundane day-to-day administration of the camps and offer little insight into the lives of the internees.

Chapter 2

The Enemy Alien and the Canadian General Election of 1917*

John Herd Thompson

I

"Many books have been written about the World War," wrote Prime Minister Robert Borden in his preface to J. Castell Hopkins' *Canada at War*, "and many more are certain to be written."[1] Time has borne out his prediction, and the war and its consequences have become an important preoccupation for generations of Canadian historians.[2] The subject has also attracted historians of Canada's Ukrainian community. Almost every book written on Ukrainians in Canada has a chapter describing the unjust treatment Ukrainian Canadians received at the hands of an English Canada inflamed by the passions of war—an unjust treatment that began with internment and culminated with the humiliation of disfranchisement under the War-time Elections Act.[3] Most of these chapters are short and not overly penetrating; many are written by "enthusiastic, well-meaning amateurs."[4] This essay examines in some detail the genesis of the War-time Elections Act and the election fought under its rules in December 1917. Although Ukrainians were not the only naturalized enemy aliens to lose the franchise, and although the act applied to all Canadian provinces, this paper is largely devoted to the experiences of Ukrainian Canadians in the three Prairie provinces for two main reasons. Most Ukrainians, whether naturalized citizens or not, lived in Manitoba, Saskatchewan and Alberta;[5] and the election of 1917 was won for the conscriptionist Union Government

*The author wishes to acknowledge funding from the Faculty of Graduate Studies and Research, McGill University.

because of the overwhelming mandate it received from the voters residing between the Red River and the Rocky Mountains.

Neither of the two principal themes of this essay should startle any serious student of Canadian history. First, the treatment afforded enemy-alien minority groups had little or no relationship to their supposed threat to Canada or to their behaviour during the war, but was instead the product of prewar nativism legitimized by an atmosphere charged with patriotism. Second, the most important "cleavage factor" (to use the term beloved of political sociologist S. D. Clark Jr.) within Canadian society has been historically what our grandfathers called "race" and we call "ethnicity."

Perhaps because the behaviour of English Canadians during the conscription crisis seems in retrospect so monstrous, some historians of the affair have sought to absolve parts of English Canadian society from responsibility. Absolution is granted in a two-step process. First, it is claimed that conscription was unpopular with two important segments of that society, the labour movement and the farm community. This assertion, best expressed by Paul Sharp and Martin Robin, has been echoed by Ukrainian author, Helen Potrebenko: "Workers and farmers in Western Canada," she maintains, "had consistently opposed conscription."[6] Once it has been established that class and regional opposition to conscription existed within English Canada, the second step in the process of absolution begins. The Union Government which enforced conscription, it is claimed, did not really represent the will of the electorate which voted for it, but gained office only through its manipulation of the votes of naturalized citizens, women and soldiers serving overseas.[7] Carried to its logical absurdity, the view maintains that conscription and disfranchisement were a plot foisted on the country by Arthur Meighen, whom everybody but Roger Graham, his biographer, seems to feel is the villain of the piece![8] Alas, for those who would remove our ancestors' crimes from this dark chapter of Canada's past, we must face squarely the events of 1917–18 and admit that they are remarkably consistent with the behaviour of the English Canadian majority toward Canadian minorities during other crises.

II

A brief exploration of the behaviour of Canada's Ukrainians between 1914 and 1918 makes it clear that they neither posed a danger to Canada's security nor opposed the national war effort. Ukrainians were undoubtedly less enthusiastic about the Allied cause than were most English Canadians, but they were not hostile to it or sympathetic toward the Central Powers. With the exception of an ill-advised and hastily-withdrawn pastoral letter (see Appendix I: 1) issued by the Ukrainian Catholic bishop Nykyta Budka, urging "all Austrian subjects who are under military obligation to return to Austria, there to be ready to defend the state," it is difficult to find evidence of Ukrainian sympathy for the Austro-Hungarian empire. Historians, in fact, have given more attention to the Budka incident than it deserves.[9] Budka presumed to speak only for Ukrainian Catholics and did not necessarily represent their feelings, even though his stance did reflect the pro-Habsburg sentiments of the Greek Catholic clergy in his native Galicia. His pastoral letter was instantly repudiated by other Ukrainian spokesmen and at a mass meeting in Winnipeg less than a week after the declaration of war, "Ukrainians unanimously pledged their loyalty to Canada and the British Empire, and promised full support for the war effort."[10] The *Manitoba Free Press* evidently accepted this view as the true sentiment of Ukrainians. In an editorial entitled "As to Slav Loyalty," J. W. Dafoe made clear that "there has never at any time been any question as to the loyalty of the majority of the Slav settlers of Manitoba or of Canada. They will be faithful sons of their adopted country."[11]

There is considerable evidence that Dafoe's conclusion was correct. Some naturalized Ukrainian Canadians—it is impossible to determine how many—enlisted in the Canadian Expeditionary Force.[12] Other examples of the almost pathetic eagerness of Ukrainians to avoid offending patriotic English Canadians can be found in the non-socialist Ukrainian-language press, which consistently urged its readers to obey the laws and regulations established by the federal government. Although the "nationalist" *Ukrainskyi holos* (Ukrainian Voice) and Catholic *Kanadyiskyi rusyn* (Canadian Ruthenian) agreed on little else, both papers supported the national registration programme begun by the Borden government in December 1916 and advised Ukrainians to fill out the information cards distributed by the Post Office. To help those without a knowledge of English, both newspapers published translations of the questions on the cards.[13] *Kanadyiskyi rusyn* went so far as to warn its readers against "English socialists" like R. A. Rigg and F. J. Dixon who urged workers of all ethnic backgrounds to oppose registration as a step in the direction of conscription. Somewhat naively it concluded that the war was no time for divisiveness; Ukrainians "should support [registration] to the fullest."[14] Even after the War-time Elections Act stripped many Ukrainian Canadians of their franchise, *Ukrainskyi holos* was prepared to urge the purchase of victory bonds:

> Ukrainian citizens should understand that it is in their own interest that the iron and despotic hand of the German Kaiser should not rule in Canada, and the loan of a few hundred dollars is . . . a show of our patriotism for our newly-adopted country.[15]

Whether such editorials were prompted by a nascent Canadian patriotism, as Ol'ha Woycenko and Michael Marunchak argue,[16] or simply by a healthy concern for the physical safety of the Ukrainian Canadian community,[17] the message is clear: Ukrainians were "not to be identified with the Austrians" but were "true Canadians and wish to remain as such."[18]

Only one element within the Ukrainian community consistently opposed the war and criticized Canada's participation in it. The Ukrainian Social Democratic Party (USDP), through its journalistic voice *Robochyi narod* (Working People), greeted the declaration of war with a rhetorical question: "Why did the capitalists make Europe a hell?" "In order to get a larger return on their capital and larger markets for their products," was the reply. Denouncing Ukrainian leaders who supported the war as "servants of capitalism," *Robochyi narod* urged all workers to use the conflict to topple capitalism and to "let a strong voice carry across the world from the working class—Down with War!!!"[19] As a result, *Robochyi narod* and the USDP vigorously condemned internment camps, opposed registration and conscription and vehemently disapproved of the War-time Elections Act. However, the USDP opposed not simply the Canadian war effort but the war itself, and did so from an international socialist rather than strictly a Ukrainian perspective.[20] Excepting official police circles, it is debatable whether the editorials were much read or understood by anyone outside the Ukrainian socialist movement, and it is perhaps surprising that the paper continued publication until the general suppression of the enemy-alien press in September 1918.

The Ukrainian Canadians therefore did nothing during the First World War that justified or explains the treatment they received. Their exemplary behaviour was described by Robert Fletcher, the supervisor for schools among foreigners in Alberta, in his 1915 annual report. "During the period of the War," he declared, "the Ruthenians have remained loyal and industrious.... Their sympathies are largely with ... [the] Allies in this great struggle."[21] Prime Minister Borden also lauded "the spirit of loyal cooperation" of Ukrainian Canadians during the war and suggested that it "deserves every commendation."[22]

III

If Ukrainians were loyal during the war, why were they treated as enemy aliens? English Canadian resentment was primarily economic in origin. During 1914 and 1915, when recession still gripped the prairie west, Ukrainians were accused of taking work which belonged by birthright to

English Canadians or immigrants from Britain. Blaming "Doukhobors and Ruthenians," an angry Calgarian wrote to the *Herald* that "working men of the British race have been going idle while the foreigner has got the jobs and the money.... Foreigners are being put to work while the British can starve."[23]

Despite such complaints, large numbers of immigrant labourers were unemployed during the first months of the war.[24] Some may have lost their jobs when "patriotic" employers decided to replace them with English Canadians, but most were simply victims of the cyclical unemployment that characterized western Canada's economy. Life was particularly difficult for unnaturalized immigrants from a country with which Canada was at war. If lucky enough to hold jobs, they were denounced for forcing the "British born...to apply to charitable institutions to support their families."[25] If unemployed, they hazarded incarceration in one of the internment camps established by the federal government in October 1914. Studies by Desmond Morton and Joseph A. Boudreau have demonstrated that the primary motivation for the policy of internment was the widespread unemployment during the winter of 1914–15, and that the enemy alien posed "no significant military threat."[26] For every Trotsky that the Canadian government guarded during the war, there were several thousand unlucky Ukrainian labourers.

By the spring of 1916, however, the war-induced expansion of prairie agriculture had combined with heavy enlistment from Manitoba, Saskatchewan and Alberta to create a strong demand for agricultural labour. Suddenly the strong backs of enemy aliens were needed to plough, sow, stook and thresh. All but a handful of the camp inmates were paroled. In a farm labour market tilted in favour of the worker,[27] the immigrant farm worker in 1916 and especially in 1917–18 was able to demand a decent wage and to pick and choose among a number of employers. English Canadian farmers, accustomed to having things their own way, were annoyed. As the *Swift Current Sun* commented during the harvest of 1916: "Alien help has never been popular on farms" since "the farmer is a man of few words and he is irritated by long explanations to a foreigner who cannot grasp the simplest language."[28]

Worse than the language barrier for most farmers was the immigrant farm worker's demand for a share of the increase in grain prices. "Austrians and other foreigners are asking exorbitant wages," complained a group of Saskatchewan farmers, unable, as were most English Canadians, to distinguish a Ukrainian from an Austrian.[29] "The alien question is beginning to look serious," wrote an Alberta farm wife to a friend. Her concern was not enemy-alien disloyalty to Canada but the fact that "these foreigners have us where the hair is short as regards wages."[30] Farmers, convinced by government propaganda campaigns that wheat production was a patriotic

duty, equated the refusal of Ukrainian farm workers to accept the lower
prewar wage rates with sympathy for the Central Powers. In a scurrilous
poem entitled "The Ferocious Farmer," a Saskatchewan weekly newspaper
made this connection: "John Reaper," a farmer, tries to hire four "Austrian"
labourers—"Bohunkis," "Ruffnek," "Hoboko" and "Tuffguysky." All are
too busy to work for him, even for the highest wages, one because he wants
to attend a party celebrating a German victory. When John Reaper
denounces the four as a "slimy collection of scum," they dance around him
singing:

> *Hoch, hoch, hoch*
> *We laugh at you, old sock;*
> *We hope your grain will freeze and rot;*
> *We hope your farm will go to pot;*
> *Us fellers, Kaiser Bill und Gott*
> *Will work at harvest for you not.*
> *The Austrians we left behind*
> *Are always present in our mind*
> *You do not like it very well*
> *But you and yours can go to hell.*[31]

"The Ferocious Farmer" is ridiculous doggerel, but the sentiments which
prompted it were very real. In April 1917 an employee of the Manitoba
Government Labour Bureau made the unfounded accusation that
"Austrian" farm workers spending the winter in Winnipeg had colluded to
drive up wages for farm help during planting. The charge was
contemptuously dismissed by *Robochyi narod*, which pointed out that
farmers "were still riding on sleighs" and that workers could scarcely
conspire "not to work on farms when snow covers the ground because then
there is no work on farms."[32] The accusation, however, typified the fears of
English Canadian farmers desperate to profit from high wartime grain
prices. Because Canada was at war, they were able to mask their
objective—a cheap and docile farm labour force—behind patriotic concern
for greater production to feed Canada's allies. Beginning during the harvest
of 1916 and continuing into the postwar period, western farmers demanded
that enemy aliens—indeed all "foreigners"—be conscripted not into the
army but as farm labourers, and that their wages be fixed at $1.10 a day,
the pay of a soldier in France.[33]

What infuriated English Canadians was not enemy-alien disloyalty, but
immigrant economic success. The years of war were years of expansion for
Ukrainian farmers, despite the hostility of their neighbours and the
repression of the Canadian government.[34] "It makes one sad to visit the

West now," an Alberta MLA told a reporter from the *Toronto Telegram* in 1918. "You see the country being cleared of our fine Anglo-Saxon stock and the alien left to fatten on war prosperity."[35] A Ukrainian woman interviewed for James S. Woodsworth's 1917 report on Ukrainian rural communities revealed the true reason behind English Canadian hostility to Ukrainians and other enemy aliens. "The English do not like us, because we came here as a poor people and now we are wealthy enough to live as we like."[36]

IV

The War-time Elections Act, like the economic prejudice against immigrant minorities, was a continuation and amplification of English Canadian prewar concern about the political influence of newly naturalized citizens from east-central Europe. This concern manifested itself in two antithetic directions. Conservatives deplored the susceptibility of the immigrant to radical ideas and warned of the danger that "these people ... will drift into Socialism." Progressive reformers, on the other hand, lamented the way in which immigrants could be deceived into voting for political machines.[37] Both opinions were based on the same assumption—that the immigrant was a political "problem" because he was incapable of exercising the franchise intelligently. As one advocate of woman's suffrage put it: "Surely my wife is more capable of voting than the ignorant Galician."[38] From this assumption it was a very short step to the conclusion that Canada "should not give the franchise too readily to immigrants who have never lived under free institutions [or] who are ignorant of the responsibilities of citizenship."[39]

War of course increased this concern about the political role of the naturalized citizen. Woman suffragists maintained that "enfranchisement of women would increase the proportion of native born electors," making it easier to deal "with the many serious problems arising from the war."[40] What John English has called "the ideology of service" was used by English Canadians both to justify their leadership of Canada in the war and to legitimize the suggestion that those who did not make an equal contribution should not have an equal voice in Canadian policy.[41] A Saskatchewan resident informed Premier Walter Scott: "Either this newly-enfranchised foreigner should equally do his duty, or ... then he should certainly be disenfranchised."[42]

Thus, when in October 1916 Arthur Meighen proposed that Borden "shift the franchise from the ... anti-British of the male sex and extend it at the same time to our patriotic women,"[43] he was confident that this would appeal to the sentiments of English Canada. What precisely prompted Meighen is unclear, but he was supported by a steady flow of resolutions and editorials, primarily from western Canada, which demanded that the franchise of naturalized enemy aliens be restricted during a wartime election. Businessmen's associations, British fraternal societies and the newly-formed organizations of returned soldiers varied in technique, but the instructions were basically the same: "The Canadian population will not stand for these foreigners having a vote and undermining Canadian National Affairs. . . . Disfranchise all those who have been born in foreign countries that we are at war with today."[44]

Thus, when Borden's government decided to act, the motivation was in part political; the fear that without restrictive legislation it would lose a wartime election. Redistribution after the prairie census of 1916 meant that Manitoba, Saskatchewan and Alberta would have forty-three seats in an election, sixteen more than in 1911. The Manitoba Tory government of Rodmond P. Roblin had been defeated in 1915, and the June 1917 provincial elections in Saskatchewan and Alberta had returned Liberal majorities. In both elections, the question of conscription for overseas service had hurt the provincial Conservatives, whose national party was piloting the Military Service Act past French Canadian opposition in the Commons. The "foreign vote" had been overwhelmingly Liberal since the two provinces entered Confederation in 1905, and as *Robochyi narod* observed, most western Liberals supported the Military Service Act and the principle of compulsory service.[45] To western Conservatives, the elections were "carried principally . . . by Anti-British sentiment," and thus in a federal contest, the Borden government would win only a handful of seats in the west "if the German and Austrian vote is allowed."[46] The only solution, grumbled a defeated Tory candidate in Calgary, was to "comb out every one of those alien enemy voters and take the franchise from them."[47]

The War-time Elections Bill (see Appendix II: 14), introduced by the Borden government in September 1917, disfranchised enemy-alien immigrants naturalized since 1902 and gave the vote to close female relatives of soldiers serving overseas. The bill met with little opposition in the Commons, and was the impetus that pushed western Liberals who supported conscription into the Union Government. One Ontario Liberal, mystified and furious, complained to N. W. Rowell that the same western Liberals who in midsummer had refused to go into Union under Borden were now agreeing to do so, even though "the only alteration that has taken place in Borden's record is that to his former blunders and political misdemeanors he has added this crime [the War-time Elections Act] above all others."[48] Rowell, who was to become a member of the Union cabinet, noted on a tour of the west during the debate on the bill, that there was "much less protest against the act" on the part of Liberals than he had anticipated.[49] Woman's suffragists in the west only protested the act's failure to extend the franchise to all English Canadian women and expressed "indignation that women born under the Union Jack should be numbered among the aliens," unable to vote if they had no close male relative serving in France!⁵⁰

The only serious English-language protests against the franchise manipulation came from Frank Oliver's *Edmonton Bulletin* and from labour newspapers. The *British Columbia Federationist* described the War-time Elections Act as "so repugnant to every principle and concept of common decency as to preclude the possibility of meeting with the approval of any decent, clean-thinking person in the land."⁵¹ Most English Canadians, however, either acquiesced in or approved of the unfair electoral tactic.

The majority of those affected by the War-time Elections Act accepted it with resignation and without protest. Because the act exempted those who lost the franchise from conscription, some Mennonites and Doukhobors even praised it.⁵² *Kanadyiskyi rusyn*, which had urged Ukrainian Canadians to live up to wartime responsibilities, was understandably bitter. Viewing the exemption from conscription as a move to "sugar-coat the pill," *Kanadyiskyi rusyn* declared that "it is honorable to die for the native land [Canada]"; there could be "no worse shame" than to be disfranchised.⁵³ *Ukrainskyi holos* hoped that the humiliation of the War-time Elections Act might "awaken in our masses, now half asleep, the memory of the already-free Ukraine" and perhaps encourage a migration back to Europe.⁵⁴ There would not, however, be any violent protest, for this was not the Ukrainian way. "If you bother a dog, the dog barks," but "if you bother a Ukrainian, he cries."⁵⁵

The same note of self-criticism can be found in some secondary works by Ukrainian authors. In *All of Baba's Children*, for example, Myrna Kostash describes the mild-voiced complaints of Ukrainians against disfranchisement as "the characteristically defensive apology of those who know their place."⁵⁶ The comment is unjust: Ukrainians could hardly affect the attitudes of the English Canadian majority, and a very real danger existed that outspoken protest would provoke a violent counter-attack by veterans' groups and other "patriots."⁵⁷ Most English Canadians felt that the enemy alien had escaped rather lightly, and that the fear of most Ukrainians was not the loss of the franchise, but conscription for military service or into a labour force for prairie agriculture at unreasonably low wages.⁵⁸ Those Ukrainians with titles to homesteads feared with some reason that their property, which the English-speaking westerners so resented, might be confiscated by the Department of Finance and sold at auction by the Alien Property Custodian.⁵⁹

One voice in the Ukrainian Canadian community that did speak out loudly against disfranchisement was *Robochyi narod*. Increasingly more Bolshevik in tone, it denounced the War-time Elections Act as something that could be expected from "capitalist political crooks [and] malicious chauvinistic elements," who would eventually "seek to deprive [enemy aliens] completely of their rights of citizenship."[60] The newspaper, however, did not dwell on the subject. Events in Ukraine and in Russia in autumn 1917 pushed Canadian politics aside, and most Ukrainians strained to follow the convoluted path of the Russian Revolution.[61]

V

The election of 1917 was virtually over before the polls opened on 17 December. The formation of the Union Government doomed critics of conscription within the English Canadian community by dividing Canada along ethnic lines. In western Canada potential Unionist candidates abounded and judicious political management was needed to prevent divisive fights over Unionist nominations.[62] Among the Laurier Liberals, on the other hand, only three sitting members contested their seats. The Unionists took six western constituencies by acclamation, and in six others the Liberals simply endorsed anti-conscription Labour candidates.[63]

The electoral campaign has been described as "a descent into the abyss of French-English violence and prejudice without precedent in Canadian history,"[64] a characterization that applies to both parties and all regions. Only Laurier and Borden tried to add a veneer of civility to the raw campaign rhetoric. As an amalgam of two parties, the Unionists lacked a coherent, centralized party organization, and electoral work was often undertaken by enthusiastic neophytes whose verbal violence was impossible to moderate.[65] Racist slurs and unfounded allegations were common in the speeches and pamphlets of both parties.[66]

Although at least one Unionist candidate promised that a Union Government would conscript enemy aliens,[67] most of the Unionist barbs were directed at the French Canadians, leaving the enemy aliens to join the disfranchised religious pacifists as "passive observers" on the sidelines.[68] One shudders to think, however, what tone the Unionist campaign might have assumed had the Laurier Liberals been able to tap their traditional electoral strength among the immigrant minorities.

A Laurier Liberal landslide in Quebec meant that the Unionists had a narrow majority of only eighteen seats in eastern and central Canada, but in western Canada they swept all before them. On the prairies, forty-one of forty-three seats went to Unionist candidates, and Unionists won more than 70 per cent of the popular vote. Those western farmers and trade unionists who had expressed doubts about conscription, or who had been worried that Union Government was high-tariff Toryism in disguise, set aside their reservations for the "call of the blood" and voted race instead of region or economic class (see Table 1).

TABLE 1 Results of the 1917 Election

	Seats		Popular Vote*			
	Unionists	Laurier Liberals		Unionists		Laurier Liberals**
Manitoba	14	1	c	83,469	c	26,134
			m	23,489	m	1,090
Saskatchewan	16	-	c	70,131	c	29,122
			m	16,230	m	690
Alberta	11	1	c	58,407	c	48,865
			m	19,534	m	1,051
Prairie West	41	2	c	212,007	c	103,121
			m	59,253	m	2,831

* c–civilian vote, m–military vote
** includes Labour vote

The most convincing demonstration of this was the disastrous showing of the seven anti-conscription Labour candidates who contested the election, all but one of whom were endorsed by the Laurier Liberals. Some trade unionists and labour-socialist politicians had criticized conscription from the beginning and had counselled workers to refuse to accept it. Advocates of compulsory military service feared that this opposition might arouse the support of naturalized Germans and Ukrainians. As the *Winnipeg Tribune* put it: "It is simply intolerable to have any note of discord sounded in our midst at this critical juncture" since such "actions and words cannot fail to have a highly pernicious influence upon the minds of the foreign masses of our population."[69] On polling day, English Canadian voters demonstrated that they shared the *Tribune*'s determination not to break ranks before the enemy alien.

Every Labour candidate lost his deposit (see Table 2). All seven constituencies—two in Manitoba, three in Saskatchewan and two in Alberta—went to the government by wide margins. William Irvine, a candidate in Calgary East, came closest to victory with 32 per cent of the vote, while R. A. Rigg in Winnipeg North and James Somerville in Moose Jaw succeeded in winning 26 per cent and 22 per cent respectively. The other candidates lost in humiliating fashion. In Winnipeg Centre, which contained half of Winnipeg's working-class population, R. S. Ward failed to win a single poll, and the British working-class district of Brooklands was lost by 319 votes to 98. In constituencies with no Labour candidates, workers supported the Unionists. In Transcona, Manitoba, a Labour stronghold, Liberal candidate G. J. Charette lost to Unionist R. L. Richardson, 632 votes to 249. While the Ukrainian population was significant in some constituencies with Labour candidates (such as Winnipeg North), it was negligible in others (such as Calgary East); it is impossible, however, to determine what proportion had been disfranchised or how those eligible actually voted.

TABLE 2 **Labour Candidates in Western Constituencies, December 1917**

Constituency	Unionist and Vote	Labour and Vote
Winnipeg Centre	G.W. Andrews	R.S. Ward
	25,580	4,650
Winnipeg North	M.R. Blake	R.A. Rigg
	9,656	3,472
Moose Jaw	J.A. Calder	James Somerville
	8,866	2,946
Saskatoon	J.R. Wilson	James W. Casey
	9,369	1,833
Regina	W.D. Cowan	Andrew MacBeth
	10,563	1,833
Calgary West	Lee Redman	William Irvine
	8,363	3,911
Red Deer	Michael Clark	Joe Knight
	6,213	701
Total	78,610	20,112

SOURCE: Canada, *Sessional Papers*, 1920, no. 13.

In an analysis in *Robochyi narod*, Danylo Lobay bemoaned the electoral trend which the results revealed. "Workers should be embarrassed," he wrote, "not us, not Ukrainian or other foreign nationalities, but English workers. It is a great disgrace, a demonstration of the lack of class-consciousness that the organized workers could not choose even one representative." Why had it happened? Because "'patriotic' workers and farmers, primarily of English background" allowed themselves to come under "the influence of the yellow press and its patriotic outburst."[70] Working-class opposition to conscription had simply not materialized, and English-language labour newspapers recognized this as well, although their comments were considerably milder. The election, said the *Voice*, had revealed "a distinct cleavage of the country on racial lines—a condition that every thoughtful citizen must regard as deplorable."[71]

In his analysis of the election results, John English found that Unionist candidates were generally more successful in rural than in urban areas.[72] Unionist majorities in Manitoba, Saskatchewan and Alberta, however, were larger in the cities than in the countryside. In the three provinces as a whole, Unionists won 76 per cent of the urban popular vote compared to 66 per cent of the rural (see Table 3). In a combined urban-rural constituency like Calgary East, for example, Unionist Lee Redman captured 70 per cent of the votes in the city and only 57 per cent of those in the surrounding farm area. How can the reduced Unionist majorities outside the prairie towns and cities be explained?

TABLE 3 Popular Vote in Rural and Urban Areas of the West, December 1917

		Union	Opposition
Manitoba	Rural	52,580	16,558
	Urban	54,257	10,638
Saskatchewan	Rural	61,478	29,059
	Urban	19,932	4,442
Alberta	Rural	34,213	30,934
	Urban	35,761	18,987
Total	Rural	148,271	76,560
	Urban	109,995	34,067

		% Union	% Opposition
Manitoba	Rural	76.0	24.0
	Urban	83.5	16.5
Saskatchewan	Rural	67.9	32.1
	Urban	77.5	22.5
Alberta	Rural	52.3	47.7
	Urban	64.5	35.5
Total	Rural	65.9	34.1
	Urban	76.3	23.7

SOURCE: Canada, *Sessional Papers*, 1920, no. 13.

The most satisfactory explanation is an ethnic one. The urban working class of Winnipeg, Brandon, Regina, Moose Jaw, Medicine Hat, Edmonton and Calgary was predominantly of British origin, while those naturalized citizens who had not lost their votes were heavily represented in the rural areas, as were the French Canadians.[73] In the only two seats the Laurier Liberals won west of the Ontario-Manitoba border, Provencher in southeastern Manitoba had a French Canadian majority and Victoria in northeastern Alberta had substantial numbers of French Canadians and naturalized Scandinavian and Ukrainian immigrants. A poll by poll examination of the results in all prairie constituencies reveals that these groups provided most of the Laurier Liberal support.

French Canadian voters in the west seem to have been even more united in their opposition to conscription than English Canadians were in their support for it. Four days before the election, Abbé P. E. Myre wrote to W. F. R. Turgeon, attorney general of Saskatchewan, that "le vote canadien français est unanime" throughout the west as in Quebec, and the results supported him.[74] In Provencher, English areas like Dominion City, Sanford and Oak Bluff gave Unionist J. R. Johns 85 per cent of their votes, but 96 per cent of the residents of French settlements like St. Jean Baptist, St. Pierre and La Broquerie voted for the winning candidate, Laurier Liberal, J. P. Malloy. In the poll in St. Malo 100 votes were cast for the Liberal candidate and only two for his Unionist opponent, while in smaller polls like

St. Labre the Unionist was shut out entirely. The pattern was repeated in the French areas of the constituencies which the Unionists won. In Edmonton East, for example, voters in Lac la Biche, Doucette, Charon and Lafond rejected the Unionists, 109 votes to 26. In Marquette constituency, T. A. Crerar's campaign workers blamed their loss in St. Lazare on "the large French and half Breed vote."[75]

Although anti-Unionist and anti-conscription sentiment was less pronounced among naturalized immigrants who still had the franchise than it was among French Canadians, Scandinavians (Icelanders, Swedes and Norwegians) reduced Unionist majorities in constituencies like Selkirk in Manitoba and Humboldt in Saskatchewan. In Victoria constituency in Alberta, Scandinavian settlers like those southeast of Camrose helped Laurier Liberal W. H. White hold the seat against the Unionist tide. Victoria constituency also contained a large number of Ukrainian settlers, and while the number of Ukrainian voters had been reduced by disfranchisement, the vote in areas where Ukrainians had arrived in the 1890s heavily favoured the Laurier Liberal candidate. At Shandro, for example, 12 of 13 votes cast (of a possible 20) went for White. In other polls, however, White received less support than his Unionist opponent (Sniatyn—0 to 2, Lwiw—0 to 3, Zawale—0 to 3, Kolomea—7 to 11), making it difficult to generalize regarding Ukrainian voting patterns.

The American-born were also a factor in several seats in Alberta and seem to have been less convinced of the importance of conscription than the British-born or English Canadian residents of the province. As a result, Unionist candidates in constituencies like Bow River and Battle River had narrower majorities, and Unionist popular vote was lower in Alberta than in Manitoba or Saskatchewan.

Any analysis of the results of the 1917 general election must consider the changes to the franchise. Besides changes through the War-time Elections Act, there was also the Military Voters' Act, which allowed soldiers in Europe to choose the constituency in which they wanted to vote, or to become "voters at large" whose votes for the "government" or the "opposition" could be applied in any constituency. The Unionists have been accused of using the special legislation to carry out "election villainy of the first order," but it seems unlikely that the overall results of the 1917 election would have been very different in Manitoba, Saskatchewan or Alberta had no such legislation existed.[76] Although the military vote was critical in changing the results in eleven constituencies in the Maritimes and Ontario, in the prairie west it overturned the civilian result in only one constituency, Frank Oliver's seat in Edmonton West. Oliver's civilian majority had been less than 100 votes, and the Edmonton area had sent thousands to war; the fact that 2,600 soldiers' votes elected Unionist W. A. Griesbach is hardly evidence of electoral fraud. In fact, had the Unionists wished to manipulate the soldiers' vote in the west, the judicious application of less than 450 ballots could have swept away the Liberal victories in Victoria and Provencher.

Was the War-time Elections Act, then, responsible for the Unionist victory in the west? A statistical analysis is impossible because precise data are not available for male voters disqualified by the act or for women voters added to the electoral list.[77] To complicate matters further, sixteen new constituencies had been created after the election of 1911. Because of the mobility of the Canadian population during that period, estimates of the election results under normal franchise laws are no more than conjecture. Joseph Boudreau's brave attempt in 1965 concluded that, without the act, eleven additional seats would have been won by Laurier Liberals—two in Manitoba, four in Saskatchewan and five in Alberta.[78] Both John English and I have taken issue with this conclusion, since it is based on the total number of enemy aliens resident in each constituency rather than on those who were naturalized, and ignores sex and age qualifications and the percentage turnouts at the polls.[79] After allowing for these factors, my conclusion is that only in Bow River, where Unionist H. H. Halliday edged out Laurier Liberal Jesse Gouge by 312 votes, could the results have been appreciably changed by the votes of the disfranchised. English is more categorical: the act "probably guaranteed not a seat." On election day new women voters added to Unionist majorities, particularly in the cities where mobility was relatively easy in a midwinter election. The staggering Unionist victories in Winnipeg, Brandon, Regina and Saskatoon were in part the result of women voters, but their presence at the polls influenced only the magnitude of the Union success, not the success itself.

The real effect of the War-time Elections Act came not on 17 December, but on 12 October, when Prime Minister Borden announced his Union cabinet. The significance of the franchise legislation is that it pushed reluctant western Liberals toward coalition. With the creation of the Union Government, the last obstacle dividing English Canadians was removed and the task at hand became clear-cut. To G. W. Allan, the Unionist candidate in Winnipeg South who received the largest majority in the country, there were only two issues facing English Canada—"first, the winning of a decisive victory over the Hun, and second, ever lambasting the Province of Quebec on the 17th of December."[80] The English Canadian majority intended to force its tribal will upon the French minority and would brook no opposition from any enemy-alien third parties.

VI

The experience of disfranchisement left its mark on those categorized as enemy aliens. The ease with which a chauvinistic campaign had welded English Canadians in the west into a solid bloc behind the Unionists was a bitter lesson. Ukrainian socialists, in particular, had expected the English Canadian working class to show stronger opposition to conscription, and were disillusioned by the election returns. In August 1917 *Robochyi narod* had predicted that it would not be easy for Borden and Meighen "to ride to office on the conscription pony."[81] In December the newspaper concluded that "English workers themselves didn't know who they were or what they wanted."[82] Events in Canada, as in Russia and Ukraine, served only to place Ukrainian socialists more firmly under Bolshevik influence, and they rejected the moderate labour socialists in the English community.[83] "Let them unite . . . with the A[merican] F[ederation] of L[abour] and its leaders like Gompers," suggested *Robochyi narod*. "Let us take our example from true workers organizations like those . . . in Russia."[84]

From those Ukrainians more influenced by nationalism than Bolshevism, the reaction was less vehement but equally profound. *Ukrainskyi holos* said little about the election result, but predicted that it would "have bad effects for Canada after the war," and that enemy aliens, "belittled by such treatment of their human dignity, will flee to their native lands and . . . shake the dust off their feet in Canadian ports."[85] Renewed warfare in eastern Europe prevented any large-scale exodus and prompted renewed migration to Canada in the 1920s, but the stain of the war years was not easily erased. Ukrainian Canadians closed ranks, more determined than ever to protect themselves. Norman F. Black, principal of Regina Collegiate, noticed this attitude in the parents of his students:

> Some—very many thought five years ago they were really becoming Canadians. . . . Owing to the war and to the questionable franchise legislation for which it is responsible, [they] are now hurt, bewildered, shy and drawing back into their half-discarded alien shells. . . . Between us and them there is arising a pestilential mist of mutual suspicion and dislike that is ominous for the future.[86]

Notes

1. J. C. Hopkins, *Canada at War: A Record of Heroism and Achievement, 1914–1918* (Toronto, 1919), 1.
2. Among the recent studies on Canada during the First World War are J. English, *The Decline of Politics: The Conservatives and the Party System 1901–20* (Toronto, 1977); J. H. Thompson, *The Harvests of War: The Prairie*

West, 1914–18 (Toronto, 1978); B. Wilson, *Ontario and the First World War 1914–1918* (Toronto, 1977); and D. Read and R. Hann, eds., *The Great War and Canadian Society* (Toronto, 1977).

3. See, for example, V. Lysenko, *Men in Sheepskin Coats: A Study in Assimilation* (Toronto, 1947), chapter 18; P. Yuzyk, *The Ukrainians in Manitoba: A Social History* (Toronto, 1953), chapter 13; H. Potrebenko, *No Streets of Gold: A Social History of Ukrainians in Alberta* (Vancouver, 1977), chapter 3; and M. Kostash, *All of Baba's Children* (Edmonton, 1977), chapter 4.

4. This phrase is from the introductory remarks of Professor Manoly R. Lupul to the symposium at which this paper was originally presented.

5. The concentration remained, although as Andrij Makuch points out in Chapter 4, the war did cause interprovincial demographic shifts in the Ukrainian Canadian population.

6. P. F. Sharp, *The Agrarian Revolt in Western Canada* (St. Paul, 1948); M. Robin, "Registration, Conscription, and Independent Labour Politics, 1916–1917," *Canadian Historical Review* 47, no. 2 (June 1966): 101–18; and Potrebenko, *No Streets of Gold*, 122.

7. See, for example, H. S. Ferns and B. Ostry, *The Age of Mackenzie King: The Rise of the Leader* (London, 1955), 242; and D. J. Goodspeed, *The Road Past Vimy* (Toronto, 1969), 124–37.

8. See Potrebenko, *No Streets of Gold*, 120–1.

9. Several authors attribute English Canadian hostility toward Ukrainians almost entirely to the pastoral letter. See, for example, Lysenko, *Men in Sheepskin Coats*, 114–15; and Kostash, *All of Baba's Children*, 46–7. Potrebenko analyses this argument in *No Streets of Gold*, 108–9. The most recent contribution to the discussion, essentially a defence of the bishop, is S. Hryniuk, "The Bishop Budka Controversy: A New Perspective," *Canadian Slavonic Papers* 23, no. 2 (June 1981): 154–65.

10. O. Woycenko, *Ukrainians in Canada* (Winnipeg, 1967), 205–6. See also T. C. Byrne, "The Ukrainian Community in North Central Alberta" (M.A. thesis, University of Alberta, 1937), 33, and *Robochyi narod*, 19 August 1914.

11. *Manitoba Free Press*, 11 August 1914.

12. For a discussion of this question, see chapter 3 by Frances Swyripa.

13. *Ukrainskyi holos*, 3 January 1917; and *Kanadyiskyi rusyn*, 3 January 1917.

14. *Kanadyiskyi rusyn*, 3 January 1917. This and other translations from the Ukrainian-language press are by Elaine Holowach-Amiot, McGill University.

15. *Ukrainskyi holos*, 7 October [*sic*] 1917. (The issue in question is dated incorrectly and should read 7 November 1917. Ed.)

16. Woycenko, *Ukrainians in Canada*, 205–6; and M. Marunchak, *Ukrainian Canadians: A Social History* (Winnipeg, 1970), 327.

17. The chief press censor, E. J. Chambers, and his western representative, Fred B. Livesay, applied steady pressure to the Ukrainian editors throughout the war. See chapter 1 by Peter Melnycky.

18. This resolution was contained in a telegram sent to Governor General H.R.H.

the Duke of Connaught by a convention of Ukrainian Canadians (reported in *Ukrainskyi holos*, 30 August 1916).

19. *Robochyi narod*, 19 August 1914.

20. See N. Makuch, "The Influence of the Ukrainian Revolution on Ukrainians in Canada, 1917–22," *Journal of Ukrainian Graduate Studies* 4, no. 1 (Spring 1979): 45.

21. Alberta, Department of Education, *Tenth Annual Report of the Department of Education, 1915* (Edmonton, 1916), 82.

22. Borden to Matthew Popovich, 16 February 1918, Sir Robert Borden Papers, OC 498, Public Archives of Canada (hereafter PAC), Ottawa, Ontario.

23. *Calgary Daily Herald*, 30 September 1914.

24. *Robochyi narod*, 21 April 1915; and Thompson, *Harvests of War*, 46–8.

25. *Winnipeg Voice*, 15 January 1915.

26. D. Morton, "Sir William Otter and Internment Operations in Canada during the First World War," *Canadian Historical Review* 55, no. 1 (March 1974): 36–8; and J. A. Boudreau, "Western Canada's 'Enemy Aliens' in World War One," *Alberta Historical Review* 12, no. 1, (Winter 1964): 2–3. Even contemporary accounts admitted that "want rather than sedition" was the rationale for internment. See R. H. Coats, "The Alien Enemy in Canada: Internment Operations," in *Canada in the Great World War*, 6 vols. (Toronto, 1917–21), 2: 148–9.

27. See Thompson, *Harvests of War*, 176, and "The Harvest Excursionists, 1890–1929," *Canadian Historical Review* 59, no. 4 (December 1978): 482.

28. *Swift Current Sun*, 8 September 1916.

29. Girvin Grain Growers to Dunning, 22 June 1918, Sir Charles Dunning Papers, 42327, Queen's University Archives, Kingston, Ontario.

30. Irene Parlby to McNaughton, 29 July 1917, Violet McNaughton Papers, D54, Saskatchewan Archives Board (hereafter SAB), Saskatoon, Saskatchewan.

31. *Turner's Weekly*, 12 October 1918.

32. *Robochyi narod*, 2 May 1917.

33. W. P. Dutton to Norris, 12 November 1917, T. C. Norris Papers, Provincial Archives of Manitoba (hereafter PAM), Winnipeg, Manitoba; *Calgary Farm and Ranch Review*, 5 December 1917; and petition of Balcarres Grain Growers, December 1916, Walter Scott Papers, SAB.

34. On economic progress, see Byrne, "Ukrainian Community," 35; J. G. MacGregor, *Vilni Zemli/Free Lands: The Ukrainian Settlement of Alberta* (Toronto, 1969), 252; C. H. Young, *The Ukrainian Canadians: A Study in Assimilation* (Toronto, 1931), 62, 80–1; and Thompson, *Harvests of War*, 85–7. The "Bohunk" comment is from A. G. Storey, *Prairie Harvest* (Toronto, 1959), 102.

35. *Toronto Telegram*, 27 April 1918, cited in Morton, "Otter and Internment," 55.

36. J. S. Woodsworth, dir., "Ukrainian Rural Communities," unpublished report of investigation by the Bureau of Social Research, governments of Manitoba, Saskatchewan and Alberta (Winnipeg, 1917), 48.

37. See, for example, C. H. Lawford, quoted in *ibid.*, 147; J. S. Woodsworth, *Strangers Within Our Gates* (Toronto, 1909), 208; W. A. Griesbach, *I Remember* (Toronto, 1946), 215–17; and Mrs. H. P. Plumptre, "Some Thoughts on the Suffrage in Canada," in *The New Era in Canada*, ed. J. O. Miller (Toronto, 1917), 322.

38. L. St. George Stubbs, quoted in the *Winnipeg Tribune*, 2 February 1912.

39. J. Willison, "Immigration and Settlement," in Miller, *New Era*, 103. See also D. W. Buchanan, *Toward Democracy* (Winnipeg, 1913), 34–5, 56–7; and R. L. Scott, *Direct Legislation* (Winnipeg, 1913), 21. In fact, Austria-Hungary had been a constitutional monarchy since 1867, which guaranteed its subjects certain basic rights. In the late nineteenth and early twentieth centuries, Ukrainian political parties in Galicia multiplied, while in 1907 universal male suffrage was introduced for elections to the Reichsrat in Vienna, and on the eve of the First World War electoral reforms to the Galician provincial diet in Lviv were passed. For a discussion of Ukrainian political life and national awakening in Galicia during this period, see I. L. Rudnytsky, "The Ukrainians in Galicia under Austrian Rule," *Austrian History Yearbook* 3, part 2 (1967): 394–429.

40. "Reasons Why Women Should be Enfranchised," 1916, and circular signed by Nellie McClung and Mrs. M.A. Lawton, 1916, McNaughton Papers, file E18, SAB.

41. English, *Decline of Politics*, chapter 6.

42. E. A. W. R. Mackenzie to Scott, 10 July 1916, Scott Papers, 14135, SAB.

43. Cited in R. Graham, *Arthur Meighen*, 3 vols. (Toronto, 1960–5), 1: 165.

44. G. M. Newton to G. H. Bradbury (copy), 18 May 1917, Borden Papers, PAC. Similar sentiments may be found elsewhere in this collection, and R.B. Bennett read a letter with much the same content to the House of Commons, 16 May 1917. Canada, *Parliamentary Debates* (Commons), 127, 2(1917): 1515.

45. *Robochyi narod*, 27 June 1917. For an examination of these elections, see J. W. Brennan, "A Political History of Saskatchewan 1905–29" (Ph.D. thesis, University of Alberta, 1976); and L. G. Thomas, *The Liberal Party in Alberta 1905–1921* (Toronto, 1959).

46. H. H. Campbell to Martin, 28 June 1917, William Martin Papers, 24339, SAB; J. H. Harvey to Meighen (copy), 22 June 1917, Borden Papers, 39768, PAC; and minutes of the Manitoba Conservative executive meeting, 10 August 1917, R. A. C. Manning Papers, PAM.

47. Thomas Tweedie, cited in the *Calgary Daily Herald*, 19 May 1917.

48. A. D. Bruce to Rowell, 17 October 1917, N. W. Rowell Papers, 2012, PAC.

49. Rowell to F. F. Pardee, 19 September 1917, Rowell Papers, 1898, PAC. See also R. Cook, *The Politics of J.W. Dafoe and the Free Press* (Toronto, 1963), 80–1.

50. Mrs. Ralph Smith, quoted in the *Manitoba Free Press*, 5 October 1917; see also *Calgary Nutcracker*, 14 September 1917.

51. Cited in A. R. McCormack, *Reformers, Rebels and Revolutionaries: The Western Canadian Radical Movement 1899–1919* (Toronto, 1977), 135.

52. A. Sawatzky, "The Mennonites of Alberta and their Assimilation" (M.A. thesis, University of Alberta, 1964), 76–7; E. K. Francis, *In Search of Utopia* (Glencoe, Illinois, 1955), 189–90; and Peter Makaroff to Meighen (copy), 6 September 1917, Sir Clifford Sifton Papers, PAC.

53. *Kanadyiskyi rusyn*, 3 October 1917.

54. *Ukrainskyi holos*, 26 September 1917.

55. *Ibid.*, 23 May 1917. In Chapter 3, Frances Swyripa notes, however, that Ukrainian contributions to wartime charities like the Patriotic Fund dropped off in response to disfranchisement.

56. Kostash, *All of Baba's Children*, 50.

57. For descriptions of such fears, see J. A. Boudreau, "The Enemy Alien Problem in Canada, 1914–1921" (Ph.D. thesis, University of California, Los Angeles, 1965), 580; and M. K. Mott, "The Foreign Peril: Nativism in Winnipeg, 1916–23" (M.A. thesis, University of Manitoba, 1970).

58. See, for example, the editorial in the *Swift Current Sun*, 7 September 1917.

59. This happened to enemy alien nationals who were interned. See M. Nordegg, *The Possibilities of Canada are Truly Great: Memoirs 1906–1924*, ed. T. D. Regehr (Toronto, 1971), 216–30; and *Canadian Annual Review* (1918): 580–1.

60. *Robochyi narod*, 5 September 1917; and O.T. Martynowych, "The Ukrainian Socialist Movement in Canada 1900–18," *Journal of Ukrainian Graduate Studies* 2, no. 1 (Spring 1977): 27–8.

61. Makuch, "Influence of the Ukrainian Revolution," 42–61.

62. Thompson, *Harvests of War*, 133–4; and English, *Decline of Politics*, 163–72.

63. This and all subsequent electoral statistics are from "Return of the Thirteenth General Election for the House of Commons," published as *Sessional Paper 13* for 1920.

64. Graham, *Meighen*, 1: 188.

65. English, *Decline of Politics*, 172–85.

66. For examples of the campaign rhetoric, see J. M. Beck, *Pendulum of Power* (Scarborough, 1968), 141–4.

67. *Robochyi narod*, 8 December 1917.

68. Boudreau, "Enemy Alien Problem," 155–6.

69. *Winnipeg Tribune*, 26 January 1917.

70. *Robochyi narod*, 19 December 1917.

71. *Winnipeg Voice*, 21 December 1917.

72. English, *Decline of Politics*, 196–7.

73. Canada, Bureau of Statistics, *Census of Prairie Provinces, 1916* (Ottawa, 1918); and *Sixth Census of Canada, 1921*, 5 vols. (Ottawa, 1924–5).

74. Myre to Turgeon, 13 December 1917, W.F.R. Turgeon Papers, SAB.

75. W. C. O'Keeffe to Crerar, 18 December 1917, Thomas Crerar Papers, Queen's University Archives.

76. This phrase is from W. T. R. Preston, *My Generation of Politics and Politicians* (Toronto, 1927), 235. The best examination of the conduct of the

soldiers' vote is D. Morton, "Polling the Soldier Vote: The Overseas Campaign in the Canadian General Election of 1917," *Journal of Canadian Studies* 10, no. 4 (November 1975): 39–58.

77. See English's comments, *Decline of Politics*, 196.
78. Boudreau, "Enemy Alien Problem," 150–3.
79. Thompson, *Harvests of War*, 143–4; and English, *Decline of Politics*, 198. Boudreau's review of the former suggests that he considers these points well-taken (*Social History/Histoire Sociale* 12, no. 24 [November 1979]: 494–5).
80. Allan to Crerar, 4 December 1917, Crerar Papers, Queen's University Archives.
81. *Robochyi narod*, 15 August 1917.
82. *Ibid.*, 19 December 1917.
83. Martynowych, "Ukrainian Socialist Movement," 28–30; and D. H. Avery, *"Dangerous Foreigners": European Immigrant Workers and Labour Radicalism in Canada, 1896–1932* (Toronto, 1979), chapter 3. The English-speaking labour movement had disappointed Ukrainian radicals before by its failure to protest the firings of Ukrainian workers by "patriotic" employers and by its support in Manitoba of unilingual education.
84. *Robochyi narod*, 19 December 1917.
85. *Ukrainskyi holos*, 26 December 1917.
86. Black to Scott, 1 July 1918, Scott Papers, SAB. For a similar comment by a Ukrainian Canadian, see W. J. Sisler, *Peaceful Invasion* (Winnipeg, 1944), 93.

Chapter 3

The Ukrainian Image:
Loyal Citizen or Disloyal Alien

Frances Swyripa

For over two decades before the First World War, Anglo-Canadian
society had viewed the Ukrainian immigrants with ambivalence—desirable
as labourers and agriculturalists but possessing "questionable" ideals and
ways of life. When these "foreigners" became enemy aliens, their new
official status reinforced an existing negative public stereotype. Together
they determined the treatment Ukrainians received from Canadian society
and its attitudes toward them over the next four years. Ukrainian loyalty
and participation in Canada's war effort were issues of concern primarily in
the three Prairie provinces where most Ukrainians lived. Here the debate in
the Anglo-Canadian press was matched by the rhetoric of Ukrainian
spokesmen representing different religious and political camps. Verbal arguments, however, were only one standard by which to measure Ukrainian
identification with the Canadian war effort. A more accurate yardstick of
sentiments at the grassroots level was the Ukrainian response to patriotic
work and military recruitment.

I

In the opening months of the war editorials in the Anglo-Canadian press
in western Canada, when they referred to the Ukrainians at all, regarded
the question of loyalty from two perspectives. The first, confident in the
superiority of British institutions, automatically assumed that the

Ukrainians supported Britain, as victory would bring to their homeland the liberties discovered in Canada. The second, harsher in tone, exacted loyalty:

> They [immigrants from Germany and Austria] have made this their country, they were welcomed with open arms, they have been admitted to all the great opportunities for material prosperity which Canada affords, and they have pursued those opportunities unhampered by conditions from which they were so anxious to escape. They have enjoyed a liberty unknown in their own country. They will not be interfered with so long as they respect the laws under which they are given protection. We cannot, however, tolerate any playing fast and loose with our hospitality.[1]

Initial doubts about Ukrainian loyalties arose primarily from suspicions aroused by the actions of prominent Ukrainians. The unfortunate pastoral letter of the recently-appointed Ukrainian Catholic bishop, Nykyta Budka, is a case in point (see Appendix I: 1–2).[2] The activities of Paul Crath (Pavlo Krat),[3] who had founded the Society for an Independent Ukraine in late July 1914, also earned the Ukrainians unwelcome publicity. Two incidents in Edmonton involving Crath are particularly interesting examples of the tactics adopted by Russophile Ukrainians to discredit the nationally conscious sector of the Ukrainian community before the Canadian public. As Austrian Ukrainians who claimed to be ethnically Russian and sought to unite Habsburg Ukrainian territories with the Russian empire, the Russophiles exploited the opportunity provided by the war to expose the traditional anti-Russian bias of most Austrian Ukrainians and to label them a danger to Canada.

The first allegation of disloyalty against Crath came in August 1914 after he had addressed a Ukrainian meeting in Edmonton to protest Budka's original letter. Edmonton's newspapers, reporting that Crath had counselled his compatriots against enlisting, cried treason; Crath's supporters retaliated by accusing "catzaps provocateurs" (that is, local Russophiles) of having sent a deliberately falsified account of the meeting to the press.[4] In September at a speech in Edmonton and Vegreville on behalf of the Society for an Independent Ukraine, Crath insisted that Ukraine had to be freed from both Austria and Russia, in essence advocating the breakup of the Russian empire, Britain's ally. This drew fresh accusations of treason and the charge that he was an Austrian agent. The *Edmonton Bulletin* warned:

> Canada is Canada, and those who become Canadian citizens are expected to limit their activities to Canada and to Canada's place and duty in the British Empire. Whether Ukraine is to become a republic, or a province of Russia or Austria is none of Canada's business, and whoever tries to carry on in Canada a propaganda for settling the political status of the Ukraine is making trouble for Canada and therefore for himself.[5]

Some reports even claimed that Crath wanted to establish a Ukrainian state in Canada; the *Vegreville Observer* noted that "Mr. Krat's argument is that now, while Great Britain is at war, is a favourable time for the Ukrainians of the west, some fifty thousand in number to throw off British rule, and to organize a Ukrainian nation here in Canada."[6] The final act in the controversy began in early October when the *Bulletin* published a translation of a circular, distributed by the Society for an Independent Ukraine before the war, suggesting it supported Austrian over Russian goals. After a dispute over the accuracy of the translation, the group responsible for giving it to the *Bulletin* and whether its aim was to discredit the Ukrainians through deliberate distortion, the newspapers abruptly dropped the entire matter.[7] Because the Edmonton press shielded its informants, charges of behind-the-scenes Russophile manipulation cannot be proven, but the vocabulary of the written evidence and the nature of the incidents strongly suggest it.

It is doubtful whether Crath's activities would have received such publicity had they not been brought to the attention of the Anglo-Canadian press, which reacted as anticipated. Apparently unaware that their attitude toward the Ukrainians had been manipulated, Anglo-Canadians were psychologically prepared to find "treason" in the new, unfamiliar situation of war and thus played into Russophile hands. Perhaps the best proof of the absence of serious doubts about Crath's loyalty is his appointment in 1915 as a translator in the office of the press censor for western Canada.

The *Bulletin*'s publication of the disputed circular sparked a spirited defence of Ukrainian loyalties by J. K. Smith, a missionary among the Ukrainians in Alberta. Provoked by insinuations of disloyalty against Mykhailo Belegay, editor of the Methodist Ukrainian-language newspaper, *Kanadyiets* (Canadian), Smith was sweeping in his assurances:

> And, furthermore, whatever may be said of the attitude of a few demagogues who seem to love agitation much more than hard work, I wish to testify that among the many, laborers of the Ruthenian people, especially among the farmers there is no lack of loyalty. Sorrowful as they are in thoughts of the suffering of the closest loved ones of the old land, who they would fain have near them now, they are still british [*sic*] to the core and openly say so.[8]

Smith was not the only Protestant clergyman to champion Ukrainian loyalty, while the Catholic Truth Society of Canada also strived to restore the reputation of Bishop Budka.[9] Canadian patriotic organizations, on the other hand, did not usually translate their concern for the foreigner's impact on Canadian national life into equal concern for his loyalty as an enemy alien—no doubt because their energies were absorbed by more urgent war work.[10]

The major domestic political issue to touch the Ukrainians during the war years was the abolition of bilingual schools in Manitoba in 1916. In the debate, the English-language press brought forth a new argument—insistence on bilingual schools was a sign of disloyalty in time of war. "Our brothers, fathers and sons are dying or being maimed on the battlefields of France and Belgium for the ideals of a British not a Galician Canada,"[11] thundered one editor in support of "English only" in Manitoba's schools. In presentations to the Norris government on behalf of the "Russians" of Manitoba, the Winnipeg Russophile community portrayed the Ukrainians as a pro-German political party conducting anti-Russian propaganda behind the walls of the Ruthenian Training School in Brandon.[12] Ukrainian hostility to the abolition of the bilingual system, the *Manitoba Free Press* explained, was due to selfish agitators exploiting wartime measures against enemy aliens to arouse a sense of grievance among the masses of loyal Ukrainians.[13]

For much of 1916, under the influence of Ukrainian-English antagonism over bilingual schools and possibly Russophile arguments, the *Manitoba Free Press* challenged the loyalty of the Ukrainian leadership. It noted that Ukrainian spies from the United States with official Austrian connections were apparently spreading propaganda among Ukrainians in western Canada. One such "spy" was George Raffalovich;[14] a second was Dr. Semen Demydczuk, a delegate of the General Ukrainian Council in Vienna to Ukrainians in America.[15] The latter, for example, was accused of inciting Ukrainian unrest to divert military attention from the task overseas and to hinder Ukrainian enlistment. He also reportedly used the bait of "a free Ukraine" to encourage the postwar repatriation of Austrian Ukrainians, in order to obtain their American wealth for reconstruction. The *Free Press* also blamed government lethargy for permitting Orest Zerebko, who had returned to Canada in 1916 after extensive travel in Europe and who was said to have ties with Raffalovich and Demydczuk, to join the staff of the influential *Ukrainskyi holos* (Ukrainian Voice). It criticized the government for failing to deal with "enemy propaganda aimed at subverting a quarter of a million loyal Canadian citizens" while "having herded the ignorant and generally innocent classes into internment camps and ... left the leaders, the brains of the organization at large."[16]

Spies aside, other incidents during the first two years of the war briefly thrust the Ukrainians onto centre stage. When a campaign launched in the spring of 1914 to aid flood victims in Galicia was transformed into a fund to assist Ukrainians in both Austria and Russia after the war, rumours spread of an active and seditious Austrian war fund in western Canada. More than one subscriber was arrested, although the arrests were due more to rival Ukrainian factions, making use of the law and public wartime uneasiness, than hysterical Anglo-Canadians. In Alberta, for example, a dispute over the proceeds from a Christmas play, originally slated for the "After the War Fund," broke out when a dissenter had the organizer arrested for collecting money for an "Austrian War Fund." The court in this case ruled that as the money was intended for the Ukrainian people, and the Ukrainians in Russia outnumbered those in Austria, the man had not acted against the British empire.[17] In Vonda, Saskatchewan, however, a subscriber to the "After the War Fund" was less fortunate. At his trial, according to the newspaper account, "various Ruthenians, Galicians and Austrians of the district" had testified that "the collection was being made by agents of the Austrian government and being forwarded to Austria through 'The Canadian Ruthenian' [the Ukrainian Catholic organ]." Following an outcry from several Anglo-Canadians against the conviction, a police investigation concluded that the report of a fund to assist the enemies of the Allies had no foundation and probably arose from "some misunderstanding."[18]

Attitudes toward enemy aliens hardened when returning veterans failed to find work. As 1917 unfolded, veterans' meetings across Canada, endorsed by patriotic organizations and a host of other groups, demanded the disfranchisement and military and labour conscription of enemy aliens. Bitterness grew when the War-time Elections Act exempted disfranchised enemy aliens from military conscription, leaving them free to profit further from wartime prosperity. In January 1918 the Great War Veterans' Association in Edmonton passed a series of anti-alien resolutions, including requests for the conscription of disfranchised enemy aliens for essential industry, monthly reporting, restriction of movement and a prohibition on enemy-alien acquisition of farm land. Greatly alarmed, Ukrainian farmers met in Vegreville to protest the resolutions and to seek assurances that their rights would be protected. After meeting with a Ukrainian delegation, Prime Minister Borden gave the desired promises. "The . . . assurances of the Government should go far toward removing the doubts and fears of the Ukrainian settlers," the *Vegreville Observer* declared, at the same time warning: "It is more than likely that in the future other causes of alarm will arise but if they keep their heads level, give no reason for offense, there is equally no doubt that the good sense of the country at large will be exerted to extend fair play and decent treatment to them."[19]

As anti-alien government measures and public sentiments escalated in Canada, the collapse of tsarist Russia altered the Ukrainian situation in Europe. Ukrainian Canadians grew more vocal on both accounts. The *Vegreville Observer*, for one, adopted a protective and advisory posture toward its Ukrainian neighbours, repeatedly counselling them to do or to say nothing to strengthen the hands of those already questioning their loyalty—polite but blunt advice to accept the repressive measures the country had imposed.[20] Elsewhere, particularly with the signing of the Treaty of Brest-Litovsk in February 1918, articles and editorials in the

Anglo-Canadian press aired the Ukrainian question.[21] In general a temporarily high international profile and local publicity resulted in greater and more accurate knowledge of Ukraine and its people. A letter to the *Edmonton Bulletin* from Mundare, in the heart of the Ukrainian bloc in Alberta, asking if there were many Ukrainians in Canada, is both highly ironic and indicative of this growing awareness of Ukrainians outside their Galician and Ruthenian guise.[22]

There was little indication, however, that the Anglo-Canadian public was any more conscious of Ukrainian-Russophile differences or how they influenced its perception of the immigrant community. The publication in western newspapers of anti-Ukrainian resolutions passed by "Russian" conventions provoked no editorial comment. The *Vegreville Observer* was unique in reprinting an English-language article from the Edmonton Russophile newspaper, *Russkii holos*, which fanned a heated controversy in its pages between the editor of *Russkii holos* and a local Ukrainian, Peter Svarich. The offending article denounced the Ukrainian Hetmanate of the spring of 1918 as a German political creation and warned English Canadians to monitor the activities of Ukrainians in Canada; according to Svarich, it had been "distributed broadcast among the veterans and mailed to prominent English publications and the Members of Parliament in order to create ill-feeling of English people against the Ukrainians." The *Observer* remained neutral in the debate, claiming ignorance, but some two months after it had begun the whole affair, censured both sides for hyphenated Canadianism.[23] Svarich's charge had considerable foundation, however, for with the collapse of the Russian empire and dual threat of Bolshevism and Ukrainian independence, the Russophile community stepped up its anti-Ukrainian agitation.

As events in Ukraine, coupled with enemy-alien status and new federal restrictions, helped to crystallize "Ukrainianness" in Canada, onlookers marked a change in Ukrainian attitudes toward Canadian society. The Ukrainians, as a discouraged Presbyterian worker in Alberta observed, were pulling back:

> Attendance at the services [1917] has not been so encouraging as in former years. Local discords have been more frequent and bitter, and indifference towards the superintendent of the mission have been added to the problems and burdens of the missionary. Since the political revolution in Russia, together with other real and imaginary grievances, many of these people have become independent and sullen towards Canadian institutions and sometimes towards Canadian people. This is augmented by the growth and increasing influence of the Ruthenian nationalist organization and its slogan "No assimilation by the English."[24]

This spontaneous withdrawal had more serious consequences for those dedicated to the prosecution of the war, for Ukrainian monetary contributions to patriotic causes fell off in 1917–18. With the change in attitude affecting the objectives of the larger society, Anglo-Canadian attacks against "nationalist agitators," exploiting wartime conditions to alienate their people, increased. For regardless of the rhetoric over Ukrainian loyalty, and in spite of their enemy-alien status, the Ukrainians were expected to participate in the Canadian war effort.

II

Throughout the war the Canadian Patriotic Fund, established to assist financially dependent relatives of men on active service, the Red Cross and the Victory Loans operated on the basis of voluntary contribution. Local branches or committees, responsible for regular canvassing and organization of work in their districts, naturally sought a broad base and in ethnically mixed areas included "enemy-alien" territory in their campaigns. Generally speaking, the Ukrainian population responded positively, if not always as generously as the Anglo-Canadian majority desired.

Ukrainian newspapers like *Ukrainskyi holos* and *Kanadyiskyi rusyn* (Canadian Ruthenian) did not identify as closely with the Patriotic Fund and the Red Cross as did the Anglo-Canadian press, although they published subscription lists and editorials on their work. The Ukrainian Protestant press, firmly under Anglo-Canadian influence, was more vocal. "Is it not our responsibility to look after ... [the soldiers' dependants] and to protect them from misery, cold and hunger?" *Kanadyiets* asked.

> If we have not gone to fight, then we must take care of these widows and poor orphans, whose fathers have gone to fight for us.
>
> In all Canada money is being collected for the Patriotic Fund for these widows and orphans. Some give money, others give in kind, but all give. AND HAVE YOU GIVEN TO THIS FUND YET? IF NOT, THEN GIVE BECAUSE THESE WIDOWS AND ORPHANS ARE WAITING FOR YOU![25]

While Ukrainian monetary contributions to the war effort were also not regular features in the English-language press, they received sufficient coverage to be noticed. Such news items often commended the tangible proof of Ukrainian loyalty; the collection of $24.30 at Vonda for the Red Cross, for instance, was described as "but another example of the loyalty of the Ruthenian population to the north of this point." "Ruthenians Give Largely to War Fund—$437 Collected at Meeting in Hafford," read another headline. Much less publicized were such donations as the fifty dollars from Ruthenian workers at Stony Mountain recorded in the books of the Manitoba division of the Red Cross Society.[26] It would appear, however, that Ukrainian participation in Patriotic Fund and Red Cross work was best documented and most publicized in Alberta.

The presence of locally influential Ukrainian "middlemen," their authority acknowledged by their own people and the Anglo-Canadian elite, ensured that Ukrainians in the large bloc settlement east of Edmonton would be mobilized behind the war effort. Shortly after patriotic work was organized in Vegreville, for example, Peter Svarich chaired a Ukrainian meeting to appoint committees to collaborate with the main Vegreville Patriotic Fund and to represent Ukrainian women in Red Cross work in the town. Besides being active in Ukrainian affairs, several committee members enjoyed ties with the Anglo-Canadian community, both Svarich and Maxim Zalizniak being closely connected with the Presbyterian Ukrainian mission in Vegreville.[27] The selection of Peter Kolmatycki as one of three men to occupy the platform when the national Fund secretary launched the 1916 campaign in Vegreville marked another instance of the intermediary function of these Ukrainians and the town's strategy to secure Ukrainian support. During the 1917 campaign, one-third of the collectors in the slackening rural areas were Ukrainians, including Svarich who covered several townships.[28] Clearly, the intent was to increase subscriptions in Ukrainian districts by using Ukrainian canvassers and assigning positions of prestige for the group's leaders, who obviously accepted and perhaps sought their role.

Anglo-Canadians were not alone in advocating this approach to stimulate Ukrainian interest in fund-raising schemes. *Ukrainskyi holos* applauded the appointment of Svarich, Kolmatycki and Nykola Nykyforuk to the Patriotic Fund subscriptions committee in Vegreville, adding that "Ukrainians should also become members of... [other similar] committees so that where matters concern our people, a Ukrainian who understands his people and whom the people understand should be in charge of affairs."[29] It was no doubt this philosophy that lay behind the profusion of Ukrainian names on Red Cross executive committees in Manitoba by mid-1918, in districts with a substantial number of Ukrainians.[30] The use of prominent Ukrainians was not restricted to the rural blocs; Andrew Shandro, elected to the Alberta legislature in 1913, attended at least one patriotic meeting in the coal mining town of Cardiff to address the local "Russian" population.[31]

Ukrainians in the Vegreville bloc contributed to the Patriotic Fund and Red Cross through established channels, held special fund-raising functions and canvassed their compatriots for direct donations. On the eve of the general election which saw many Ukrainians disfranchised, a correspondent to the *Vegreville Observer* noted tersely: "Red Cross Day at Mundare netted $250. Who said the Ruthenians were unpatriotic?"[32] In spite of such evidence that voluntary Ukrainian support was both forthcoming and acknowledged in Anglo-Canadian circles, the Department of Extension at the University of Alberta expended considerable energy to loosen Ukrainian purse strings; its evening entertainment packages of lantern slide shows and war lectures to raise money for the Patriotic Fund and the Red Cross were regular features in the bloc colony.[33]

For Patriotic Fund purposes, northern and southern Alberta were organized by electoral district under the sitting member; the province's portion of the total amount required annually by the Fund was raised by assessing for each unit a sum determined by its affluence and population. Thus, whether willing or not and regardless of their enemy-alien status, the Ukrainians were automatically included in Patriotic Fund activities, especially in constituencies where they made up a significant proportion of the residents. The greatest mobilization of the Ukrainians behind the war effort occurred in the electoral district of Whitford, where Andrew Shandro represented his countrymen. It was here in particular that the Ukrainians' response to the Patriotic Fund was lauded as proof of their loyalty.

Most of the Slavs in Whitford constituency were Ukrainians from Galicia and Bukovyna, but many belonged to the Orthodox church (manned in Canada by Russian missionaries from the United States) and had pro-Russian leanings. Until early 1917 the Bukovynian-born Shandro was also a Russophile. In the spring of 1916, when he assured the Alberta legislature of the loyalty of the "300,000 Russo-Austrians" in Canada, he stated that

> he had been born in Austria, but was of Russian nationality,... [and] could not understand why the people of Canada called them Ruthenians. That was the German name for Russians, and it was part of the scheme of the Germanization of the Austrian Empire that the people of Bukowina, where he and his countrymen came from, were given that name.[34]

Although the Mundare-based *Postup* (Progress) attacked Shandro's statement,[35] no Ukrainians responded in the English-language press where the impact would have been greater. Although Shandro later recanted his Russophilism in *Ukrainskyi holos* (3 January 1917), he did not do so in the English newspapers or the legislature in Alberta. Neither did he explain or withdraw his earlier comments, the like of which were used to accuse the Ukrainians of disloyalty and Austrianism. Letters in *Ukrainskyi holos* criticized his failure to censure the Russophiles.[36]

Anxious to demonstrate his own loyalty and that of the "Russo-Austrians," Shandro flung himself into Patriotic Fund work. He launched an ambitious personal campaign in 1916, conducting thirty-seven schoolhouse meetings in less than one month. He later told the legislature that "at three Christmas parties he had collected $430 ... from Russian laborers who were not even naturalized," and that "his countrymen willingly contributed what they could, as they valued the privilege of living under the British flag and in a free country."[37] Shandro's organization of his constituency for the 1917 campaign, when growing numbers of Albertans were clamouring for the Patriotic Fund to be raised by taxation, was more thorough. In September 1916 the Canadian Patriotic Fund, Whitford Branch, was established with Shandro as president and Arthur M. Boutillier as secretary. The councillors (mostly Ukrainians) of each improvement district formed the executive in their jurisdiction, with the secretary-treasurer serving as local Fund treasurer. It was "respectfully requested that all clergymen, school teachers, school treasurers and trustees in Whitford district attach themselves to this executive, and assist it greatly by their ardent cooperation."[38] A circular letter, stressing the importance of the Fund in "Russian," English and Romanian, went to everyone in the constituency and each quarter section was assessed the sum of five dollars.

By this means Whitford exceeded its assessed levy of $4,000 by $2,700.[39] The official bulletin of the Patriotic Fund praised Shandro as "an enthusiastic supporter of the Fund since its beginnings ... anxious to see his people realize the privileges they enjoy under the Canadian flag."[40] Not all "Shandro's people," however, were equally enthusiastic. Workers reported occasional indifference or refusal to pay. One individual had to be told "that those unfriendly to the Patriotic Fund are unfriendly to the country and by being so give comfort to the enemy—which is treason." Others were said to give their five dollars grudgingly while "smilingly tak[ing] 10 and 10½ cents per pound for their hogs."[41]

To those who saw Ukrainian contributions to the Patriotic Fund and Red Cross as proof of their loyalty and thus right to fair treatment, the War-time Elections Act was a blow. Disfranchisement became an obstacle to fund-raising in Ukrainian settlements. The *Vegreville Observer* explained:

> The War Franchise Act is another rap at the Patriotic Fund ... the Ruthenians of Whitford have been fairly generous in their support of the Fund; perhaps not overwhelmingly generous but fairly so. Now that the government has questioned their loyalty, has deprived them of their votes, has treated them more scurvily than any people were ever before treated in this country, it is too much to expect from them that they will rally as heretofore in loyal support of the Patriotic Fund.[42]

At a meeting of the Northern Alberta Branch of the Canadian Patriotic Fund in late September 1917, Shandro charged that Prussianism had followed his people to Canada. George P. Smith, MLA for Camrose, a constituency with a large Ukrainian population that had contributed twice its assessed amount to the Fund, also spoke:

> We have worked year after year with these people, ... and had at last got them to realize what British liberty and British institutions stood for. They had become loyal citizens and contributed loyally and generously to the Patriotic Fund. Now all our work has been swept away in an instant.[43]

Facing escalating demands on all fronts to abandon the voluntary system in favour of taxation, the meeting argued that the War-time Elections Act would hurt collections and asked the federal government to assume immediate responsibility for the Fund. Thus, ironically, an anticipated decrease in its voluntary support base—with the alienation of a largely Ukrainian disfranchised and enemy-alien population—became the official justification for Northern Alberta's demand to change the status of the Canadian Patriotic Fund.

Its fears regarding future Ukrainian contributions to patriotic work were not groundless. As the War-time Elections Act was implemented and some veterans vented their frustrations on enemy aliens, others marked a growing distance between the Ukrainians and Canadian activities. In 1918, for example, in the wake of the anti-alien resolutions passed by the Great War Veterans' Association in Edmonton, Boutillier warned Ottawa that rumours of new repressive measures were affecting Red Cross and other war-related collections in the Whitford area. Locally, Boutillier tried to cajole the Ukrainians into good behaviour and continued support of the war effort. He pointed out that residence in Canada had saved them from three and one-half years of "misery, ruin and desolation":

> They sure will become anxious to show their keen appreciation and thankfulness by seeking and doing those things that are for our national welfare.
>
> What is more in the national interest at the present time, and more pleasing to the authorities than our subscriptions to the Canadian Red Cross Society? Let us make generous donations and from whole hearts. Let each and every man do his share. Then depend upon it, the authorities will have nothing but good-will toward us, and will be glad to express their pleasure.[44]

Outside Alberta, Ukrainian participation in patriotic fund raising drives also wavered. In Saskatchewan in late 1918, with a new Victory Loan in the offing, the Reverend Sigmund Bychinsky of Canora proposed to Premier Martin that Ukrainian committees be established to canvass among Saskatchewan Ukrainians. They "could do more efficient work than committees of English speaking people who do not understand and very little know the Ukrainian farmer as was proven in last year's campaign," he argued. No doubt the former Independent Greek priest's status as a Presbyterian minister, which placed him under Anglo-Canadian influence, affected Bychinsky's desire to see his fellow Ukrainians support the Victory Loan. In yet another alliance between Anglo-Canadian and Ukrainian to promote Ukrainian patriotic work, the Reverend G. A. Hackney urged Martin to help Bychinsky and his group to prove their loyalty. Martin, for his part, when he informed the prime minister of Bychinsky's request, identified the Ukrainian as a "man of good type" with "the proper view with regard to the Canadianizing of our new settlers."[45]

III

There was one more certain test of loyalty than participation in the Patriotic Fund, Red Cross and other war-related ventures, and that was to offer one's life for Canada and the British empire. The number of Ukrainians who served in the Canadian armed forces during the Great War is unknown. Shortly before Armistice, Budka claimed that some two thousand had volunteered and fought under the British flag, but as he had quoted the same figure two years earlier, it loses its authority. Other contemporary estimates placed Ukrainian enlistment by 1916 at 750 in Winnipeg and 450 in Alberta (mostly from the Edmonton and Vermilion districts). The *Manitoba Free Press* maintained that a large number of Ukrainian volunteers came from the small Protestantized sector of the community, under direct Anglo-Canadian influence.[46] A total figure of 10,000 Ukrainian servicemen, including two thousand from Russian Ukraine, has been generally accepted. Given the confusion of nationality, the Canadian military's laxness in recording the birthplaces or ethnic origins of the nation's soldiers and the present inaccessibility of individual personnel records, perhaps no greater accuracy can be expected.[47]

Ukrainian enlistment in the Canadian Expeditionary Force served two purposes. To Ukrainians, it justified their right to better treatment from Canadian society and removal of the enemy-alien stigma. Second, it provided ammunition for those Anglo-Canadians who believed in the Ukrainians' loyalty as Canadians and British subjects and wished to convince others likewise.

The fact that significant numbers of their young men had volunteered for overseas service augmented the sense of grievance in many Ukrainian Canadian circles. In the summer of 1916, following its adoption by a mass meeting in Winnipeg, six Ukrainian newspapers issued an "Address to the Canadian People," demanding the release of Ukrainian internees and abolition of enemy-alien status. "Thousands of our Ukrainian boys have enlisted with the Canadian overseas force, and many have already lost their lives fighting beside their English brethren on the battlefields of France," it argued, "and as the price of their blood we have the right to ask the Canadian people for better treatment of the Canadian Ukrainians" (see Appendix I: 3). These sentiments were echoed the following year when a resolution of the Second National Convention in Saskatoon requested the restoration of Ukrainian rights and privileges because the Ukrainians "have sent voluntarily thousands of their young men to the front, who are now fighting and dying for the cause of the Allies" (see Appendix I: 4). While these resolutions used Ukrainian enlistment to appeal to Canadian sympathies, other community spokesmen urged their compatriots to enlist as their duty to the land that gave them liberty. Budka, for one, repeatedly admonished his rural flock to do its bit for the victory of democracy—on the battlefield and in agricultural productivity and patriotic work at home.[48] In other instances, fighting for Canada became entwined with fighting to avenge loved ones in Galicia.

Prominent among Anglo-Canadians who saw military enlistment as proof of Ukrainian loyalty were those who had worked among Ukrainians and felt qualified to comment on the Ukrainian character. Missionary C. W. W. Ross spoke with conviction when he told the 1918 Alberta Conference of the Methodist Church: "I could raise regiments out there in the colony to fight for the king and country. They are loyal citizens."[49] Other statements showed that Ukrainian protests did not always fall on deaf ears. With its publication of the "Address to the Canadian People," the *Manitoba Free Press* ran an editorial which, although again blaming nationalist agitators for bringing the group into disrepute, conceded:

> The plain fact is that, because of their Austrian birth, these people have been too hastily classed by Government officials and others as alien enemies.... The great mass of them are entirely out of sympathy with Austria. Many have volunteered for service with the Canadian overseas battalions, and left to themselves, they have no desire but to be loyal and industrious Canadians.[50]

Early in the war, Ottawa announced that all naturalized Canadian citizens with German or Austrian names could enlist for service.[51] The *Edmonton Bulletin* felt that "the correction, or change of policy, is right enough. There is no reason why a husky Canadian of German or Austrian descent who wants to keep free the land of his forefathers from slavery to militarism should not be allowed to do so."[52] Although the ruling did not include registered enemy aliens, an unknown number of enemy-alien volunteers were accepted into the Canadian armed forces and served overseas. Others were turned away or discharged later when their identity was discovered.

Some Austrian Ukrainians changed their names or tried to pass as Poles or Russians in order to enlist, as the recruitment campaign for the 77th Battalion in Ottawa revealed:

> A considerable number of Austrians bent on shouldering a musket at any cost applied. They were quite displeased in some cases when not accepted, and could not understand why their Russian brethren ... were accepted and they were not. Father Sinnoneski, who acts as their interpreter, detected several who were passing themselves off as Russians, and warned the recruiting officer.[53]

Other Austrian Ukrainians adopted a Russian camouflage simply to receive better treatment from Canadian society; still others flatly refused to enlist or pass as Russians or to accept Russia, the oppressor of their European compatriots and conquerer of Galicia, as Canada's ally. In late 1916 one Ukrainian claimed that more Ukrainians would have enlisted if the military authorities had recognized their opposition to both Austria and Russia and permitted them to volunteer as Ukrainians.[54]

In the summer of 1915 Ottawa announced that with the blessing of the Russian consulate in Montreal, Russians in Canada (including Ukrainian immigrants from Russian Ukraine) were to be accepted into Canada's armed forces, adding that "the 77th of Ottawa, now being organized ... contains over 50, while the 59th Regt. of Kingston has also quite a proportion of the big fellows."[55] Russian volunteers had to produce a certificate of nationality, issued by the consul general after presentation of identification papers and a photograph. This regulation, faithfully observed, would have prevented Austrian Ukrainians from enlisting under Russian guise. The acceptance of Russian recruits, or those posing as Russians, often created new problems. Ignorance of English among Russians in one battalion led to charges that they were "useless in the ranks as they were mere cogs in the military wheel" and the demand that all future Russian volunteers understand English as well as bear certification of "the genuineness of their nationality."[56]

Unnaturalized Russophile Ukrainians from Galicia and Bukovyna considered their position to be particularly unjust. Although they identified fully with "mother" Russia in the war and hoped to see Austrian Ukrainian territories incorporated into the Russian empire, they had been born on Austrian soil and thus, as enemy aliens, were barred from enlistment. Lay and religious Russophile leaders encouraged the naturalized among them to enlist, although they tended to subordinate assistance to the British empire to support of Russia. During 1917 the Russophiles publicly re-emphasized their loyalty. In February, Canadian "Russians" voted to petition the military authorities to permit the enlistment of Galician-born Russian Orthodox Slavs (Russophile Ukrainians) on the warranty of a priest, claiming that of 75,000 Galicians in this category, 5,000 would immediately join. Their resolution to Prime Minister Borden read in part:

> We solemnly protest against the fictitious mention of the name Ukrainians and Ruthenians, as in fact it means not a nation, but a political clique organized by German propaganda to divide the united Russian nation in parts. We pray the Canadian government that in the event of their sending representatives to a peace convention that they do not consider the Ukrainian or Ruthenian question, as it has no historical basis, but appears to be exclusively a low German political falsification.[57]

In mid-1918 a "Russian" delegation representing "several hundred thousand Carpatho-Russians" in western Canada asked Borden to remove its people from enemy-alien status and include them in the conscription law so that they could assist in "the securing of freedom to their enslaved nation."[58] Finally, in the closing months of the war, efforts were made to organize voluntary "Russian" units in Canada and the United States from among the Carpatho-Russians (immigrants from Galicia, Bukovyna and Transcarpathia) to help fight the Bolsheviks.[59]

In late 1916 rumours circulated that the formation of a Ukrainian battalion was imminent. Budka informed Ottawa that his people, although initially averse to fighting their kinfolk in Austria, were loyal Canadians ready to do their duty.[60] Rumours were followed in February 1917 by an announcement in the Ukrainian Canadian press:

> Mr. Shandro, an officer in the 218th battalion, has been entrusted to recruit a Ukrainian battalion with Ukrainians residing in western Canada.
>
> This battalion will not go into fire, because it will consist of former subjects of Austria, but will only be used in building railways, bridges, etc. behind the fighting line.[61]

The decision to place Ukrainians in a non-combatant unit reflected concern in military and political circles over both the wisdom of placing former enemy nationals in the trenches and the status of captured Ukrainians. It also marked official recognition of the wealth of navvy experience Ukrainians would bring into labour battalions. Nor is it insignificant that the Ukrainian battalion was to be recruited in Alberta, where Andrew Shandro had a reputation for rallying Ukrainians behind the war effort.

On 21 March 1917 the attorney general of Alberta appointed Anton Kuprowski of Mundare and Roman Kremar of Edmonton military justices of the peace, forestry battalion, for recruiting purposes. Kremar was Shandro's long-time political opponent and a popular advocate of bilingual schools, which had often brought him into conflict with Alberta's Liberal government. His commission, which he accepted as "Lieut., The Officer Commanding, Ruthenian Forestry Draft, C.E.F.," was cancelled on 16 March 1918.[62] Evidently, in the face of increasing manpower needs on the front, Ukrainian enlistment was to be encouraged through the strategic placement of prominent Ukrainians. Subsequent Ukrainian sources, however, have attributed Kremar's military career not to the designs of Canadian war leaders but to his own pro-Ukrainian motives. Anticipating the disintegration of the Russian empire, they maintain, Kremar saw that Ukraine would need a military force to establish an independent state, and with this in mind

> in 1917 joined the Canadian army with the rank of lieutenant, receiving permission from the Department of National Defence to recruit a Ukrainian legion—with secret plans—so that when the time came he would succeed in going to Ukraine with this legion and there contribute to the establishment of our state.[63]

According to this account Kremar lost his army commission when the Russophiles succeeded in branding him an Austrian agent.

Was Andrew Shandro, who had shown no prior inclination to enlist, officially encouraged to join the 218th Battalion to stimulate recruiting among Alberta Ukrainians? He joined (as a private but soon acquiring officer rank) only in 1917, after his break with the Russophile camp. "His enlistment bespeaks his personal loyalty to his King and country," the *Bulletin* wrote, "and is ... another illustration that the class of our citizens whom he represents are willing to do their bit in this time of crisis for the land in which they have made their homes."[64] When the 218th Battalion left Edmonton in February 1917, Shandro remained in the city to continue recruiting among his countrymen. The effect of his recent realignment and past record on his efforts is uncertain.

The 218th Battalion, or "Irish Guards" as they were popularly called, was recruited in northern Alberta for railway construction at the front. As far as can be determined from the nominal roll of officers, non-commissioned officers and men who embarked at Halifax on 17 February 1917, approximately 27 per cent were Slavs, the great majority of whom gave Russia as their birthplace. The *Edmonton Journal* considered the recruits to be Ruthenians, although "some ... enlisted as Poles or Russians, perhaps with a view to concealing their Austrian birth." Budka's claim that they were Ukrainians, however, drew an angry denial from the "Russians" of Alberta and Saskatchewan. While it is difficult to determine the accuracy of information from the nominal roll, there is little doubt that Ukrainians were well represented. Distinctly Ukrainian names (such as those ending in "enko," "iuk" and "chuk") abound, and approximately one-third of the Slavic recruits were born in the Russian Ukrainian provinces of Kiev and Podillia. There is even some proof of volunteers' juggling the truth in order to enlist; one soldier, for example, gave his birthplace as Chernowich, Russia, when in fact Chernowich (Chernivtsi) was the major city in Bukovyna.[65]

Published references to Ukrainian participation in the Canadian military during the First World War are brief and scattered. One Ukrainian Canadian soldier from the Great War did receive recognition in his day and lasting fame. Filip Konowal, an Ottawa labourer and native of Russian Ukraine, joined the 77th Battalion in 1915. Transferred to the 47th Battalion in England, the veteran of the Imperial Russian army fought on the continent and for "conspicuous bravery and leadership" received the British empire's highest military honour, the Victory Cross (see Appendix II: 13). To contemporary Anglo-Canadians, Konowal was a "Russo-Canadian"; the contemporary Ukrainian press paid passing attention to his heroics, but his achievement has since been adopted by "symbol makers" within the Ukrainian group to argue that it has earned a niche in Canada's national life.[66]

Wartime writings give some insight into the situation of the Ukrainian serviceman and attitudes toward his enlistment. Not all Ukrainians craved a khaki uniform, either for adventure or to "prove their loyalty." In the summer of 1918 a group in Winnipeg sought a court ruling on whether Galicians could be forced to perform military duty outside Canada, as naturalization protected them as British subjects only in the country and captured soldiers risked punishment as Austrian traitors.[67] Ukrainians who did enlist received some compliments from their military superiors and comrades in arms. Colonel Cornwall, recruiting for the "Irish Guards" among Ukrainians at Mundare, considered "his volunteers of this nationality as among the pick of his effective recruits," while "their fellow soldiers of English blood pay them the tribute of being good, strong, capable fighting men, and as thoroughly patriotic as any."[68] A Ukrainian immigrant, however, saw the situation differently:

> Look here! Our boys respond to the call of this country and enlist. But do you think that the English respect them. Not at all. They point at them with their fingers and say, "look, there is a Galician in the uniform of a British soldier" and laugh at them. I don't know why we should fight for them if they laugh at us.[69]

As for performance in the field, the Canadian military commanders in

France gave special recognition on one occasion to the Alberta railway construction battalion, consisting largely of Ruthenians, for bravery under fire.[70] One last effect of military service on the Ukrainian peasant-turned-soldier was noted in the society columns of his local newspaper, announcing that he had come home from the war with an English bride.[71]

IV

In spite of the periodic concern over Ukrainian loyalties during the First World War, it never became a serious popular issue among Anglo-Canadians. It is even evident that some of the negative publicity originated with a small faction within the Ukrainian community. In fact, the Ukrainians had their defenders among Anglo-Canadians on philosophical grounds, while their visible support of the Canadian war effort, perhaps more than could have been rightfully expected under the circumstances, won grudging admiration.

Notes

1. *Saskatoon Phoenix*, 4 November 1914.
2. Budka was never fully trusted and he was watched throughout the war. In July 1918 religious squabbles within the Ukrainian community rather than Anglo-Canadian alarmism led to his arrest on a sedition charge, but the case was dismissed. In 1919, after pressure from the Great War Veterans' Association, a court inquiry in Winnipeg investigated Budka's loyalty and the possibility of internment and deportation, but he was cleared of any wrongdoing.
3. An immigrant from Russian Ukraine, Crath was editor of the Ukrainian Social Democratic Party organ, *Robochyi narod*, in 1914, but his activities were becoming increasingly unacceptable to the movement and his days in it were numbered. In 1915 Crath enrolled in theology at the University of Saskatchewan and in 1917 was ordained into the Presbyterian ministry. There has been one study of Crath: N. O. M. Kazymyra, "The Defiant Pavlo Krat and the Early Socialist Movement in Canada," *Canadian Ethnic Studies* 12, no. 2 (1978): 38–54.
4. *Edmonton Capital*, 8 August 1914; the article, "Ukrainian Protest Arouses Ire Slav Population Here," is essentially a Russophile document, supporting the charge that local Russophiles were behind the negative Ukrainian publicity. See also *Edmonton Bulletin*, 18 and 19 August 1914.
5. *Edmonton Bulletin*, 6 October 1914. The Society for an Independent Ukraine

was criticized by the Ukrainian community as well. *Novyny* in Edmonton reiterated the *Bulletin*'s sentiments when it declared that "we can detest Russia as much as we like. Not all Englishmen look upon this alliance with Russia with pleasure. However, as long as the war lasts, we have no right or privilege to hostile acts against Russia" (8 October 1914).

6. *Vegreville Observer*, 23 September 1914.
7. The whole "Independent Ukraine" episode sparked a flurry of articles, editorials and letters to the editor in the Edmonton and Vegreville newspapers as all sides explained their positions. The issue can be followed in the *Edmonton Bulletin*, 22, 24, 25 and 28 September, 5 and 6 October 1914; and in the *Vegreville Observer*, 23 and 30 September, 7 and 14 October 1914.
8. *Edmonton Bulletin*, 6 October 1914.
9. See, for example, letters to the editor in the *Manitoba Free Press*, 7 and 9 March 1916; and *The Vindication of Bishop Budka* (Toronto, 1919).
10. Wherever their work among immigrants was not suspended or curtailed during the war, these groups regarded it as part of their home-front responsibilities to ensure that "the ideals of our national life, for which ... [our men] have been fighting and for which such sacrifices have been made, ... [do not] to a great extent disappear ... because the aliens ... have not been instructed in Canadian ideals" (minutes, 9 November 1916, Edmonton Municipal Chapter, Imperial Order of the Daughters of the Empire Records, Provincial Archives of Alberta [hereafter PAA], Edmonton, Alberta).
11. *Edmonton Bulletin*, 29 July 1915.
12. T. C. Norris Papers, 42–5, Provincial Archives of Manitoba (hereafter PAM), Winnipeg, Manitoba.
13. See *Manitoba Free Press*, 20 June 1916. The Ukrainian community did not let pass unchallenged charges that their opposition to the abolition of bilingual schools was being manipulated by their leaders; see *ibid.*, 10 March 1916, for a rebuttal by Taras Ferley to the Manitoba legislature to such accusations against Budka.
14. See *ibid.*, 29 November 1916, for full particulars of the *Free Press* case against Raffalovich, including the incident that exposed him as a "spy." Raffalovich's escapades are discussed in the article by David Saunders in this volume.
15. Formed in Vienna in 1915 as the official Ukrainian liaison with the Central Powers, the General Ukrainian Council supported an independent Ukrainian state in Russian Ukraine and territorial-national autonomy for Ukrainians in Galicia. It dissolved in late 1917, disillusioned by Austrian policies in Eastern Galicia.
16. *Manitoba Free Press*, 3 April 1916. See also *ibid.*, 18 February, 3 April and 20 June 1916, for its case against Demydczuk. Ottawa, however, was not quite as indifferent as the *Free Press* charged to fears that unwelcome agitation was reaching the Ukrainian Canadian community from the United States; in January 1916 it had banned the Ukrainian Catholic newspaper *Svoboda* from Canada as an instrument of pro-German propaganda.
17. *Novyny*, 2 February 1915.

18. The Vonda case received considerable publicity in the Saskatoon press through articles, editorials and letters to the editors. See *Saskatoon Phoenix*, 7, 14 and 17 May 1915.

19. *Vegreville Observer*, 6 March 1918. See also *Edmonton Bulletin*, 18 January 1918; and *Vegreville Observer*, 23 and 30 January, 20 February 1918. The Ukrainian deputation that met with Borden contained a number of highly influential persons; besides the Ukrainians A. S. Shandro, P. Svarich, H. Slipchenko and T. Petrushevich, there were J. S. McCallum (MLA for Vegreville), Alberta Premier Stewart and the former premier of the province, A. L. Sifton.

20. See, for example, *Vegreville Observer*, 25 July 1917 and 24 July 1918.

21. The *Manitoba Free Press* alone produced some half dozen editorials at this time; see *Manitoba Free Press*, 21 January, 4, 13, 16 and 18 February, 18 March and 7 May 1918.

22. *Vegreville Observer*, 20 February 1918. The reporter was not impressed: "The *Bulletin* gives him a lot of information out of the Encyclopedia Britannica, and says there are many settlements of them, especially in the western provinces. It doesn't tell him that Mundare is the exuberant culmination of their supreme apothesis and that he can't set foot on his own sidewalk without treading on the tails of their coats."

23. See *Vegreville Observer*, 29 May, 5 and 6 June, 10 and 17 July 1918.

24. W. Simons, "Northern Alberta," in *Acts and Proceedings of the Forty-Fourth General Assembly of the Presbyterian Church in Canada* (1918), 34. Simons' sentiments, reiterated the following year, were also echoed by workers in Saskatchewan and Manitoba; see *Acts and Proceedings of the Forty-Fifth General Assembly of the Presbyterian Church in Canada* (1919), 27, 32–3, 35.

25. *Kanadyiets*, 1 October 1915.

26. *Saskatoon Phoenix*, 16 October 1914 and 13 May 1916; and minutes, [October 1914], Canadian Red Cross Society (Manitoba Division) Records, PAM.

27. In addition to Svarich and Zalizniak, D. Prystash, P. Melnyk and P. Kolmatycki sat on the Patriotic Fund committee, while Mrs. Svarich and Mrs. Zalizniak were the Ukrainian representatives to the Vegreville Red Cross.

28. *Vegreville Observer*, 8 November 1916.

29. *Ukrainskyi holos*, 17 November 1915.

30. *Manitoba Free Press*, 14 June 1918.

31. *Edmonton Bulletin*, 28 November 1916.

32. *Vegreville Observer*, 14 November 1917.

33. For an account of one such evening at Zawale school in aid of the Patriotic Fund, see M. Elston, "The Canadian Slav and the War," *Graphic* (1917): n.p. (see PAA 65.55). Several Anglo-Canadians expressed interest in having this contact with the Ukrainian settlers maintained by the Department of Extension after the war, requesting a special Extension official for community work in the Ukrainian bloc. See F. L. Tilson to A. E. Ottewell, 6 September 1919, and A. E. Archer to H. M. Tory, 27 October 1919, Henry Marshall Tory

Papers, 68–9/801B, University of Alberta Archives, Edmonton, Alberta.

34. *Edmonton Bulletin*, 1 March 1916. The *Bulletin*'s accuracy did not improve with time; on 29 January 1917 it identified Shandro as "of Ruthenian descent, having been born in Russia."

35. *Postup*, 7 March 1916.

36. One letter complained that "Mr. Shandro neither at this time, nor in the English Liberal press, nor in the Alberta legislature, made a vigorous protest against the catsap leaders, calumniators and their work" (*Ukrainskyi holos*, 14 March 1917).

37. *Edmonton Bulletin*, 1 March 1916.

38. *Vegreville Observer*, 11 October 1916.

39. P. H. Morris, comp. and ed., *The Canadian Patriotic Fund: A Record of Its Activities from 1914 to 1919* (n.p., n.d.), 57.

40. Cited in *Vegreville Observer*, 27 December 1916.

41. *Ibid.*, 3 January 1917.

42. *Ibid.*, 26 September 1917.

43. *Edmonton Bulletin*, 29 September 1917; the meeting was also reported in the *Vegreville Observer*, 3 October 1917.

44. *Vegreville Observer*, 6 March 1918.

45. William Martin Papers, 1742-52, Saskatchewan Archives Board, Saskatoon, Saskatchewan. Bychinsky also asked if it would be possible to organize a Ukrainian regiment in the Canadian army.

46. See *Vegreville Observer*, 11 September 1918; *Edmonton Journal*, 30 November 1916; and *Manitoba Free Press*, 3 April 1916 and 18 February 1918.

47. Research by the late Vladimir J. Kaye-Kysilewsky might prove the contrary; his extensive work on Ukrainian participation in the Canadian military during both world wars has not yet been made public, however.

48. See *Vegreville Observer*, 30 May and 11 September 1917, for Budka's speeches to Ukrainian Catholic gatherings at Copernick, Alberta, and Rama, Saskatchewan. The second article, handed to the *Observer* by a Ukrainian, illustrates the concern in Ukrainian circles that the Anglo-Canadian community have a positive picture of Ukrainian wartime loyalty.

49. *Edmonton Bulletin*, 1 June 1918.

50. *Manitoba Free Press*, 17 July 1916.

51. See *Edmonton Bulletin*, 2 December 1914. Ottawa made the announcement to quell rumours from Salisbury Plain that the British war office had ordered all Canadian volunteers with German names arrested and examined. *Ibid.*, 26 November 1914.

52. *Ibid.*, 2 December 1914.

53. *Saskatoon Phoenix*, 27 July 1915.

54. *Manitoba Free Press*, 6 November 1916.

55. *Winnipeg Tribune*, 2 August 1915.

56. *Saskatoon Phoenix*, 9 August 1915.

57. *Manitoba Free Press*, 10 February 1917. As early as 1915 the Russophile community in Alberta moved to petition the authorities to permit "Russians from Galicia and Bukovyna" to enlist. See *Russkii holos*, 31 August/13 September and 21 September/4 October 1915. (*Russkii holos* used both Old and New Styles to date its publication.)

58. *Regina Morning Leader*, 8 April 1918.

59. *Manitoba Free Press*, 26 August, and 16 September 1918.

60. *Edmonton Journal*, 30 November 1916.

61. *Ukrainskyi holos*, 21 February 1917; and *Kanadyiets*, 14 February 1917.

62. Justice of the Peace Files, 69.2308, PAA. See also OC 379/17 and OC 348/18. The official record gives no reason for cancelling Kremar's commission.

63. *Ukrainskyi pionir*, no. 4 (January 1955): 10–11. A more recent biography of Kremar (in *Ukrainians in Alberta* [Edmonton, 1981], 2: 166–71) indicates that Kremar had repeatedly approached Ottawa in the matter of Ukrainian enlistment and stresses that his involvement in recruiting a forestry battalion was independent of Shandro's enlistment activities.

64. *Edmonton Bulletin*, 29 January 1917; see also *Vegreville Observer*, 31 January 1917.

65. *Canadian Expeditionary Force, 218th Battalion, Nominal Roll of Officers, Non-Commissioned Officers and Men* (issued with Militia Orders, 1917). See also *Edmonton Journal*, 30 November 1916; *Saskatoon Phoenix*, 18 December 1916; and *Edmonton Bulletin*, 20 January 1917. The emphasis on the 218th Battalion is not meant to imply that it was the only military unit with a large Ukrainian component. The 190th and 184th Battalions recruited in Winnipeg also had significant numbers of Ukrainians. See M. H. Marunchak, *The Ukrainian Canadians: A History* (Winnipeg, 1970), 254–5.

66. See, for example, P. Yuzyk, *Ukrainian Canadians: Their Place and Role in Canadian Life* (Toronto, 1967), 34.

67. *Manitoba Free Press*, 27 July 1918. Lawyers Jaroslaw Arsenych and Fred Heap were retained to argue the test case in the courts.

68. *Edmonton Journal*, 20 July and 30 November 1916.

69. J. S. Woodsworth, dir., "Ukrainian Rural Communities," report for the Bureau of Social Research, governments of Manitoba, Saskatchewan and Alberta (Winnipeg, 1917), 128.

70. *Ukrainskyi holos*, 7 October [*sic*] 1917. (The issue is dated incorrectly and should read 7 November.)

71. *Lamont Gazette*, 27 September 1919.

Chapter 4

Ukrainian Canadians
and the Wartime Economy

Andrij Makuch

Between 1914 and 1918 the Canadian economy was severely tested. Not only did the young Dominion have to equip an army of over 600,000, but it also became a major source of foodstuffs and munitions for Britain and occasionally the other Allies. The great increase in manufactured exports, industrial output and seeded acreage reflected the economic growth as the country met its obligations.[1] Like other Canadians, Ukrainian Canadians benefited from these developments. But their position as enemy aliens, denied the privilege of enlisting, led to accusations of selfish profiteering while native-born sons shed their blood overseas. When the economic activities of Ukrainian Canadians during the war years are placed in perspective, however, it becomes clear that such charges were largely groundless. The war did accelerate existing trends within the Ukrainian community—the growing tendency for immigrants to seek industrial or labouring jobs, the movement of established farmers out of subsistence agriculture, a change in demographic distribution—but it did not dramatically alter Ukrainian occupational patterns or bring sudden prosperity.

I

The emergence of distinct groups of farmers and labourers was not anticipated by the agriculturally-focused immigration policy that first brought the Ukrainians to Canada. Until 1905 Ukrainian immigrants were primarily peasant-settlers who worked as seasonal labourers only long

enough to raise the capital necessary for homesteading.[2] The expansion of
secondary and resource industries, particularly in Ontario, which
accompanied the wheat boom of 1900–14, brought about significant
changes. These labour-intensive enterprises required a large pool of cheap,
reliable workers, and the immigrant-settler who entered the job market only
periodically no longer sufficed, despite his proverbial capabilities as a
human beast of burden. As domestic sources could not provide sufficient
labourers, Canadian immigration policy, beginning during Frank Oliver's
term as minister of the interior, shifted away from agricultural settlers to
industrial labourers.[3] The implications for Ukrainian immigrants were clear.
Not only did Ukrainian immigration almost double after 1905 (increasing
greatly in the three years preceding the war), but the proportion of
immigrants going to the Prairie provinces fell from 80 per cent in 1904–6 to
54 per cent in 1914. In the latter year almost 45 per cent of the arrivals
gave Quebec, Ontario or British Columbia as their destination.[4] The
preponderance of males in provinces outside the Prairies illustrates the
economic attractions offered to the labourer (see Table 1). The sort of work

TABLE 1 **Ukrainian population by province, according to sex, as a
percentage of the total, 1911 and 1921**

	Total Ukrainian population		Percentage of males		Percentage of females	
	1911	1921	1911	1921	1911	1921
Manitoba	30,584	44,129	54.9	53.1	45.1	46.9
Saskatchewan	22,276	28,097	55.8	54.0	44.2	46.0
Alberta	17,584	23,827	57.5	54.0	42.5	46.0
Nova Scotia	292	389	71.6	62.2	28.4	37.8
Quebec	458	1,176	76.2	57.3	23.8	42.7
Ontario	3,078	8,307	82.5	59.6	17.5	40.4
British Columbia	682	793	89.7	65.2	10.3	34.8
Prince Edward Island	4	—	100.0	—	0.0	—
Total (Canada)	74,963	106,721	57.4	54.2	42.6	45.8

SOURCE: Darcovich and Yuzyk, *Statistical Compendium*, 41–4.

performed by these immigrants is demonstrated by their concentration in
primary industrial and heavy manufacturing regions. In 1911, for example,
287 of 292 Ukrainians in Nova Scotia lived in Cape Breton county and 431
of 458 Ukrainians in Quebec lived in the vicinity of Montreal; in Ontario
sixteen of fifty-three census districts contained over 90 per cent of the
Ukrainian population.[5]

During the war the trend toward entering the wage labour market
continued. The number of Ukrainians outside the Prairie provinces more
than doubled (4,519 to 10,668) in the decade prior to 1921, while the urban
Ukrainian population within the Prairie provinces also rose (8,721 to

13,471). By 1921 the proportion of Ukrainian Canadians who were not rural prairie residents, and therefore not farmers, had risen to 22.6 per cent.[6] This figure is perhaps a conservative reflection of the demographic change within the Ukrainian population as many migrant labourers, constantly on the move in search of work, were omitted by the census takers.[7] Census statistics reflect two additional changes in the Ukrainian demographic structure between 1911 and 1921—a significant increase in the number and proportion of women in communities outside the Prairies (see Table 1) and in the proportion of Ukrainians in Ontario who resided in the southern half of the province.[8] While the former represented a stabilization of community life as sojourners put down permanent roots, the latter denoted a shifting emphasis from the primary industry of the northern shield to the secondary heavy industries of the south, industries stimulated by the wartime demand for munitions.

II

Ukrainian Canadian agriculture was sufficiently established by the eve of the First World War for the subsequent period to be viewed as one of reaping the first modest fruits of a long-awaited harvest. As the 1917 Woodsworth survey pointed out, prosperity largely depended on the nature of the land settled, while the length of time a farmer had been working his land tended to determine the degree of improvement.[9] In a report on the Alberta bloc settlement written in 1911, Peter Svarich had reached similar conclusions: those who had been on the land more than a decade had stock, land, buildings and machinery worth between five and ten thousand dollars; those on the land from five to ten years had assets from one to five thousand dollars; and those in operation less than five years had assets under one thousand dollars.[10] At the outbreak of the war, most Ukrainian farmers had small operations and fell into one of Svarich's two latter categories; a wartime sample of farms in Ukrainian districts in Alberta, Saskatchewan and Manitoba showed that the quarter-section farm was still the overwhelming norm.[11]

Ukrainians generally were able to improve and expand their operations during the war as a result of high prices. In Alberta, for example, the total seeded acreage in the largely Ukrainian districts of Victoria and Whitford increased significantly between 1913 and 1918 (see Table 2). In both districts the growth was indicative of a new productive capacity among Ukrainians in Alberta, but it is unproven that the increase in total acreage sown was proportionately greater than increases for the province as a whole. In fact, the proportion of the total Alberta seeded acreage represented by each district tended to fluctuate considerably throughout the war years. As

TABLE 2 Acreage cultivated in two Ukrainian crop districts in Alberta,
        1913–18

	Total acreage*		Percentage of total Alberta acreage sown*	
	Whitford	Victoria	Whitford	Victoria
1913	27,542	58,766	0.9	2.1
1914	30,942	63,453	1.2	2.45
1915	51,039	66,439	1.45	1.8
1916	45,274	59,857	1.2	1.6
1918	61,409	99,558	0.8	1.3

* Based on seven crops: spring wheat, winter wheat, oats, barley, flax, rye and mixed grains.
SOURCE: Alberta, Department of Agriculture, *Annual Report,* 1913–18.

sown acreage in Alberta was increasing more rapidly than in the Prairies
generally,[12] the increases in Victoria and Whitford districts were
proportionately greater than for the Prairie provinces as a whole. The
figures for total improved acreage in several predominantly Ukrainian local
improvement districts in Alberta also show a percentage increase greater
than on the Prairies as a whole, although less than in Alberta (see Table 3).

TABLE 3 Improved acreage in nine predominantly Ukrainian local
        improvement districts in Alberta, 1916 and 1921

Local Improvement District	Improved acreage		Increase in
	1916	1921	percentage
Ukrainia (#513)	15,829	22,311	41.0
Sobor (#514)	17,806	23,961	34.6
Norma (#515)	41,910	63,565	51.7
The Pines (#516)	34,768	48,066	38.3
Eagle (#545)	35,982	51,567	43.3
Wostok (#546)	35,399	45,594	28.8
Leslie (#547)	39,348	54,902	39.5
Wasel (#575)	19,115	24,941	30.5
Smoky Lake (#576)	17,486	24,211	38.5
Alberta	7,510,303	11,141,985	48.4
Prairies	34,330,246	44,863,266	30.7

SOURCE: Canada, Bureau of Statistics, *Census of Prairie Provinces, 1916* (Ottawa, 1918),
        338, 348, and *Sixth Census of Canada, 1921,* 5 vols. (Ottawa, 1924–5), 5:
        424–8; and Thompson, *Harvests of War,* 177.

These two sets of figures illustrate that Ukrainians took advantage of the
opportunities offered by wartime conditions as well as or even better than
other Prairie farmers. Were they guilty of profiteering or did other factors
come into play? Several characteristic features of Ukrainian pioneer
agriculture in western Canada suggest that the latter was the case. First,
Ukrainian farms were less mechanized, more reliant on family over hired
labour and more self-sufficient than the average Canadian farm. These

factors reduced operating expenses for Ukrainian farmers and increased their real profits. Emphasis on mixed agriculture and reluctance to speculate in cash crops·also prevented sudden losses due to market shifts.[13] In addition, although not always on the best soil, Ukrainian farms were almost all located in the parkland belt; as a result they received adequate moisture during the partial droughts of 1917–19 and were able to grow good crops to sell at high prices. Lastly, Ukrainians often managed both to work their own farms and to hire themselves out during harvest season, adding one more source of income to their operations. Toward the end of the war, when high profit levels made it more worthwhile for Ukrainians to remain on their own farms, this practice declined while the price demanded by those who continued to hire themselves out rose. Much of the outcry against Ukrainians and other "foreigners" came from the increased wages of farm workers—sometimes giving rise to conspiracy theories to explain why farm help was becoming so expensive and to charges of Ukrainian disloyalty.[14]

The war years were a turning point for many Ukrainian farmers, with high prices and good weather combining to help them along the road to progress. Growth often proved to be a mixed blessing, however, and in the early 1920s the Ukrainian-language press began to record bankruptcies among Ukrainian farmers who had spent their money foolishly or over-expanded during the war years.[15] Ukrainian farmers had become accustomed to a higher standard of living; items whose price they had once not dared to ask became ordinary purchases. This precipitated their transition from subsistence to commercial farming and increased operating costs for mechanization, costs not always matched by the unstable returns for their products. In other words, the war years saw the integration of many Ukrainians into the mainstream of Canadian agriculture.

III

Enemy-alien status obviously created difficulties for Ukrainian Canadians trying to earn a living. Farmers were perhaps less affected than labourers, but government regulations reached even the remotest areas. The order in council prohibiting enemy aliens from possessing firearms or explosives (see Appendix II: 9–10), for example, prevented Ukrainian farmers from shooting game to supplement their diets. The suspension of naturalization for immigrants from enemy countries was more serious, since Austrian Ukrainians were unable to acquire title to the lands on which they had settled.

The sector of the Ukrainian Canadian population most affected by the wartime regulations, however, was clearly the labourers. Registration limited their mobility, both within Canada and in migrating to the United

States, and the restrictions on explosives theoretically excluded them from working in munitions plants and certain mining jobs.[16] A greater stumbling block for Ukrainian Canadian workers was that they had been classified as enemy aliens, and faced the brunt of rising nativism, at a time when jobs were at a premium and the prewar depression had already caused widespread unemployment among them. Their sense of injustice was well summed up by a comment in the weekly, *Robochyi narod* (Working People), the official organ of the Ukrainian Social Democratic Party and the most influential publication among Ukrainian Canadian workers: "Like it or not, they count you as an enemy and they don't ask why you had the misfortune to be born in Austria and not some other place—even Russia."[17] *Robochyi narod* reacted to the war in predictable fashion: it was a war of capitalists and imperialists waged at the expense of the working class. Nevertheless, the newspaper recognized that the war would bring temporary economic instability as finance and export markets were disrupted, and realized that the jobs created by the war, which required skilled labour, would not benefit the Ukrainians.

Although *Robochyi narod* remained loyal to the principle of labour solidarity, such solidarity was largely illusory as Anglo-Canadian and other allied workers closed ranks against their enemy-alien comrades. Dismissals brought instability and the threat of internment to Ukrainian Canadian workers. The precariousness of their position was reflected in the reduced organizational activities of the Ukrainian Social Democratic Party, which was also hurt by arrests among its members, despite the severity of the crisis. By August 1915 *Robochyi narod* had been reduced to a monthly; many local party branches either closed temporarily or suffered a sharp decline in membership as labourers moved in search of work.[18]

The employment situation for enemy aliens improved in 1916 when the increased need for labour overrode the practice of exclusion on the basis of nationality. *Ukrainskyi holos* (Ukrainian Voice) remarked: "Even though certain firms and companies previously had been choosy about the people they employed—for example, they would not accept 'Austrians' (whether someone was actually 'Austrian' was immaterial), they do not discriminate at all any more—just as long as they can find anyone to work."[19]

As prospects brightened for Ukrainian workers, the Ukrainian Social Democratic Party revived; *Robochyi narod* soon returned to a weekly format and late in 1916 Matthew Popovich made a successful tour of eastern Canada to collect funds for the party press.[20] By 1917 conditions were such that the *Canadian Annual Review* reported the entry of Ukrainians and other "foreigners" into once-sensitive areas of employment, noting that "the labour shortage everywhere [has] resulted in the employ of Austrian and German aliens in work of all kinds—the Imperial Munitions Board, the Lindsay Arsenal and many munitions and other industrial plants."[21]

Near-full employment did not end the problems of Ukrainian Canadian workers. While the economy was doing well and wages were rising, so too were prices, and like all workers in Canada, Ukrainians felt the pinch of inflation. By 1917 wages became the major issue in a series of strikes involving Ukrainians, most notably in the Crowsnest mining district. The return of growing numbers of veterans, inflamed by what they considered the delicate treatment afforded "foreigners" and the openly-seditious activities of labour unions, fed an already-tense situation. With demobilization and the postwar economic recession, veteran demands for the dismissal of "foreigners" from jobs "rightfully" belonging to Canadians found many a sympathetic ear. Undoubtedly, many Ukrainian workers could empathize with the sentiments of the immortal Shtif Tabachniuk, a popular cartoon character of the time, "Nema rykhtu na sviti—there's no justice in this world!"

IV

The question of wartime profiteering by Ukrainian and other enemy-alien workers and farmers has been raised repeatedly by historians of both the Great War and ethnic groups in Canada.[22] During the war itself, tolerance was low. The remarks of Alberta MLA, Roberta MacAdams, in 1918 reflect the prevailing view:

> It makes one feel very sad to visit the West now. You see the country being cleared of our fine, Anglo-Saxon stock and the alien left to fatten on war prosperity. It is most disheartening. Out there aliens are getting as high as $16 a day. Some of them won't even loan their war earnings to the country. They bury it in the ground rather than do so. It's all very well for people to say that a great number of those aliens will develop into good Canadian citizens. But they should be sharing the sacrifice and service of today.[23]

Such sentiments fueled public agitation for either the forced labour of enemy aliens at $1.10 daily (the wage of a Canadian soldier) or their internment. At the war's end there were more radical demands for the deportation of "parasitic" aliens. As a bitter Winnipeg clergyman who had lost a son in Flanders posed it, the "burning question of today" is "shall the aliens go?":

> How the heroic British-Canadian returns from cleaning up Central Europe, broken in health, with a pittance of a pension, and not a foot of land to his name to find the Austro-Hun, brother of the creature he has been fighting, on his Canadian heritage. Here is a displacement any sane man can see is wrong. How would you make the matter right? Just send the Hun home, and let the

Canadian soldier in.

For his own sake the Hun should be allowed to go. As in England and all over the world the Austro-Hun has forfeited the right to dwell among decent people. He is depreciated and held in suspicion everywhere.[24]

Statements like these arose as much from racism and prejudice as from any accurate perception of the wartime prosperity of enemy-alien minorities. This chapter has attempted to demonstrate that even more temperate judgments of war-based economic progress are perhaps overstated. The Great War did not drastically alter Ukrainian Canadian economic patterns; what it did do was accelerate the pace of those changes already begun. The tendency for a greater proportion of Ukrainians to find industrial rather than agricultural employment, producing demographic shifts, is one example. While Ukrainian wage earners found regular employment an improvement over the depressed conditions of 1913–14, they remained in unskilled occupations, their real wages were eroded by the rapid inflation of 1917–19 and they were among the first to suffer during the postwar recession. Ukrainian farmers emerged from subsistence-level agriculture in significant numbers, but it was traditional peasant practices such as self-sufficiency and family labour, as well as good harvests, that made it possible for them to capitalize on the increase in agricultural prices induced by the war. Neither farmer nor worker was a "war profiteer," despite the angry accusations of nativist Anglo-Canadians. Instead, both tried to survive, to make a living and a better life in a most difficult time.

Notes

1. R. C. Brown and R. Cook, *Canada 1896–1921: A Nation Transformed* (Toronto, 1976), chap. 12.
2. The typical picture is of a man in a sheepskin coat who arrived in the spring, took up a homestead and hired his eldest son out as a farm hand, his daughter as a domestic, and himself as a railway worker, leaving his wife and the younger children in a primitive earthen dugout; the three salaries were combined to finance a modest beginning on the farm the following year. For an early example of this "type," see "Tymko Havryliuk," a short story by the Reverend Nestor Dmytriw published in *Svoboda* between 2 September and 21 October 1897.
3. See D. H. Avery, *"Dangerous Foreigners": European Immigrant Workers and Labour Radicalism in Canada, 1896–1932* (Toronto, 1979), 25–33.
4. See W. Darcovich and P. Yuzyk, eds., *A Statistical Compendium on the Ukrainians in Canada, 1891–1976* (Ottawa, 1980), 507, 514, 517.
5. The sixteen districts, the majority in southern Ontario, were Algoma, Brant, Carleton, Cochrane, Essex, Kenora, Kent, Lincoln, Ontario, Sudbury, Thunder

Bay, Waterloo, Welland, Wentworth and York. The situation in all three provinces had changed little by 1921. See *ibid.*, 60–4.

6. *Ibid.*, 41–4, 130.

7. The failure to record all transient workers helps to explain the discrepancy between the official figure of 106,721 Ukrainians in Canada in 1921 and an estimated figure of over 200,000. While a 1917 survey indicated that 15,000 Ukrainians in Alberta lived either in the cities or mining communities, and another 12,000 to 15,000 lived in Winnipeg, the 1921 census showed only 7,001 and 547 Ukrainians in Winnipeg and Edmonton respectively. See J. S. Woodsworth, dir., "Ukrainian Rural Communities," unpublished report of investigation by the Bureau of Social Research, governments of Manitoba, Saskatchewan and Alberta (Winnipeg, 1917), 3; and Darcovich and Yuzyk, *Statistical Compendium*, 66.

8. Darcovich and Yuzyk, *Statistical Compendium*, 62–4.

9. Woodsworth, "Ukrainian Rural Communities," 4. See also the findings of the individual reports.

10. *Ukrainskyi holos*, 8 March 1911.

11. See Woodsworth, "Ukrainian Rural Communities," individual reports.

12. The difference was approximately 30 per cent. See J. H. Thompson, *The Harvests of War: The Prairie West, 1914–1918* (Toronto, 1978), 177.

13. See *ibid.*, 85–7.

14. See, for example, *Ukrainskyi holos*, 4 April 1917.

15. See, for example, *Nash postup*, 25 December 1923 and 1 January 1924.

16. See, for example, the correspondence between the Rothwell Coal Company and the deputy minister of justice, Department of Justice Records, vol. 207, file 1900, Public Archives of Canada, Ottawa, Ontario.

17. *Robochyi narod*, 9 June 1915.

18. See *ibid.*, 14 July 1915 and 15 March, 15 April 1916.

19. *Ukrainskyi holos*, 3 May 1916. See also *Canadian Annual Review* (1916): 431.

20. *Robochyi narod*, 21 November 1916.

21. *Canadian Annual Review* (1917): 438.

22. A number of the more general, often early accounts of Ukrainian life in Canada support the view that Ukrainians and others did profit economically as a result of wartime conditions while Anglo-Canadians were fighting overseas. See, for example, C. H. Young, *The Ukrainian Canadians: A Study in Assimilation* (Toronto, 1931), 60, 80–2; T. C. Byrne, "The Ukrainian Community in North Central Alberta" (M.A. thesis, University of Alberta, 1937), 34–6; and J. G. MacGregor, *Vilni Zemli/Free Lands: Ukrainian Settlement in Alberta* (Toronto, 1969), 252.

23. *Toronto Telegram*, 27 April 1918, cited in *Canadian Annual Review*, (1918): 580.

24. J. W. Bridgman, *Breaking Prairie Sod: The Story of a Pioneer Preacher in the Eighties, with a Discussion on the Burning Question of Today—Shall the Alien Go?* (Toronto, 1920), 188–9.

Chapter 5

Ethnic and Class Tensions in Canada, 1918-20:

Anglo-Canadians and the Alien Worker

Donald H. Avery

Ukrainian workers did not figure prominently in the policies of Canadian businessmen or government officials between 1918 and 1920. As unskilled and semi-skilled workers in the extractive industries and urban processing plants, especially in western Canada and northern Ontario, they were not insignificant, but most Anglo-Canadians were unclear as to their identity and used a variety of terms—foreigner, alien, Slav, Austrian, Ruthenian—to describe them.[1] After the Russian Revolution of 1917 and the intensification of industrial unrest in Canada, the Anglo-Canadian press and security agencies often branded Ukrainian workers as "Bolshevik."* Police surveillance and intimidation threatened not only those who had been enemy aliens during the war, but others who had been "friendly" aliens as emigrants from Russia.

Individuals and groups were deemed loyal or disloyal, law-abiding or revolutionary, according to how their behaviour conformed to the values and norms of the middle class Anglo-Canadian community.[2] The Ukrainian worker experience between 1918 and 1920 must be understood within the context of the hostility and suspicion then facing all East European immigrants, particularly in regions where industrial conflict prevailed. In the spring of 1919, as Canada moved toward the brink of serious class conflict, Ukrainian workers became increasingly vulnerable. Veterans and other "loyal" Canadians issued widespread demands for "patriotic"

---

*The *Toronto Globe* (21 December 1918) defined Bolshevism as "a label for any act or tendency which happens to offend our beliefs and prejudices."

dismissals, often backing up their words with displays of force. Canadian security agencies monitored "radical" alien organizations, pointing to the growing number of "dangerous foreigners" arrested and deported to justify their activities.

I

The opening months of the First World War had seriously affected Ukrainian workers in Canada. Massive layoffs by railway, mining and lumber companies swelled the ranks of the unemployed, especially in centres like Winnipeg, Edmonton and Vancouver. Depleted savings and difficulty in obtaining relief created considerable bitterness, particularly among the "sojourners" who were unable to rejoin their families in Europe after July 1914.[3] The socialist *Robochyi narod* (Working People) expressed the prevailing frustration with economic conditions before the outbreak of war: "Hundreds of unemployed Ukrainian workers groan from the blow of hunger, and those who have luckily found work suffer unheard-of cruel treatment and mockery from employer benefactors."[4] Not surprisingly, then, there was widespread concern among Anglo-Canadian businessmen and government officials over the possiblity of immigrant labour unrest. It was reinforced in May 1914 when "2000 unemployed workers, mostly Ukrainians, marched through the streets of Winnipeg with shovels demanding 'work or bread'."[5] Three months into the war J. A. M. Aikins, a prominent member of the Winnipeg establishment, warned Prime Minister Robert Borden that the "foreigners" in the North End might take advantage of the war "for the destruction of property, public and private [and other]... crazy wicked things."[6]

Although only 8,579 of approximately 540,000 enemy aliens were interned, the threat of imprisonment was felt by the whole group. Indeed, so great was anti-alien sentiment that the federal government frequently had to justify its hesitancy to launch large-scale "round-ups."[7] Canadian workers were also caught up in the wartime hysteria, although in the early stages of the war, their demands that enemy aliens be dismissed and interned often conflicted with the interests of employers anxious to retain their traditional cheap labour. On several occasions this clash of priorities between Canadian owners and Canadian workers intensified industrial unrest.[8]

One of the most bitter confrontations occurred in the coal mining regions of Alberta and British Columbia (District 18) in the spring of 1915. Despite the presence of many enemy aliens in the locals of the United Mine Workers of America (UMWA), Anglo-Canadian and "allied alien" workers demanded that the labour force be purged.[9] Eventually, the threat of strikes and possible violence forced both the companies and the federal government to give way: over three hundred "Austrian" miners were dismissed and temporarily interned. Although *Robochyi narod* praised the efforts of the UMWA executive to combat "radical chauvinism,"[10] the incident demonstrated that trade-union membership did not necessarily guarantee fair treatment. Throughout the war the executive of the Trades and Labor Congress (TLC) accepted the need for "patriotic" dismissals and was not overly concerned about the use of interned enemy aliens as "forced labour" as long as they did not displace Anglo-Canadian workers.[11] Complaints of dangerous working conditions and unsanitary living conditions were generally ignored by the TLC, and the mining and railway companies continued to impose severe restrictions on their "conscripted" labour.[12]

The war also intensified the long-standing campaign by large industrial concerns for labour stability, especially as military requirements withdrew thousands of Anglo-Canadians from the labour force. After 1916 alien and enemy-alien workers were regarded as essential to maintain a high level of manufacturing and agricultural productivity. To ensure that they performed adequately, economic incentives were reinforced by a series of state regulations. In August 1916 everyone over sixteen years of age was required to register with the Canadian Registration Board, while in April 1918 the so-called "anti-loafing act" stipulated that "every male person residing in the Dominion of Canada should be regularly engaged in some useful occupation."[13]

Prior to 1917 employers and security officials alike, especially in the ethnically diverse regions of western Canada, welcomed the changes. Reporting on previously militant groups in the Kootenay mining regions to the superintendent of the British Columbia Provincial Police in 1916, a local chief constable observed:

> From a police point of view there has been less trouble amongst them [Slavs] since the beginning of the war than previously, the fact that several of them were sent to internment camps...seemed to have a good effect on the remainder.... In my opinion, if there is ever any trouble over the employment of enemy aliens, it will be after the war is over and our people have returned.[14]

II

Although government and Anglo-Canadian public suspicion of the enemy-alien population increased between 1918 and 1920, the most severe reaction against "alien" dissenters occurred in the latter stages of the war—when victory was within the grasp of the Allies. In some regions, the label "alien" became synonymous with traitor and revolutionary.[15] The most dramatic official manifestations of the "hard-line" approach were the orders in council of 25 September 1918 prohibiting enemy publications and certain organizations (see Appendix II, 15–16). Under PC2381 the censorship powers of the federal government were enormously expanded, while the definition of "enemy-alien language" for publications purposes was broadened to include "German, Austrian, Hungarian, Bulgarian, Turkish, Romanian, Russian, Ukrainian, Finnish, Estonian, Syrian, Croatian, Ruthenian and Livonian." Under PC 2384 the use of "enemy-alien languages" was curtailed further: German, Austrian, Hungarian, Bulgarian, Turkish, *and* "the languages of Russia, Ukraine, or Finland" were banned from all public meetings excluding religious services. In addition, fourteen organizations were outlawed, among them the Ukrainian Social Democratic Party, the Russian Workers Union, the Industrial Workers of the World (IWW) and the Social Democratic Party. According to C. H. Cahan, in many respects the author of these repressive measures, the IWW and the Social Democratic Party posed the greatest threat as their membership combined ruthless aliens with Anglo-Canadian renegades and demagogues.[16]

Nor were these measures merely a warning to the foreign-born population. Magistrates were authorized to impose severe sentences—five years imprisonment and fines of five thousand dollars—for violations; and Canadian security forces received extensive powers of search and apprehension "at any time of the day or night." The Dominion Police in eastern Canada and the Royal North West Mounted Police in western Canada were now assisted in their work by other federal security agencies, most notably military intelligence and the Public Safety Branch under Cahan.[17] Most members of the Unionist cabinet appear to have approved of the bans. Sir George Foster, minister of trade and commerce, noted in his diary on 30 September that "the Council [had] disposed of some very important matters.... The prosecution of revolutionary and anarchist societies will be gratifying to the public and useful as well."[18] Dominion security officials shared Foster's enthusiasm, the more so since their expanded scope of operation justified additional funding. Between September 1918 and June 1919 the federal government was deluged with reports of alien worker subversive activity. Many of these reports were exaggerated and even contradictory, but there was a growing tendency for the cabinet to believe the worst about alien radicals. The federal government was, nevertheless, forced to back down on both measures. In October 1918, PC 2384 was modified, under pressure from the Trades and Labour Congress, to permit the use of "such languages as may be necessary" to conduct a legitimate meeting; in November the editors of the foreign-language press managed to have the censorship regulations modified to grant publication permits to responsible newspapers (*Robochyi narod* was not included), providing they printed verbatim translations in English or French in parallel columns.[19]

Canadian courts also shared the siege mentality, and many aliens experienced the full weight of Canadian justice, although the severity of sentences varied with the province and magistrate. In 1914 Ontario courts had already greatly reduced the ability of enemy aliens to seek judicial review with the decision that a person "may not sue in a British court unless he enjoys the protection of licence of the Crown."[20] This "hard-line" approach in Ontario persisted in the enforcement of PC's 2381 and 2384, particularly in centres like Sault Ste. Marie, Cobalt, Port Arthur, Brantford and Toronto. In a number of instances local magistrates rejected the option of a fine instead of a long prison sentence; when a fine was imposed, it was often of such magnitude that the defendant had no choice but to accept the alternative of prison.[21] Significantly, there was little Anglo-Canadian opposition to the two measures. Most English-language dailies in the country did not even comment on their enactment, although the *Toronto Globe* warned that "some of these [foreign] organizations are utterly incompatible with positive Canadian citizenship. Their menace exists now, and will continue to grow."[22]

The end of hostilities and the beginning of demobilization forced the federal government to adopt a more conciliatory attitude toward dissent. In a letter to R. L. Richardson, Manitoba MLA and editor of the *Winnipeg Tribune*, Arthur Meighen described how the government intended to proceed during the spring of 1919:

> We have ... recently modified the restrictive laws that had been in effect by reason of war conditions but in doing so, we have been careful not to relax farther than the present semi-peace conditions require. I [am] ... not much of a believer myself in the efficacy of forbidding the preaching of political doctrines, however foolish these doctrines may be. Any attempt, however, to stir up people to the use of force, to incite revolution is, of course, forbidden and will continue to be forbidden.[23]

This "tolerance" led to considerable consternation among those security officials who believed that almost all organizational activity and propaganda on the part of the alien population was revolutionary. In January 1919 C. H. Cahan had been so incensed over the limitations placed on the Public Safety Branch that he had submitted his resignation to the acting prime minister, Sir Thomas White.[24] Colonel Ernest Chambers, chief press censor, shared Cahan's dismay, particularly as the more permissive policy coincided with the appearance of even more radical newspapers: *Red Flag* (Vancouver), *Soviet* (Edmonton), *Western Labour News* (Winnipeg) and *Ukrainski robitnychi visty* (Ukrainian Labour News) (Winnipeg). In April 1919, during an unsuccessful attempt to suppress *Ukrainski robitnychi visty*, (which succeeded *Robochyi narod*), the western press censor, Fred Livesay, had argued:

It is true that the Western Labor News . . . is about on a par [with *Ukrainski robitnychi visty*]. But that paper [*Western Labour News*] is published and circulated entirely among English speaking people, who have in the English press a means of correcting mis-statements and false impressions. One may suppose that it would be extremely difficult to put this paper out of business. It might provoke industrial disturbances. But the Ukrainian Labour News . . . is on a different footing. As a foreign language paper it cannot enlist the general sympathy of the laboring classes. . . . This is not a case for supervision but for ruthless suppression.[25]

Other self-appointed crusaders for Anglo-Canadian supremacy, such as D. A. Ross, the erratic MLA for St. Clements, Manitoba, were even more aroused "over spineless governments . . . protecting the disloyal and the enemy aliens." In a letter to Arthur Meighen, then acting minister of justice, Ross ominously warned that "the English-speaking people of this province have put up with this nonsense as long as they are going to. The returned soldier is back."[26]

And back he was, with three thousand more veterans arriving every month. Their return created a unique situation in Canada's history—the presence in society of large numbers of unemployed men, from all classes, trained to fight. During the spring of 1919 the main target for veteran frustration was the enemy-alien population: violent assaults occurred in Sudbury, Port Arthur, Calgary, Drumheller and Winnipeg.[27] In many ways the 26–7 January "race riots" in Winnipeg were the most shocking, because of the extent to which some Anglo-Canadians in the city were prepared to accept mob justice. Moreover, local police and military security officials made no attempt to protect the "foreigners." At the provincial level Premier Norris' response to the violence was not to punish the rioters but to establish an Alien Investigation Board. Presided over by Judge Myers, it was instructed to issue registration cards only to those enemy aliens who were considered "loyal"; their cards would enable "loyal" aliens to secure employment and, ostensibly, protected them from physical intimidation. In practice, however, the hearings of the board often degenerated into virtual "kangaroo" courts with the aliens being harassed by members of the board and crowds of hostile veterans who gathered daily at the Registration Hall. Many of the aliens declared disloyal were subsequently scheduled for deportation along with interned enemy aliens.[28]

But even these measures did not satisfy Anglo-Canadian demagogues like Ross. Despite clear evidence to the contrary, Ross claimed that the entire Ukrainian community in Manitoba was dominated by Bishop Budka, and that this sinister prelate was deeply involved in a Bolshevik conspiracy. Ukrainians throughout the province, so Ross maintained, "had machine guns, rifles and ammunition to start a revolution in May," and intended "to divide up property equally among everybody."[29]

In the early months of 1919 the Unionist government was deluged with petitions from patriotic societies, veterans' organizations, boards of trade, and municipal and provincial governments demanding the mass deportation of enemy aliens. Department of Justice surveys revealed that there were still 88,000 enemy aliens registered, 2,222 of them in internment camps. There were also 63,784 Russian subjects in Canada, many of whom, officials in Ottawa believed, were potentially subversive. A policy of mass deportation was rejected, however, for two reasons: the likely international repercussions and the demands it would make on the country's transportation facilities at a time when troops were returning from Europe. But "selective" deportations continued. In May 1919 the commander of the Kapuskasing internment camp informed Major General Otter, director of Internment Operations, that he had designated one hundred undesirables for immediate "repatriation"; these men, Major Date explained, were "socialists and IWW agitators [and] the type of man found around city pool halls, making an easy living."[30]

Patriotic sentiments, mounting labour unrest and the possibility that veteran violence might also be directed against corporate "profiteers" convinced many companies to dismiss their foreign employees. By February 1919 the British Columbia Employers' Association and the British Columbia Loggers' Association, for example, had both announced that their members were prepared to offer employment to returned soldiers by dismissing alien enemies. Similar promises were made in northern Ontario and in the coal mining regions of Alberta. Even the Canadian Pacific Railway joined the patriotic crusade of dismissals; as Vice-President D. C. Coleman put it: "The aliens who had been on the land when the war broke out and who went to work in the cities and towns, taking the jobs of the men who went to the front . . . [should] go back to their old jobs on the land."[31] The *Winnipeg Telegram*, one of the most virulent anti-alien newspapers in the country, called upon Anglo-Canadians to reassess their national priorities: "Are we to assume that Canadians have reached that state of luxury-loving that we should import a race of inferior beings to do our work."[32] In April and May 1919 the hearings of the Royal Commission on Industrial Relations (the Mathers Commission) gave Canadian businessmen the opportunity to take up the *Telegram*'s challenge. In general, corporate spokesmen expressed their willingness to reassess their involvement in alien worker employment, despite lingering doubts whether returned soldiers would be willing to take "the more arduous and less highly paid jobs."[33]

The Winnipeg General Strike of May 1919, sympathetic strikes in other centres and a major confrontation in the coal fields of District 18 turned an already ugly situation into a national crisis. In Winnipeg the self-appointed defender of civic law and order was the Citizens' Committee of One Thousand. In the pages of the *Winnipeg Telegram*, the *Manitoba Free Press* and its own publication, the *Citizen*, it carried on a systematic campaign against alien workers, who, it alleged, were the "shock troops" in the incipient revolutionary movement. Fortified by reports from the district military commander, Major General H. D. B. Ketchen; Arthur Meighen, who as acting minister of justice controlled the RNWMP; and A. J. Andrews, an active member of the Citizens' Committee of One Thousand, the federal government felt justified in dealing decisively with the strikers. Deportation was regarded as a particularly effective weapon, especially against "foreign-born radicals." In fact, the government had prepared the machinery for such action in April 1919 with an amendment to section 41 of the Immigration Act, providing for the deportation not only of self-proclaimed anarchists but also of "any person other than a Canadian citizen" who advocated revolution or who belonged to "any organization entertaining or teaching disbelief in or opposition to organized government." On 4 June 1919 the Naturalization Act was amended so that Bolshevik aliens could be denaturalized and deported under section 41. These measures, however, satisfied neither the Citizens' Committee of One Thousand nor security officials in Winnipeg who argued vigorously that British-born radicals should also be liable to deportation. Accordingly, section 41 was changed a second time in an amendment rushed through Parliament in less than an hour, under which British-born radicals could expect the same fate as their foreign-born comrades.[34]

In practice the government maintained a double standard, as British-born radicals were not brought before immigration tribunals but were processed through normal judicial channels. In Winnipeg it was the "mythical" alien leadership of the Central Strike Committee—Charitinoff, Alamazoff, Blumenberg and Schopelrie—who were subjected to deportation hearings under the authority of section 41. An even more unpleasant fate awaited those aliens arrested during the Winnipeg riots of 21 June: the majority were deported without a formal hearing.[35] In July 1919 members of the Russian Workers' Party were arrested in Vancouver for seditious activity; after a prolonged enquiry, fourteen were ordered "repatriated" to Vladivostok even though the government was warned that the men would be "murdered in cold blood by either the Japanese or the White Guard." It was only after the British Columbia Federation of Labour had launched a vigorous defence campaign and threatened a dock strike that the order was rescinded.[36] But Canadian immigration officials were not easily deterred: in December 1919 they attempted to place the Russians on the S.S. *Buford*, the famous Soviet Ark, which was about to sail for Russia with over three hundred American socialists and anarchists on board.[37]

Officials of the Department of Immigration and Colonization tended to brand certain European immigrant groups in particular as potentially dangerous. In the fall of 1919 F. C. Blair, departmental secretary, informed several employers that immigration from Finland was being discouraged because a "number of Finnish people seem to be very busy spreading IWW propaganda." Ukrainians and Russians, especially those who lived in Soviet-controlled territory, were seen in similar light. Even Italians were suspect, not only for an alleged propensity for crime, but also because the Bolshevik threat had spread to their country.[38]

By the end of 1919 immigrant socialists and syndicalists found themselves in desperate straits. Arrests and deportations had continued throughout the year, justified by RNWMP reports that "early in November [1919] ... revolutionaries will probably resort to ... 'open violence'." Certain segments of the Anglo-Canadian press continued to exploit the "Red Scare," particularly since lurid stories of Bolshevik intrigue enhanced sales.[39] Moreover, many employers fed anti-alien hysteria for their own purposes. This strategy was well evident in District 18 where the Western Coal Operators found themselves in an unusual alliance with the international trustees of the United Mine Workers of America and the federal government to crush the One Big Union. Their task was facilitated by the ability to turn the veteran against the alien striker.[40] Ethnic pogroms of this kind shocked many Anglo-Canadians who sought to heal the wounds of war, but tolerance was not a popular sentiment in postwar Canada. Thomas A. Crerar, the Unionist minister of agriculture, caught the mood of the times in this revealing comment:

> A great majority of the [Canadian] people, as a result of the times we have lived through in the last four years ... are not quite back to normal judgement. It is emphasized by the low nature of appealing to the prejudices of the returned soldiers ... Canadian psychology in the mass today has in it some of the elements of Bolshevism in embryo, only do not tell anyone I have said so.[41]

III

How does one account for the intensity of anti-alien sentiment among Anglo-Canadians which Crerar and others found so disturbing? How does one explain government harassment of those persons who were designated enemy aliens or "radical" aliens? And why were Ukrainian Canadians subjected to such a high degree of suspicion and hostility between 1918 and 1920?

One explanation would be to regard the nativist sentiment as merely an intensification of prewar bias. Prior to 1914 negative stereotypes of east and south European immigrants were widespread. Even such social reformers as the Reverend Charles W. Gordon (Ralph Connor) and James S. Woodsworth tended to equate poverty with immorality and ethnic festivals with debauchery and violence.[42] RNWMP reports from western Canada also stressed the tendency of foreign workers to take the law into their own hands; according to these accounts, the prevalence of knives and guns could turn even a minor disagreement into violent confrontation. During the 1906 Lethbridge coal strike, for example, the district superintendent of the RNWMP insisted upon the maximum deployment of police units in order to control Slavic and Italian miners: "These people have been ruled in force for generations [and] ... in consequence, it now requires forces to keep them in order." The RNWMP were also distressed by their inability to apprehend labour agitators and "criminals," largely because ethnic communities often viewed the Law as "the enemy."[43] Police authorities were particularly concerned about this conspiracy of silence in large ethnic "ghettos" like North End Winnipeg and in the single enterprise industrial communities of western Canada. In 1913 the Chief Constables' Association stressed the difficulty in dealing with European immigrant workers, especially those who attempted "to perpetuate customs which are foreign to us and which, if established here, would not be in the moral or material interests of our people."[44]

Yet another prewar stereotype was the spectre of the foreign agitator who sought to disrupt Canadian society on behalf of sinister goals. Industrial unrest among immigrant workers was usually blamed on anarchists, socialists and syndicalists who, it was alleged, were able to mobilize the latent violence of the foreign workers.[45] Anglo-Canadian reformers also charged that the Canadian political system, especially in the west, was being subverted by "foreign demagogues." During the 1914 Manitoba provincial election, for example, John W. Dafoe, the influential editor of the *Manitoba Free Press*, had branded the alliance between Roblin's Conservatives and members of the local Ukrainian elite, most notably Bishop Budka, as "un-Canadian"; ironically, a decade earlier, when Clifford Sifton had been Liberal minister of the interior, Dafoe had "delivered" the Ukrainian, Polish and German vote in the province to his employer.[46] What had changed? An obvious factor was that the provincial Conservatives had become more efficient than the Liberals in recruiting the immigrant vote. Of even greater consequence was the fact that, by 1914, Ukrainian lay and religious leaders were demanding a higher price for their political alliance. The development of the Ruthenian Training School for teachers, the growing influence of Ukrainian school trustees and the 1912 Coldwell amendment to the Manitoba School Act (which further facilitated the establishment of bilingual schools) had also persuaded many Anglo-Canadians that cultural concessions and political expediency were interrelated in a most sordid way.[47] Nor did Dafoe and other critics of Manitoba's ethnic pluralism respond favourably to the Ukrainian point of view, especially when couched in language such as that used by Petro Karmansky in *Kanadyiskyi rusyn* (Canadian Ruthenian) in early 1914:

> It is not everybody who looks upon culture from the standpoint of the Canadian art lover. The latter loves the wild yells of the prairie cowboy, symbol of ox-like satisfaction. It is charged that Galicians look upon Canada as an absolute savage country, a country of holdups and thieves and devoid of ideals and ethics. Do they? Well, then prove that they are mistaken.[48]

The First World War intensified the deeply entrenched hostility toward Ukrainians and other East Europeans classified as enemy aliens. Throughout 1914 and 1915 there were reports of German and Austrian agents infiltrating key defence installations and sabotaging Canadian war production. After 1916 such reports increasingly focused on the destructive activities of the IWW among enemy-alien workers, as syndicalists, socialists and anarchists came to be regarded as the main agents of the Central Powers in Canada. Moreover, as the war dragged on and casualties escalated, propaganda about the Central Powers became more and more vicious; by 1917 "most Canadians...believed that they were fighting a people that innoculated its captives with tuberculosis, decorated its dwellings with human skin, crucified Canadian soldiers, and enforced a national policy of compulsory polygamy on its virgins."[49]

Canadian residents of German origin, and immigrants from the Austro-Hungarian empire, were subjected to state harassment and public ostracism. In addition to internment, Germans faced property confiscation and press regulation; even the German Lutheran Church became suspect.[50] A December 1917 report by a government official in Winnipeg, for example, accused many of the local Lutheran clergy of acting "as paid or unpaid agents of the Kaiser...Teutonmaniacs whether by connection or persuasion." Certain German-language editors were also considered dangerous and threatened with internment. At times Anglo-Canadians took matters into their own hands; in April 1917 a mob destroyed the Regina offices of *Der Courier*, a German newspaper which gained notoriety for its defence of German cultural rights in western Canada. A similar fate befell other German newspapers and cultural associations during 1918 and 1919.[51] Yet a grudging respect for the superior qualities of German immigrants seems to have survived everything. In the spring of 1919, during a parliamentary review of the Immigration Act, the Unionist government blocked the imposition of a statutory prohibition of German immigration;

while German immigrants were temporarily excluded, power to remove the ban lay with the Immigration Branch.[52] The immigration debates of 1919 also showed that German immigrants were not regarded as potential Bolsheviks. Security officials did not seem to fear German Canadian industrial workers, and significantly no German organizations had been specifically outlawed by the order in council of 25 September 1918. Nor were German-language newspapers regarded as advocates of revolution and industrial unrest.[53]

The situation of Ukrainian Canadians was quite different, especially after 1916. Despite abundant evidence that Ukrainians and other non-Germans from the Austro-Hungarian empire were unwilling belligerents, they were more distrusted than their German Canadian counterparts. One reason was that the "Austrians" were recent arrivals; in 1911, 60 per cent of Ukrainians in the Prairie provinces were foreign-born.[54] Cultural issues also placed the Ukrainian community in confrontation with Anglo-Canadians; the determined Ukrainian resistance to the abolition of bilingual schools in Manitoba, for example, stirred deep hostility among Anglo-Canadians in the province. The western press censor, Fred Livesay, went so far as to interpret the temporary alliance between *Kanadyiskyi rusyn* and *Ukrainskyi holos* (Ukrainian Voice) on the matter of Ukrainian language rights as part of a German/Austrian conspiracy to disrupt the Canadian war effort. This stereotype of a homogeneous Ukrainian community on the Prairies, manipulated by a disloyal and demagogic elite, gained even more credence among Anglo-Canadians during the election of December 1917. It assumed its most insidious form, however, when concern over Bolshevik conspiracy gripped elements of the Anglo-Canadian community throughout 1918 and 1919.[55]

Canadian reaction to the Russian Revolution went through several stages. Initially, there was widespread support for the overthrow of the tsar, in part, at least, because of the belief that the authoritarian character of imperial government impeded Russia's war effort. In March 1917 the *Toronto Globe* claimed that the Russian people "had revolted against the idea of fighting the battle of human freedom while they themselves were slaves of Romanov despotism" and that now Russia's leaders would share in the struggle for democracy over autocracy. By November, however, the paper was denouncing their Bolshevik replacements as "cutthroats and bandits" whose policies were a "danger to civilization." Anti-Bolshevik sentiment continued to grow during 1918 and the decision to send Canadian troops to aid anti-Soviet forces in Siberia was popular.[56]

If Anglo-Canadians did not understand the implications of the Russian Revolution, their appreciation of the impact of the Ukrainian Revolution on Ukrainians in Canada was even more limited. Before the war Anglo-Canadians rarely had been able to distinguish the different ideological groupings within the Ukrainian community; after March 1917 the situation became even more complicated. In the fall of 1917 *Robochyi narod* called upon all Canadian Ukrainians to emphasize their common identity and national purpose; now was the time, it argued, to let "our neighbours in Canada know clearly who and what we are: that we are not 'Austrian,' or 'Galician,' or a wild, uneducated people as portrayed by 'our own native' undercover agents, who have sold out and are traitors to our people." In December, however, it vigorously denounced the Ukrainian Central Rada and the prospects of a bourgeois independent Ukraine.[57] As differences between the Ukrainian Social Democratic Party and the remainder of the Ukrainian immigrant community became irreconcilable, those opposed to the Bolsheviks often appealed to Canadian security agencies, supplying information about Ukrainian socialists in return.[58] In September 1918 the chief press censor concluded that Budka was not a security risk and could be utilized as a source of information:

> The Bishop states that there is a distinct and well organized revolutionary Bolshevik movement in Canada, looking to the overthrow of all established authority and to the introduction into Canada of the chaotic conditions of affairs which exist today in Russia. He mentioned the *Robotchy Narod* and *Rabotchy Narod* as being mouthpieces of those who are engineering this revolutionary movement.[59]

Yet despite Budka's assistance to the authorities against the Ukrainian socialists, his position remained precarious. He was twice charged with seditious activity in 1918, and in February 1919 was the subject of an inquiry by the Great War Veterans' Association. Budka's loyalty was vindicated, but the episode did little to enhance his popularity among Anglo-Canadians in western Canada.[60]

Veteran militancy deeply affected industrial and ethnic relations throughout the country, especially in heterogeneous communities. Most companies were able to deflect veteran animosity through large-scale dismissals of enemy-alien workers; some, however, such as Swift's Meat Packing Plant at Elmwood, Manitoba, had to be forcibly reminded that "unpatriotic" employment practices could be considered war profiteering. The *Manitoba Veteran* left little doubt about its attitude toward corporate opportunism: in June 1919 it called upon the federal government to treat "these profiteers, and all men who belong to their treasonable brood . . . in a manner exactly similar to that employed against Bolshevists, traitors and conspirators."[61] The serious strikes of 1918 and 1919 gave worried Canadian businessmen ample opportunity to placate the veterans.[62] In some centres returned soldiers were regarded as potential strike-breakers and shock troops who could be used against alien radicals and trade-union militants.

Wartime conditioning to hate the Hun, resentment of the neighbourhood "bohunk" who had apparently prospered on the home front and the anti-socialist position of the executive of the Great War Veterans' Association were usually sufficient to place the veteran on the side of law, order and property.[63] But not always. In Winnipeg, for example, many of the same veterans who had battered enemy aliens in January 1918 were to be found at strike rallies and protest marches alongside their former adversaries in 1919. C. Rice-Jones, general manager of the United Grain Growers' Company and confidant of T. A. Crerar, candidly assessed this growing detente between veterans and trade unions:

> The dreams of the Manufacturers' Association and professional politicians that they could line up the returned soldiers by appealing to their patriotism and trying to prejudice them against any one of foreign birth are apparently being dashed to the ground in the Winnipeg strike, and it is only a matter of time before a large majority of the returned men line up with labor.[64]

Undoubtedly the vicious anti-alien propaganda issued by citizens' committees in Winnipeg, Port Arthur and Vancouver was a desperate attempt to keep the returned soldiers out of the socialist trade union.

Of course, businessmen were not alone in fostering anti-alien sentiment. Demagogic politicians like D. A. Ross and newspapers like the *Winnipeg Telegram* had their own reasons for riding the nativist horse; but ride it they did, without danger of censorship or libel suits.[65] Perhaps most distressing was the tendency of certain federal security officials to legitimize allegations about a radical alien conspiracy. The performances of C. H. Cahan, Colonel Chambers and Major General H. D. B. Ketchen reveal the danger of entrusting amateurs with the important task of operating a security system. Not only were they poorly qualified for such important work, but they also tended to have an exaggerated sense of their own role in protecting the nation. Reports from the Public Safety Branch, the Office of the Chief Press Censor and the Winnipeg Military District illustrate the great difficulty these officials and their subordinates had in differentiating between rumour and fact, hyperbole and sedition.[66]

In the spring of 1919 the "Red Scare" greatly enhanced the authority of those advocating stern measures against radical aliens. Within the Unionist cabinet even such "liberals" as Thomas Crerar and Newton Rowell were deeply affected by national and international reports of Bolshevik subversive activity and by the scale of industrial unrest in the country.[67] Indeed, in the tumultuous months of May and June 1919 many "liberal" Anglo-Canadians were prepared to condone the approach which police magistrate Hugh John Macdonald subsequently recommended to the acting justice minister, Arthur Meighen:

I should like to impress upon you ... the desirability of getting rid of as many undesirable aliens as possible and I venture to do so because, as Police Magistrate, I have seen to what a large extent Bolsheviki ideas are held by the Ruthenian, Russian and Polish people whom we have in our midst and how large a section of the Russian and German Jews hold similar views.... [F]ear is the only agency that can successfuly be employed to keep them within the law and I have no doubt that if the Dominion Government persists in the course that it is adopting the foreign element here will soon be as gentle and as easily controlled as a lot of sheep.... When I speak of the foreign element, I allude only to men of the races I have above mentioned, as here we find those coming from other countries no harder to handle and keep in order than our own people.[68]

Notes

1. O. T. Martynowych, "The Ukrainian Socialist Movement in Canada, 1900–1918," *Journal of Ukrainian Graduate Studies* 1, no. 1 (Fall 1976): 27–44, indicates that prior to 1914 there was no strong sense of common Ukrainian identity in Canada, even among the socialists. This viewpoint has been emphasized by others as well: "Although the intelligentsia, both in Canada and Ukraine, had long exhorted the peasants to shed their 'Bukovynian,' 'Galician,' or 'Ruthenian' identities and to recognize themselves as part of the 'soporific' Ukrainian nation, their efforts were often not rewarded" (N. Makuch, "The Influence of the Ukrainian Revolution on Ukrainians in Canada, 1917–22," *ibid.* 4, no. 1 [Spring 1979]: 43–4). Makuch also points out that while the "liberal intelligentsia" associated with *Ukrainskyi holos* were strongly committed to developing national consciousness and used the term "Ukrainian" in the title of their newspaper in 1909 (1910—Ed.), the organ of the Greek Catholic Church, *Kanadyiskyi rusyn*, became *Kanadyiskyi ukrainets* only in 1919.

2. D. H. Avery, *"Dangerous Foreigners": European Immigrant Workers and Labour Radicalism in Canada, 1896–1932* (Toronto, 1979), 65–79; and A. R. McCormack, *Reformers, Rebels and Revolutionaries: The Western Canadian Radical Movement 1899–1919* (Toronto, 1977), 160–85.

3. P. Wathner to McBride, 10 September 1914, Sir Richard McBride Papers, Box 166, Provincial Archives of British Columbia (hereafter PABC), Victoria, British Columbia.

4. *Robochyi narod*, 14 March 1914.

5. Martynowych, "Ukrainian Socialist Movement," 32. A disturbance in Edmonton saw about six hundred unemployed workers, "many of whom were said to be Russian, Polish or Ukrainian," give public vent to their sense of alienation; arrests were made, particularly of demonstrators believed to be

members of the Industrial Workers of the World. See H. Potrebenko, *No Streets of Gold: A Social History of Ukrainians in Alberta* (Vancouver, 1977), 92–7.

6. Aikins to Borden, 12 November 1914, Sir Robert Borden Papers, 106322, Public Archives of Canada (hereafter PAC), Ottawa, Ontario.

7. W.D. Otter, *Internment Operations, 1914–1920* (Ottawa, 1921), 6; and D. Morton, "Sir William Otter and Internment Operations in Canada during The First World War," *Canadian Historical Review* 55, no. 1 (March 1974): 32–58.

8. Avery, *"Dangerous Foreigners"*, 67–70.

9. The Hillcrest mine disaster of June 1914 which killed 189 men, including twenty Ukrainians, contributed considerably to the fear of alien sabotage. Potrebenko, *No Streets of Gold*, 96.

10. *Robochyi narod*, 23 June 1915. The same issue reported the arrest of fourteen members of the Ukrainian Social Democratic Party in Fernie and another twenty-eight in Michel.

11. *Canadian Annual Review* (1916): 325–8.

12. *Ibid.* (1915): 354; and W.D. Otter to F.L. Wanklyn (Canadian Pacific Railway), 12 June 1916, and John Aronee (prisoner of war) to Otter, 14 May 1917, Internment Operations Files, file 3326, Secretary of State Papers, PAC.

13. Canada, *Statutes*, 9 and 10 Geo. 5, xc iii.

14. John Simpson to Colin Campbell, 26 June 1916, British Columbia Provincial Police Records, file 1355–7, PABC.

15. See, for example, M. Bliss, "The Methodist Church and World War I," *Canadian Historical Review* 49, no. 3 (September 1968): 220–2.

16. Cahan to Borden, 14 September 1918, Borden Papers, PAC.

17. S.W. Horrall, "The Royal North-West Mounted Police and Labour Unrest in Western Canada, 1919," *Canadian Historical Review* 61, no. 2 (June 1980): 169–90.

18. Diary of Sir George Foster, 30 September 1918, PAC.

19. Cahan to Borden, 20 October 1918, Borden Papers, 48169, PAC.

20. *Bassi v. Sullivan*, 32 *Ontario Law Reports*, 1914, 14. The ruling by Judge Hodgins interpreted the federal proclamation of 15 August 1914 very narrowly in that it placed the burden of proof on the enemy alien to establish that he was not hostile to the Crown. In contrast, a Manitoba court had, in a similar case, interpreted the proclamation more broadly and concluded that an enemy alien did have the right to bring suit in a Canadian court (*Pescovitch v. Western Canada Flour Co.*, 7 *Western Weekly Reports*, 1914, 454). This ambivalence remained until the end of the war since neither case was appealed to the Supreme Court. See C. Cole, "The War Measures Act, 1914" (M.A. thesis, University of Western Ontario, 1980).

21. Memorandum, Borden to the solicitor general, 20 June 1919, Borden Papers, 60974, PAC.

22. See, for example, *Manitoba Free Press*, 20–28 September 1918; *Edmonton Journal*, 20–28 September 1918; *Vancouver Sun*, 20–28 September 1918; and

Toronto Globe, 27 September 1918.

23. Meighen to Richardson, 3 April 1919, Arthur Meighen Papers, 000267, PAC.

24. Cahan to Major General Gwatkin, 3 January 1919, Department of Militia and Defence Records, file C-2051(2), PAC.

25. Livesay to Chambers, 17 April 1919, Chief Press Censor Files, 144–A–1, vol. 27, PAC.

26. Ross to Meighen, 16 April 1919, Meighen Papers, 000279, PAC.

27. D. Morton, "'Kicking and Complaining': Demobilization Riots in the Canadian Expeditionary Force, 1918–19," *Canadian Historical Review* 61, no. 3 (September 1980): 334–60; and J. A. Stevenson to Meighen, 24 February 1919, Meighen Papers, 000256, PAC. In Sudbury a group of Ukrainians who had been assaulted appealed to the Borden government for assistance to return to Europe; Albert Cawdron, Acting Commissioner of the Dominion Police, to the Minister of Justice, 28 July 1919, Department of Justice Records, file 2266, 1919, PAC.

28. D. H. Avery, "The Radical Alien and the Winnipeg General Strike of 1919," in *The West and the Nation: Essays in Honour of W. L. Morton*, ed. C. Berger and R. Cook (Toronto, 1976), 209–31. By PC 332 of 4 February 1919 the federal government conferred the authority upon county court judges to order the internment of "persons of alien nationality residing or being within a designated locality." Comptroller to Commissioner Perry, 20 March 1919, Royal Canadian Mounted Police (RCMP) Records, PAC.

29. Ross to Meighen, 16 April 1919, Meighen Papers, 000279, PAC. In April 1919 the efficiency of the Alien Investigation Board became a matter of national controversy when H.A. Mackie, Unionist member for Edmonton East, charged in the House of Commons that the Norris government was utilizing the board for partisan purposes. Liberal organizers, he alleged, were working closely with Ukrainian nationalists in dispensing this new and insidious form of patronage. The flurry of counter-charges from Premier Norris, Judge Myers, D. A. Ross, Bishop Budka and the Ukrainian Canadian Citizens' Committee tended to destroy public confidence in both the board and the Manitoba government's willingness to deal with the "alien enemy problem." Moreover, in May 1919 the Ukrainian Canadian Citizens' Committee initiated legal action in order to test the constitutionality of the board. *Winnipeg Tribune*, 10 May 1919.

30. Avery, *"Dangerous Foreigners"*, 676–82; and Date to Otter, 12 May 1919, Internment Operations Files, file 6712(2), PAC.

31. *Vancouver Sun*, 1 and 3 February 1919; *Montreal Gazette* 14 June 1919; and *Canadian Mining Journal*, 15 November 1919.

32. *Winnipeg Telegram*, 10 February 1919.

33. Mathers Royal Commission on Industrial Relations, 1919, "Evidence" (Dept. of Labour Library), Victoria Hearings, 28 April 1919.

34. Avery, "Radical Alien," 219–26. Hugh Guthrie, the federal solicitor general, emphasized that since Germans, Austrians and Russians maintained dual nationality they could be easily denaturalized. Canada, *Parliamentary Debates*

(Commons), 138, 5 (1919): 4122.

35. Avery, "Radical Alien," 223–4.

36. F. C. Blair to J. A. Calder, 25 February 1920, Immigration Branch Records, 969713, PAC; and A. S. Wells to Meighen, 26 July 1920, Meighen Papers, 071232, PAC.

37. Blair to Calder, 24 November 1919, and John Clark to Blair, 19 June 1919, Immigration Branch Records, 961162(2) PAC.

38. Blair to McFadden and McMillan Lumber Co., Fort William, 27 August 1919, Immigration Branch Records, 651(3), PAC; and Blair to the president of the Algoma Steel Co., 20 September 1920, Immigration Branch Records, 28885(5), PAC.

39. Report of Commissioner Perry, cited in Gwatkin to S. D. Mewburn, 9 August 1919, Militia and Defence Records, C–2817, PAC; and *Maclean's Magazine*, August 1919.

40. Avery, *"Dangerous Foreigners"*, 86–7; and A. Woywitka, "Drumheller Strike of 1919," *Alberta History* 21, no. 1 (Winter 1973): 1–7. During periods of industrial unrest in the 1920s mine owners and officials of the Alberta Provincial Police frequently requested that the Immigration Branch deport immigrant radicals; see, for example, Commissioner to Premier Brownlee, 25 July 1925, Alberta Provincial Police Records, Provincial Archives of Alberta, Edmonton, Alberta.

41. Crerar to George Chipman, 15 April 1919, Thomas Crerar Papers, Queen's University Archives, Kingston, Ontario.

42. See J. S. Woodsworth, *Strangers Within Our Gates* (Toronto, 1909); C. W. Gordon [Ralph Connor], *The Foreigner* (Toronto, 1909); and C. A. Magrath, *Canada's Growth and Some Problems Affecting It* (Ottawa, 1910).

43. Inspector E. J. Camies to J. O. Wilson, Supt. 'K' Division, 7 April 1906, RCMP Records, file 790, PAC. See also annual reports of Commissioner A. Bowen Perry in the *Sessional Papers* for 1904, 1910, 1912 and 1914.

44. *Address to the Chief Constables' Association of Canada, Ninth Annual Convention*, Halifax, 25–7 June 1913, Immigration Branch Records, 813739(1), PAC.

45. Reaction to the proposed visit of Emma Goldman, the famous anarchist, to Winnipeg in 1908 clearly revealed this sense of paranoia on the part of the Anglo-Canadian community. See Avery, "Radical Alien," 212.

46. During the 1904 election Dafoe co-ordinated the electoral activities of the various immigration officials. In April 1904 he advised Sifton to place all eligible Ukrainians on the federal voters' list so that these "new" Canadians would realize "to whom they are indebted to for the privilege of the franchise" (Clifford Sifton Papers, 127153, PAC).

47. See M. Donnelly, *Dafoe of the Free Press* (Toronto, 1968), 57, 71; P. Yuzyk, *The Ukrainians in Manitoba: A Social History* (Toronto, 1953) 144–8; J. Skwarok, *The Ukrainian Settlers in Canada and Their Schools 1891–1921* (Toronto, 1959). 60–70; and *Manitoba Free Press*, 21 May and 3 August 1914.

48. Cited in *Manitoba Free Press*, 5 March 1914. Possessing a teaching diploma from Lviv University, Karmansky had come to Canada in 1913 to lecture at the Ruthenian Training School. An intransigent personality who alienated many in the immigrant community, he wrote for both the Catholic *Kanadyiskyi rusyn* and the short-lived conservative *Kanada*. Karmansky rapidly became disillusioned with Canada and returned to Galicia shortly before the war. He was noted as a journalist.

49. Avery, *"Dangerous Foreigners"*, 65–76; and Bliss, "Methodist Church," 220.

50. See M. Nordegg, *The Possibilities of Canada are Truly Great; Memoirs 1906–1924*, ed. T. D. Regehr (Toronto, 1971), 215; and H. K. Kalbfleisch, *The History of the Pioneer German Language Press in Ontario* (Toronto, 1968), 105–14.

51. Report of Agent No. 50, 30 December 1917, Militia and Defence Records, C–965(24), PAC; Chambers to C. E. Eymann, 24 November 1915, Chief Press Censor Files, 119–C–1, vol. 19, PAC; and *Canadian Annual Review*, (1915): 355–6, and (1918): 585–7.

52. Canada, *Parliamentary Debates* (Commons), 134, 1 (1919): 771; *ibid.*, 135, 2 (1919): 1867–73; and Canada, *Statutes*, 9 and 10 Geo. 5, chap. 25.

53. Cahan to Borden, 14 September 1918, Borden Papers, 56676, PAC; Cahan to Borden, 21 October 1918, Borden Papers, 56698, PAC; and Gwatkin to Cahan, 4 January 1919, Militia and Defence Records, C–20–51, PAC.

54. Canada, Bureau of Statistics, *Census of Prairie Provinces, 1916* (Ottawa, 1918), 220–2.

55. *Manitoba Free Press*, 29 February and 1 March, 1916; Livesay to Chambers, 12 July 1916, Chief Press Censor Files, 196–4, vol. 444, PAC; and *Manitoba Free Press*, 10 December 1917. Just prior to the 1917 federal election *Kanadyiskyi rusyn* complained bitterly about the tendency of the Anglo-Canadian community to seek scapegoats: "It is the custom in Canada during the war that when anything happens or goes wrong the failure is put on those inhabitants of Canada who come from enemy countries.... If the wheat crop doesn't turn out, it is the fault of the enemy alien; a train jumping its tracks, fire and strike are all the fault of the enemy alien" (*Kanadyiskyi rusyn*, 10 December 1917).

56. *Toronto Globe* 17 March and 25 November 1917; *Manitoba Free Press*, 22 December 1917, 19 July 1918; and J. Swettenham, *Allied Intervention in Russia, 1918–1919, and the Part Played By Canada* (London, 1967).

57. Makuch, "Influence of the Ukrainian Revolution," 44, 49.

58. The Czech Frank Dojacek, publisher of *Kanadyiskyi farmer*, was used extensively because he disassociated himself from Ukrainian nationalists and socialists alike. In March 1920 Dojacek was criticized by the editor of *Kanadyiskyi ukrainets* at the convention of the Ukrainian National Council in St. Boniface, Manitoba; he was charged in particular with being a collaborator during the war and betraying Ukrainian interests "before the authorities in Ottawa" (Dojacek to Chambers, 4 March 1920, Chief Press Censor Files, 196–1, PAC).

59. Chambers to Martin Burrell, 20 September 1918, Chief Press Censor Files, 144–A–1, PAC. At this time *Robochyi narod* was edited by Matthew Popovich and the Russian-language *Rabitchy narod* by Michael Charitinoff; in October 1918 Charitinoff was sentenced to three years imprisonment and fined one thousand dollars for possession of illegal literature. The campaign to secure his release united Anglo-Canadian and Ukrainian socialists throughout western Canada. Avery, "Radical Alien," 216–17.

60. Canada, *Parliamentary Debates* (Commons), 134, 1 (1919): 646; *ibid.*, 135, 2 (1919): 1936–9; and *Toronto Star*, 22 March 1919.

61. *Manitoba Veteran*, 21 June 1919.

62. Mathers Commission, "Evidence", Calgary Hearings, 3 May 1919.

63. Avery, "Radical Alien," 218–22; Mathers Commission, "Evidence," Edmonton Hearings, 6 May 1919. In British Columbia Italian workers were also the target of veterans' organizations because of their alleged indifference to the war effort; see *Vancouver Sun*, 4 February 1919. In Winnipeg many of the reports of undercover RNWMP operations were distinctly anti-semitic; see report, 11 June 1919, Borden Papers, 62037, PAC.

64. Rice-Jones to Crerar, 22 May 1919, Crerar Papers, PAC.

65. In an editorial of 29 January 1919 the *Winnipeg Telegram* denounced the *Winnipeg Tribune* for being "a toady to Bolshevism." The attack stemmed from the *Tribune*'s criticism of the *Telegram* for justifying the use of violence against aliens during the Winnipeg riots of 26–7 January.

66. The role of federal security officials during the First World War has never been thoroughly analysed. The author has, however, conducted a systematic study of the activities of the Press Censorship Branch, the Public Safety Branch, the Department of Justice, the Royal North West Mounted Police and military intelligence.

67. See A. Marwick, *The Deluge: British Society and the First World War* (New York, 1965); D. Mitchell, *1919: Red Mirage* (New York, 1970); and W. Rodney, *Soldiers of the International* (Toronto, 1969). M. Prang, in *N.W. Rowell: Ontario Nationalist* (Toronto, 1975), has indicated that during the Winnipeg General Strike Rowell and Crerar were "in substantial agreement with the Citizens' Committee of One Thousand" (299).

68. Macdonald to Meighen, 3 July 1919, Meighen Papers, 002537, PAC.

Chapter 6

Aliens in Britain and the Empire During the First World War*

David Saunders

Aliens loom large at the beginning and end of wars. At the beginning the public is xenophobic and the government worried about fifth-columnists. At the end the people are afraid that resident foreigners will keep returning soldiers out of jobs, while the government is forced both to relax existing controls and to tighten legislation to increase security in the future. In the middle, once controls have been introduced, the problem of aliens may lie fallow. It refused to do so in Britain between 1914 and 1918. For reasons other than the German threat, aliens were a contentious issue before the outbreak of hostilities. Britain's domestic politics and its international economic standing had been changing in ways which made the treatment of aliens particularly difficult. When a world war supervened, a war fought against not only Germany but also Austria-Hungary, a war in which Russian support created as many problems as it solved, and a war which raised questions of imperial as well as domestic policy, an administration already troubled by aliens was troubled still further.

The treatment of Britain's German aliens followed a predictable pattern

*I am extremely grateful to my friends and colleagues, Tony Badger, David French and Martin Pugh, for their comments on an earlier version of this paper. Remaining errors of fact and interpretation are my own. I should like to thank the Research Committee of the University of Newcastle upon Tyne for financing research in London. Crown copyright in documents at the Public Record Office, London, is vested in the Controller of Her Majesty's Stationery Office.

during the First World War: internment soon after the outbreak of hostilities followed by restrictions on future immigration in 1918. The treatment of other aliens, however, was more complicated. Hostility toward Germans had been growing since the turn of the century,[1] but it constituted no more than a fraction of the total hostility toward foreigners. Britain had experienced Irish immigration in the first half of the nineteenth century and Jewish immigration since the 1870s. The second of these waves produced radical changes in British attitudes toward foreigners. The Victorians' self-confidence, meanwhile, had evaporated. With the growth of the electorate the government had to be more responsive to public opinion. With the passing of Britain's economic supremacy its open-handedness toward the outside world contracted. Before 1914 the Liberal government was already adapting its values to meet the needs of changing circumstances. Between 1914 and 1918 different administrations found themselves having to adapt still further. The treatment of aliens shows the process of adaptation at work. In what follows I shall review aliens policy before 1914, consider the position of aliens during and just after the war and look at three aspects of the question in detail: "friendly enemies" and "enemy friends," the imperial dimension, and Britain's Ukrainians—a case study in the complexity of aliens control during the First World War.

I

Between the end of the Napoleonic Wars and the passage of the Aliens Act in 1905 Britain kept an open house. From 1823 to 1906 no foreigner was prevented from entering the country or forced to leave it.[2] In 1968, by contrast, even certain citizens of the United Kingdom and colonies were prevented from taking up residence in the mother country.[3] The transition from the liberal to the narrow view of immigration began with the vast influx of Jews from eastern Europe in the late nineteenth century. In 1887 Arnold White, a leading right-wing radical,[4] wrote a letter to the *Times* which will serve as a text for that hostility toward East European immigrants which characterized so much of the following twenty years in England. "At the present time," he wrote,

> and since the Russian persecutions of 1880, the burden of maintaining the traditions of England in regard to hospitality to oppressed foreigners has been borne, not by that portion of the community able to indulge in the luxury of sentiment as to the "traditions of England," but by those poor workers for whom the wolf is always waiting at the door. Until 1880 the occasional visit of a few religious or political refugees enabled us to reflect not only that we are not as other men are, but that our virtue was not at variance with our financial interest [for earlier immigrants—the Huguenots—had benefited England

economically].... But there is no similarity between the habits, training, knowledge, skill, and means of the Huguenot silk weavers of two centuries back and the ignorant Russians and Poles driven from their own country and refused asylum in the United States who are allowed to settle in England without restriction.[5]

By "ignorant Russians and Poles" White meant Jews. "The splendid benefactions of the Rothschilds and other leaders of the Jewish community to their coreligionists in the East-end," he continued, "are as a lamp set on a hill to those in Eastern Europe who are tormented by the agents of resolute government until they consent to emigrate."[6] White wanted immigration stopped:

If we have neither power to quell the flame of religious strife in Eastern Europe nor to determine the period of its outbreak, surely the wiser course for our rulers is to see that England is no longer the rubbish heap on which discarded elements of Continental societies may be shot with impunity.[7]

Eighteen-eighty-seven marked the beginning of the long agitation which led to the passage of the Aliens Act of 1905.[8] Limiting immigration went against the grain for English politicians who prided themselves on preserving freedom. In opposing the Aliens Bill of 1904, for example, Winston Churchill commented:

The simple immigrant, the political refugee, the helpless and the poor—these are the folk who will be caught in the trammels of the bill and may be harassed and hustled at the pleasure of petty officials without the smallest right of appeal to the broad justice of the English courts.[9]

In view of such opposition it was not surprising, perhaps, that the 1904 bill failed to pass or that eighteen years elapsed between White's protest of 1887 and the eventual carrying of the Aliens Act. But in 1905 the measure reached the statute book.[10]

Expulsions began under the new law,[11] but it left untouched the right of asylum. Jews were able to enter the country by claiming to be political or religious refugees. Public disquiet therefore persisted. Three Russian Jews, for example, were admitted at Grimsby in 1906, after having been turned away by the United States on health grounds. Sir Howard Vincent, disturbed by their entry into Britain, asked about them in the House of Commons. He described their rejection by the United States, "as suffering from trachoma and being otherwise undesirable associates for the citizens of the Republic," and requested the Home Office to "explain the reasons for the course adopted [in Britain], and say how many of His Majesty's subjects have since been infected with the contagious disorders from which these aliens were suffering."[12] Vincent's parliamentary question illustrated the way in which hostility toward aliens continued after the passage of the 1905 act.

As the international situation grew more tense, the government, concerned for security, became as worried about aliens as the general public. The disquiet expressed by Vincent in 1906 found more wide-ranging expression in an official document of 1913, the "Report and Proceedings of the Standing Sub-Committee of the Committee of Imperial Defence on the Treatment of Aliens in Time of War."[13] The sub-committee described its "essential objects" as "to protect vulnerable points or natural resources against ill-disposed persons; to prevent the communication to an enemy Government of information of military value; and to hinder resident enemy aliens from rendering assistance to a hostile force which has landed in this country."[14] The General Staff had called for an investigation into the wartime treatment of aliens. It proposed the amendment of the 1889 Official Secrets Act "to give powers of arrest [of aliens] without previous reference to the Attorney-General, and power of search"; the "registration at all times of all aliens arriving in this country"; and the granting to the executive of such wartime powers as had been conferred during the Napoleonic Wars in 1803.[15] These proposals, particularly the second, went beyond what seemed necessary to achieve the subcommittee's goals, but all three were accepted. The first was implemented in the Official Secrets Act of 1911, when the subcommittee was sitting.[16] The second, registration of aliens, took effect unofficially.[17] The third found embodiment in appendices of the 1913 report, which included a draft bill to impose restrictions on aliens in time of war or crisis and a draft order in council for its enactment. The government envisaged taking powers to order aliens to reside in certain areas, to oblige aliens to register and to prevent alien enemies travelling more than five miles from the address at which they were registered.[18] These were the guidelines that were to serve Britain during the war.

II

When war broke out, the powers outlined in the report of 1913 took effect under the Aliens Restriction Act of 5 August 1914.[19] Although the Liberal home secretary, Reginald McKenna, made himself unpopular with the Unionist opposition for acting slowly with respect to aliens,[20] and although it was not until May 1915 that internment of adult male enemies became the rule[21] and a "policy . . . of the deportation or repatriation of alien enemies other than males of military age" began to be enforced,[22] action was taken to deal with aliens as soon as hostilities began. The Registrar-General of England and Wales outlined the history of this action in a memorandum of 1917. Since early August 1914, he wrote, "all alien enemies wherever resident, and all aliens residing in prohibited areas were required to register with the local police...and to report any changes of residence or any alterations in the particulars registered within 48 hours." In December 1914 the Belgians who had been flocking into the country since the outbreak of war, although not enemy aliens, were placed under the same obligations; "and in addition to local registration with the Police a Central Register was established to be kept by the Registrar-General." In February 1916, after the internment of enemy aliens became general, the control of aliens was greatly increased and all aliens, whether friendly or enemy, were required to register with the police. "A temporary exception was made for the Metropolitan Police District" but it was "gradually withdrawn," and by 1917 "only female alien friends who were resident in London on or before the 14th February, 1916," did not have to register.[23]

Dealing merely with enemy aliens was a sufficiently daunting problem. In 1911 Britain's inhabitants included 32,400 male Germans and 9,400 male citizens of Austria-Hungary.[24] In July 1916 there were "about 32,000 male enemy aliens interned as civilian prisoners of war," while another 20,000 had applied for exemption from internment.[25] A year later the War Office estimated that the "original enemy colony" of about 75,000 had been reduced to 23,000 "remaining at large," the rest having been interned or repatriated.[26]

But the British authorities did not confine their activities to enemy aliens. During the First World War Britain collected more or less complete data on all alien inhabitants of the country—a considerable undertaking, for the 1911 census gave the total alien population of England and Wales as 284,830.[27] Britain seems to have taken advantage of the war to produce its first comprehensive aliens policy, hiding the "leaf" of enemy aliens in the "forest" of aliens as a whole. Even at the outbreak of hostilities enemy aliens seem to have constituted not much more than a quarter of the total alien population.[28] By the time the Aliens Committee of the Ministry of Reconstruction was considering what to do about aliens after the war's end, enemy aliens made up less than a ninth of the total number of aliens at liberty. The committee reported that on 1 July 1917 there were 24,053 adult alien enemies in the country, 164,448 allied aliens, and 37,929 neutral and other aliens.[29]

As the war progressed, then, British authorities looked at all aliens, not merely enemies. They came to think in terms that went beyond the logic of the wartime conflict. The Aliens Committee of the Ministry of Reconstruction was required to consider three points:

1. The questions which will arise at the end of the war in connection with the presence in this country of persons of enemy nationality, and whether the repatriation of such persons is desirable, and if so in what cases.

2. What restrictions, if any, should be imposed after the war on the admission of aliens into this country and their residence here.

3. Whether any changes in the law or practice of naturalization have been shown by the experience of the war to be required in the public interest.[30]

Thus, the committee had to review the provisions of the Aliens Restriction Act of 1914 and the Aliens Act of 1905. In redefining British immigration policy it concluded, harshly, that interned enemy aliens were to be compulsorily repatriated; that the cases of uninterned enemy aliens were to be reviewed at the end of the war with those "who cannot without disadvantages to this country be permitted to remain" to be repatriated; that "a general system of alien registration ... [was to] ... be established at the end of the war"; that naturalization was to be made harder, especially for Germans; and that certificates of naturalization should be revoked for "disloyalty or criminality." It also laid down which considerations were to be important in the hearing of appeals against repatriation and discussed how to effect "total exclusion ... of the subjects of the present enemy countries" if the government were to decide upon such a far-reaching step.[31] With the implementation of the committee's recommendations,[32] Britain greatly extended the control of aliens which it had introduced in 1905.

In 1918 and 1919 hostility toward aliens seems to have been widespread and indiscriminate. The War Office wanted to repatriate all alien enemies, whether combatant, civilian, interned or uninterned. The *Daily Mail* and the *Manchester Guardian* wanted to prevent future German immigration. The separate administration of the Isle of Man tried to stop a friendly alien, a Russian, from setting up business on the island. Several London borough councils urged the central government to enforce the laws on immigration and registration of foreigners because returning soldiers, in their view, were finding it hard to get work owing to the size of the alien population.[33] A. J. P. Taylor argued that "the war left few permanent marks on British life," but that three "inventions" made during the course of it lived on afterwards: daylight saving time (the only pleasant one of the three), the closing of public houses in the afternoon and extensive alien controls.[34] At the outbreak of the Second World War Britain declared that it would treat aliens more gently than in 1914–18, but after the fall of Norway, it again engaged in vigorous internment.[35] At the end of the war Britain made no bones about the forcible repatriation of displaced Russians.[36] British administrators seemed to be expressing implicit approval, in retrospect, of the severity with which their predecessors had treated aliens between 1914 and 1918.

III

Since Britain concerned itself during the First World War not merely with interning enemy aliens but with the wider dimensions of the aliens question, it faced problems which went far beyond the location and imprisonment of Germans. The following sections will consider three of them: the problem of deciding which aliens were for, and which against, the war effort; the difficulties arising from aliens in the imperial context; and Britain's Ukrainian community.

Aliens could not simply be classified as "friendly" or "unfriendly" according to their citizenship. Citizens of Germany, Austria-Hungary, Bulgaria and Turkey were all technically enemies. But in fact Alsatians, Slavs from Austria-Hungary and Armenians from Turkey tended to support the British and their allies. Russian Jews, on the other hand—much the largest alien minority in Britain[37]—were unsympathetic to the Allied cause owing to their experiences at the hands of the tsarist regime. The administrative headaches to which these complications gave rise did not, perhaps, encourage British authorities to be generous toward aliens after the war.

The Czechs seem to have experienced least difficulty in establishing that, although technically enemy aliens, they were not hostile to the Allies.[38] The Home Office informed Chief Constables in December 1914 that the War Office had authorized "the London Bohemian (Czech) Committee" to visit internment camps and pick out their fellow-countrymen. The government was "anxious that where there are no grounds for suspicion against such persons they should not be interned or, if already interned, should be released."[39] The Home Office did not wholly exempt Czechs from the provisions of the Aliens Restriction Order but applied the latter as leniently as possible.[40] The War Office, too, was relatively well disposed toward the Czechs. An Army Council Instruction of 18 August 1916 defined very narrowly which classes of enemy alien could enlist in British forces, but three months later the War Office officially exempted Czechs from its restrictions.[41] The British authorities seem to have accepted the "friendly" status of the Czechs more readily than they did that of other alien minorities. Eduard Beneš explained why they were justified in so doing when in May 1918 he wrote to the foreign secretary asking for British recognition of the Czechoslovak National Council. He pointed out that the Czech army was larger than that of any other oppressed minority; that Czech sympathy with the Allies was "much more clearly and decisively manifested than in the case of other Central European peoples"; that the Czechs were "more united, more homogenous [*sic*] and much better organized than others" in their situation; and that the Czech National Council did not suffer from internal division as, for example, did the Polish National Committee.[42]

The southern Slavs established their claim to special consideration with greater difficulty. In June 1915, six months after steps had been taken to release the Czechs, the Serbian Minister in London applied to the foreign secretary for the release from internment of "a number of ... Austro-Hungarian subjects of Serbian (or, what is the same, Creat [*sic*] and Slovene) nationality."[43] Steps were taken to grant the request, but problems arose. The Serbian Minister had asserted that the Austro-Hungarian subjects of whom he spoke were sympathetic toward the Allies, but the Home Office was convinced neither of this nor that all southern Slavs were sympathetic toward the Kingdom of Serbia (which the Serbian Minister had implied by speaking for them). In November 1915 a Home Office official wrote a memorandum drawing on three sources: the Serbian Legation, the " Jugo-Slav Committee" (a body designed to work for "a united independent Serbo-Croat nation") and the Italian Information Committee (which was hostile to southern Slav independence owing to Italian interest in the head of the Adriatic).[44] The author of the memorandum, R. S. Nolan, quoted one of the Italian representatives as saying that most southern Slavs wanted "rather ... autonomy within the Austro-Hungarian Empire than ... incorporation within the Kingdom of Serbia." Although Nolan felt that the Italian might well have been right, he believed that it would be safe enough to release southern Slavs from internment; but he remained "afraid that sufficient ground is not shown for believing that these persons are heart and soul with us."

In February 1916 Nolan expressed further doubts about southern Slavs after a discussion with Todorović of the Serbian Legation.[45] Many of them, he pointed out, had only recently come to Britain, "some having been taken prisoners off ships, and consequently little can be known about them here." They tended to "belong to a humble class the sympathies of which are probably in many cases difficult to gauge." The Jugo-Slav Committee too readily assumed that their sympathies were pro-Serbian, while turning them against their former masters might lead to the maltreatment of British prisoners by the enemy.[46] In 1916 and 1917 British authorities went on pressing Yugoslavs to join the Serbian colours,[47] but they had a shrewd appreciation of the problems involved in handling southern Slav aliens and perceived that the men with whom they were dealing were by no means as united as the Czechs.

With regard to the Poles the authorities were less perceptive. They backed the wrong horse in accepting the anti-semitic and land-hungry Dmowski as principal Polish spokesman.[48] Although Polish emigre leaders disagreed with one another far more extensively than did their Czech counterparts, the British allowed themselves to be convinced by a single faction. The Poles, in fact, were officially recognized as alien friends six months before the Czechs.[49] Beneš commented on this injustice.[50] Confronted with Polish factionalism, the British seem to have lost their nerve and chosen to support a single group for the sake of simplicity. It was a measure, perhaps, of the frustration induced by the complexity of the aliens question.[51]

Dealing with Russian Jews, however, was the most intractable problem posed by aliens in wartime Britain. Just as mass Jewish immigration had been the reason for the Aliens Act of 1905, so Jewish reluctance to contribute to the war effort strengthened animosity toward foreigners between 1914 and 1918. The problem became intense in 1916 when Britain began to press resident citizens of Allied powers into military service.[52] After the introduction of conscription for British citizens in January 1916 it was unreasonable to suppose that friendly aliens would be allowed to retain their civilian status. On 29 June 1916 Sir Herbert Samuel, home secretary, announced that Russian aliens in particular would henceforth be expected to contribute to the war effort.[53] In doing so he stirred up a hornets' nest. The only sanction which he could apply to Russian Jews who refused to enlist was that of deportation, but the Jews were determined not to return whence they had come—and the Russian government did not want them back. By trying to satisfy British public opinion, which demanded that aliens fight or be summarily dealt with, the government created problems which lasted until the end of the war.

The plan to enlist Russian Jews seems to have been devised without the full understanding of the Russian authorities. On 13 August 1916 the Russian consul general asked a Home Office official "how the Russian enlistment stood, as both he and the Embassy were in the dark about it." The official replied "that the policy was that Russians of military age ought to be doing service either here or in Russia, and that the only way of applying pressure was to say that if a man refused to serve here without good reason, he should not be allowed to stay here." The Russian embassy had apparently agreed in June to this policy of forced enlistment or deportation, but in August it stated that the Chief of the Russian Staff had recently been in Britain "and told the Consul not to waste money on sending defaulters back to Russia: they were not likely to be much use, they might spread disaffection in the Army, and they were not wanted."[54] Despite the Russians' lack of enthusiasm, the British authorities persisted in their policy. They encountered opposition both from opponents of the principle of conscription[55] and from the resident Russian community. The Committee of Delegates of the Russian Socialist Groups in London printed a thirty-two-page pamphlet entitled *An Appeal to Public Opinion: Should the Russian Refugees be Deported?*[56] Pointing out that the British Home Secretary had said that "it would be a monstrous thing" to treat Armenians resident in Britain as if they were Turks, the pamphlet asked: "Is it less monstrous for the Home Secretary to deport Jews, members of other nationalities, and political emigrants who had fled to this country from the terrible Russian oppression?"[57] The implication was that Britain employed dual standards in its treatment of aliens.

Questions were asked in the House of Commons about the alarm felt by Russian aliens,"[58] and on 22 August the home secretary announced significant changes in the policy he had put forward two months earlier. Russian Jews who enlisted voluntarily before 30 September were to be given the right of naturalization without charge after three months' service and were to be allowed to serve together.[59] Few Russian Jews, however, took advantage of the opportunity to enlist voluntarily,[60] and the problems arising from the attempt to get them into the British army persisted well into 1918.[61] Britain's most substantial alien minority loomed larger in the public eye at the end of the war than it had at the beginning. The Aliens Act of 1905 made it more difficult for foreigners to come to Britain, but those who had already entered the country were sufficient in number to create administrative confusion. Having been the principal reason for the 1905 act, Russian Jews contributed in no small measure to the passage of the new Aliens Restriction (Amendment) Act of 1919.

IV

The imperial dimension of the aliens question tended not to encourage British sympathy with non-nationals. The treatment of aliens in Canada and Australia was determined locally rather than in London, but the centre and peripheries of the empire corresponded on the question, and not all their considerable interaction tended to improve the temper of the London government.

Inhabitants of the dominions and colonies sometimes increased London's work load with respect to aliens. Although Canada possessed considerable independence in these matters, her residents occasionally complained to Britain rather than to Ottawa. In January 1916, for example, Andrew Bone wrote from Elcan, Alberta, complaining about the sums of money made by Austrian and German miners at a time when Canadian men were fighting. If it was essential to employ them, he argued, "why not do the same with them as they do with the unfortunate Russians and our own poor fellows in Germany and Austria. If they are not required for work why not intern them, and if they have any nonsense about it line them up and give them what they deserve."[62] The Colonial Office merely referred this anti-alien hysteria to the Canadian government. In some instances, evidence of the subsequent investigation survives.[63] These complaints from Canada were not significant in themselves, but they increased the volume of aliens business at a time when Britain had enough of its own.

The mother country did not want to become unduly involved with aliens in the empire. When London was considering whether to recognize Poles as alien friends, a Home Office minute pointed out that it was "clear that the British Government can only take responsibility for Poles in the United Kingdom."[64] Britain's recognition of the Czechs as friends, later in 1918, similarly applied only to those in the United Kingdom. When Czechs in Canada began applying for certificates of naturalization in light of the change in British policy, the Canadian official concerned had to ask the governor-general for guidance.[65] In 1915 the Serbian Minister in London asked for the release of Serbs interned not only in Britain but also in South Africa, Australia and Canada; he seems to have received help only in connection with those in Britain.[66] Sometimes the different parts of the British empire appear to have been completely out of step with one another in their treatment of aliens. Early in 1918, for example, Austria-Hungary (via neutral Sweden) inquired of the British Foreign Office about an order issued by the government of India, threatening to repatriate all Austro-Hungarian subjects at the end of the war if they had not applied for exemption by 1 May 1918. The Home Office, to whom the inquiry was passed, professed ignorance; so far as the home secretary was aware, no such measure had been enacted in India or in "any other self-governing Dominion," and certainly nothing of the kind existed in Great Britain.[67] Although other evidence indicated a greater degree of imperial interaction on the question of aliens,[68] Britain never attempted to impose uniformity.

The War Office alone took an interventionist line on the imperial aspect of the aliens problem. At a conference held in March 1918 on "The Disposal of Enemy Prisoners of War on the Conclusion of Hostilities," General Belfield of the Prisoners of War Department asked "to what extent ... the recommendations of the Aliens Committee should apply to India, the Dominions and Colonies, where a large number of prisoners-of-war and enemy aliens are interned." The Home Office representative replied that the recommendations were intended only for the United Kingdom but that copies of them would be sent to the India Office and the Colonial Office "for such action as might be thought proper."[69] This was too faint-hearted for the War Office. In October it circulated a hard-hitting memorandum to the Foreign, Colonial and India Offices, envisaging repatriation of all aliens. It clearly hoped to stamp its views on the empire as a whole. Home Office anger with the War Office, which had been growing for more than two years on the question of enlisting aliens in the British army,[70] reached a new peak. Many aliens, the Home Office pointed out, had been subjected to scrutiny and allowed to remain at liberty during the war. "It is little short of ludicrous," wrote a Home Office official, "to suggest that such persons are in any way a danger to the British Empire and their forced repatriation at the end of the war will in most cases be a senseless piece of cruelty which would be the reverse of creditable to the nation as a whole."[71]

Apart from the War Office, therefore, British government departments did not attempt to coerce aliens in the dominions and colonies. Self-interest rather than moderation dictated their policy. Aliens who were repatriated to Europe from far-flung quarters of the empire tended to be repatriated via Britain and could be held up there instead of proceeding to their destinations. Britain was anxious to prevent interrupted journeys that increased domestic confusion. In September 1914 it urged that deportation of "criminal and undesirable aliens" from Canada be brought to an end. "This country," wrote the Home Office,

> always stands in considerable danger of being made the resting-place of persons of this class who would not come here except for the fact that they are being sent from Canada to Europe; but in ordinary circumstances arrangements are made,... At the present time, however, it is practically impossible for Germans, Austrians, Hungarians or Russians to be sent back from the United Kingdom to their native countries.[72]

Recognizing British concern, the Canadian authorities reported that they had deported no aliens since the beginning of the war and did not intend to do so "while existing conditions continue."[73] A month later, however, Sir Robert Borden complained:

> Situation with regard to Germans and Austrians particularly Austrians very difficult. From fifty to one hundred thousand will be out of employment during coming winter as employers are dismissing them everywhere under compulsion of public opinion.

Borden wanted either to "let them go, provide them with work or feed them, otherwise they will become desperate and resort to crime." The Colonial Office responded that, despite the expense, Canada must keep its alien immigrants; only thus could it "preclude the practical certainty of any Germans or Austrian drifting, by way of the United States of America, back to the enemy's firing line."[74] At least on this occasion London based its argument on considerations of security rather than on the fear that aliens would be "dumped" in Britain, but given the charge on public funds which Britain was forcing the Canadian government to assume, it could hardly be said to have had the best interests of the empire at heart. Non-interventionism in colonial aliens policy wore thin when that policy threatened to disturb the international balance. In April 1915, however, financially hard-pressed, Canada permitted "a considerable number of aliens" to leave Vancouver for the United States.[75] Britain did not always get its own way.

At the end of the war, as at the beginning, Britain showed relatively little sympathy for the dominions' and colonies' problems regarding aliens. The fear of "dumping" predominated again. Soon after Armistice the Home Office asked the Colonial Office not to sanction large-scale repatriation of aliens from the empire via Britain.[76] Three weeks later it agreed to take batches of up to a hundred,[77] but it remained uneasy. In the first half of 1919 the governor-general of Australia asked London if he could deport some troublesome Russians. The Home Office admitted that Britain was itself in the process of deporting unwanted Russian radicals, but said there was no certainty about where in Russia they could be landed. "In no circumstances," the Australian governor-general was informed, "should Russian deportees be sent from Australia to the United Kingdom for transhipment to Russia."[78] Britain seemed to be less concerned about possible subversion in Australia than about minimizing the aliens problem at home. It was not even enthusiastic about Whites returning to non-Bolshevik Russia at their own expense. When the Russian embassy in London enquired on behalf of some Russians in Canada, the Foreign Office granted them permission to enter Britain en route, but insisted that they support themselves and expressed pessimism about their prospects of completing the journey.[79] In 1918 and 1919 British authorities were tired of their own aliens; those from beyond the seas wearied them still further.

Although Britain did not take responsibility for aliens in the empire, neither did it wash its hands of them. Prudence, in wartime, dictated that it keep a watching brief; and self-interest led it to make use of the empire to reduce some of its own problems with aliens. Perhaps the strain of needing and yet not wanting to know about the empire's aliens tended to increase British anti-alienism.

Before the war began, Britain was kept informed about aliens in the dominions and colonies. In December 1913, for example, Canadian intelligence reported an increase in Japanese immigration into Canada, and in January 1914 it sent total Canadian immigration figures for 1912 and 1913.[80] When, in July 1914, the Canadian High Commission in London reported that for the present Canada had "enough artisans, and skilled and unskilled labourers," the British government co-operated in attempting to discourage new immigration from Austria-Hungary and western Russia.[81] After war broke out, reports from Canada advised the Colonial Office of Major General Sir W. D. Otter's appointment as director of Canadian Internment Operations, of the progress of alien registration, the number of internees in Canada, of a German's abortive attempt to blow up a bridge between New Brunswick and Maine and of apparently German-inspired dynamite outrages in Ontario.[82] Mindful of possible subversion from south of the border, Canadian intelligence reported "the number of people of foreign birth living in the United States" and distinguished the citizens of

Germany and Austria-Hungary from the rest.[83] Britain thus made good use of Canada in extending its knowledge of enemy aliens.

It used Canada, too, to increase its capacity for dealing with aliens. In 1918 eight hundred of Canada's remaining internees, about a third of the total, "came from the West Indies and are held by us. at the request of the imperial authorities."[84] The British took advantage of Canada in another respect. In late 1916 they were trying to persuade an interned Pole to join a labour battalion. When Miss Laurence Alma Tadema, representative of Polish Exiles Protection (PEP), said that "the Canadian War Office had sanctioned the raising of a Polish Legion in Canada . . . and asked whether fit Poles in this country might not join such a body," the British Home Office jumped at the suggestion.[85] Britain welcomed a means of reducing the number of aliens for whom it was responsible.

The disadvantages of a pan-imperial aliens policy, however, outweighed the advantages. Such a policy threatened unwanted complications in British politics. Two incidents brought out the difficulties inherent in imperial interaction on the question of aliens. In 1913 the Australian high commissioner inquired "whether the British Government asks Foreign Representatives to keep them supplied with lists of their nationals, or whether any other steps are taken to obtain complete lists of foreigners resident in Great Britain."[86] Such lists were to be one of the fruits of the war, but in 1913 they existed only sub rosa.[87] In replying to the Australian inquiry, therefore, Britain experienced a conflict of interest. On the one hand, it wanted as much information as possible about aliens, in the empire as well as at home; on the other hand, in order to prevent both domestic and international repercussions, Britain did not want it widely known that it was taking steps to increase supervision. Was Australia to be advised to follow its example and draw up lists of foreigners? The British Security Service noted that "it would be of considerable mutual assistance if a periodical interchange of lists of undesirable aliens could be effected between us and the Commonwealth of Australia," but it urged that "any reply sent should not disclose more information than is contained in the attached draft." Following Security's lead, the Home Office instructed the Foreign Office to reply to Australia that only unofficial lists were kept but that they afforded "some indication of the number and distribution of Aliens throughout the country—special attention being paid to areas of Naval and Military importance"; the matter was to be regarded as secret.[88]

Britain succeeded in preventing the Australian inquiry from becoming an embarrassment. In 1919, however, when Canadian action on aliens briefly inflamed a British parliamentary debate, the imperial tail seemed to be wagging the dog. Member of parliament Sir John Butcher asked the British home secretary to "lay upon the Table of the House a copy of the Order in Council recently issued by the Canadian Government for the deportation and exclusion of Germans and other undesirable aliens from the Dominion of Canada."[89] The request was unusual. Dominion orders in council were not normally brought to the attention of the House of Commons, but because aliens were so much in the public eye in Britain, Butcher pressed his suit and in mid-August received copies of Canadian orders in council of 14 March and 9 June.[90] Before Butcher's inquiry the Colonial Office had been aware only of the order of 14 February, by which the Canadian government had assumed stronger powers to intern enemy aliens. Under the later orders Canada prohibited the immigration of Germans, Austro-Hungarians, Bulgarians and Turks (excluding citizens of newly-recognized independent states). Clearly Canada's severity could provide an anti-alien British MP with useful ammunition. Clearly, too, in the light of Butcher's question, the British government's reluctance to attempt an imperial aliens policy was undesirable. If the dominions were moving against aliens faster than the motherland, Britain's political initiative could be undermined.

Neither the Australian incident of 1913 nor the Canadian incident of 1919 posed insuperable problems for the British government, but both were symptomatic of the complexities of the aliens question during the First World War. In view of the emotions and administrative headaches to which the war gave rise, controlling aliens in Britain was difficult enough. The imperial dimension made the question of aliens still more intractable.

V

Ukrainians figured little in British minds between 1914 and 1918, but on the few occasions they attracted attention they provided further illustration of the problems posed by aliens. They were particularly confusing for Britain's administrators in that they included separatists and supporters of both Austria-Hungary and Russia. Britain expected Austro-Hungarian minorities to be friendly to the Allies, but found that the principal Russian minority with which it was concerned (the Jews) tended to be hostile. Which category Ukrainians belonged to was not clear. Poles also straddled the frontiers of eastern Europe, but as Russia promised them autonomy early in the war the British were prepared to believe that they were sympathetic toward the Allied effort. Ukrainians had received no such promise. Early in 1915 Joseph King, a prominent critic of the war and the one British MP with any knowledge of the Ukrainian question,[91] drew attention to the inconsistency in Russia's treatment of Poles and Ukrainians.

[He] asked the Secretary of State for Foreign Affairs whether he is aware that a large proportion of the population of Galicia, which has recently been annexed by Russia, is purely Ukrainian (Ruthenian); whether the Russian offer of autonomy to Poland is to be construed as involving an offer of autonomy to the Ukrainian population also; and, if this is so, whether that offer has been extended to the Ukrainian population of Northern Bukovina and of the Carpathian districts of Hungary?[92]

No doubt its ignorance of the Ukrainian question prevented the Foreign Office from answering King. Other departments of the British government, better informed, expressed various attitudes toward Ukrainians.

Andrew Bonar Law at the Colonial Office was firm in his hostility. On 30 September 1915 King spoke to him about the Ukrainian national cause "and its relation to Canada" and on 4 November sent him a copy of the Ukrainian newspaper *Svoboda*, published in New Jersey.[93] Although King maintained that the paper had a large circulation and displayed "nothing disloyal . . . to our cause," Bonar Law disagreed and in reply to King quoted a virulently anti-Russian passage from *Svoboda*. It appeared that King had done Ukrainians a disservice.[94]

Officials of the Home Office, who had most to do with Ukrainians during the war, were by no means as certain as Bonar Law that they were anti-Russian and therefore anti-Ally. Although for the first two years of the war the Home Office was evidently unaware of a Ukrainian problem,[95] it then tried rather hard to find out about it. In June 1915 Henryk Sienkiewicz pleaded for both Poles and Ruthenians interned in Britain,[96] but at that time the distinction meant little to British officials. The political orientation of Ukrainians in Britain seems to have become a question only in September 1916, when PEP was deciding which Poles qualified for certificates granting exemption from internment. W. Czapski, the Canadian Pole who did nearly all PEP's work on the ground,[97] sent seventeen reports on persons in Manchester, nine of whom were Ruthenians. "With regard to the Ruthenians," he wrote, "we are satisfied that they do not consider themselves Poles, and the Committee therefore cannot grant them certificates. So far as we know, they are decidedly adherents of the separatist movement, whose centre was in Lemberg [Lviv], Galicia."[98] J. B. Wainewright of the Home Office felt that the separatist inclinations of the Ruthenians made little difference to the question of their exemption from internment. He suggested on 2 October that they be treated "as if the P.E.P. had granted certificates."[99] His superior, Nolan, was more cautious. On 3 October he wrote a memorandum on the question:

There has long been a feud between the Poles and the Ruthenes in Galicia, the cause of the latter being assiduously championed by Russia, as against the Poles.

The Ruthenes may be divided into two parties. Firstly, the Ukrainians, who seek the autonomy of the Ukraine and the Ruthenian people—a movement which is vigorously opposed by Russia, who regards Ruthenians as being Russians, and does not recognize their Church, i.e. the Greek Catholic Church. Secondly, there are those who accord with the Russian view and would be willing for incorporation with Russia.

It would be difficult to ascertain the relative numbers of the two parties. M. Dmowski, on the occasion of his recent visit, stated that the latter party is about one third of the Ruthenian population. Mr. Kopecky of the Czech Committee stated to me, nearly a year ago, that he had noticed very strong Ukrainian, and consequently anti-Russian, sentiments among Ruthenian Prisoners of War in the Isle of Man, who, for that reason, inclined to Austrian sympathies. The very few whom I interviewed at the Alexandra Palace recently ... professed no pro-Ally sentiments and no objection to German or Austrian surroundings.[100]

Nolan's argument seemed to be leading him to conclusions different from those reached by Wainewright. If the bulk of Britain's Ruthenians were anti-Russian, they ought not to be treated as if they had been granted certificates of exemption from internment by PEP. They were likely to be unsympathetic toward the Allied war effort. Surprisingly, however, Nolan concluded that "prima facie, a Ruthene would be more likely to be pro-Ally than a Pole." He felt that it was necessary merely "to have some enquiry into their sentiments in each case." Presumably he believed that because they were so much worse off within Austria-Hungary than the Poles, Ruthenians would be hostile to Vienna. He seems to have overlooked the possibility that, in some cases at least, they looked to Vienna for help against their immediate masters.

Nolan persuaded PEP to look into the cases of three hundred Ruthenians in Manchester, to consider the possibility of creating a Ruthenian organization separate from PEP and to "take steps to come into touch with" Ruthenians in London.[101] On 20 October 1916, Laurence Alma Tadema reported on her visit to Manchester. She found that the Ruthenians were for the most part not hostile to the Poles and were willing to be vetted by PEP, provided their certificates of exemption from internment stated that they were Ruthenians from Galicia rather than Poles. Nolan felt that she had missed the point. "For us," he observed, "the important point was not whether the Ruthenes were of Polish sentiments but whether they had pro-Ally sympathies." He suggested "that possibly some of them might be followers of the Ukrainian movement," and Tadema promised to ask the Polish priest in Manchester to find out.[102] The Ruthenians' political orientation remained uncertain.

At this point the Ukrainian question briefly hit the headlines. On the same day that Tadema was reporting to the Home Office, Joseph King was fined one hundred pounds with twenty-five guineas costs at Bow Street for sending "information with respect to the supply and condition of certain war material...in a letter, dated August 22, 1916, addressed to one George Raffalovich, New York, contrary to the Defence of the Realm Act."[103] The offence was relatively minor, in that King had merely repeated in his letter information he had used in a parliamentary speech and which had been published in Hansard. On 23 October the *Evening Standard* said that "nobody doubted the good faith of the M.P., but much more might have been said of Mr. George Rafaelovitch [*sic*], to whom the letter was sent."[104] This article, and another two days later,[105] gave details of Raffalovich's activities. Between 1912 and 1915 he had been responsible for promoting the Ukrainian cause in Britain.[106] Subsequently he continued his work in America,[107] and he had no doubt sent King the copy of *Svoboda* that had reached Bonar Law. The journalists who described Raffalovich's Ukrainian nationalism in 1916 painted it in a lurid light, suggesting that it made him pro-German. "If by some process of induction, or deduction," wrote Helen Sevrez,

> an undisguised contempt for the "political swashbucklers" of Russia may be made to include active pro-German sympathies, then the vista opened up before us is wide indeed, and sufficiently damning to the reputation of the man by whom such sentiments were freely uttered.[108]

In his prewar journalism Raffalovich had certainly shown greater sympathy for Austria-Hungary than for Russia. In 1913 he had written:

> If the Russian Government imitate Austria and give their Ukrainian subjects their due, the longing on the part of many of these to fall under the rule of the Hapsburg may be assuaged. If they do not, the longing will increase and spread.[109]

In 1916 such remarks were turned against their author. Sevrez, quoting Raffalovich on the possibility of Ukraine's twentieth-century return to statehood, concluded: "Financed by German funds? That is the question asked tentatively by the 'Evening Standard'."[110] Sevrez took advantage of Raffalovich to deepen the general prejudice against aliens which was growing in Britain during the war. "It is time we envisaged with greater seriousness," she wrote, "the banishment from our shores of that type of political intriguer and adventurer who in the past has penetrated behind the scenes."[111] Raffalovich was turned into a stalking-horse.

The Home Office included a copy of Sevrez's article on Raffalovich in the file on Ruthenians.[112] The King case cannot have increased Ukrainian chances of achieving respectability in the eyes of British officialdom. Early in November 1916 those chances were further reduced, as Nolan made clear in a letter to Tadema:

I am afraid your already difficult task in judging the political sentiments of Ruthenians has now been rendered more difficult still.

According to the press there has been a Ruthene protest in Vienna against the grant of autonomy to Galicia. This seems to clearly to proceed [*sic*] from their feud with the Poles, preferring to be directed under Austria than under a Polish Home Rule Government. In one sense it may be regarded as an indication of Austrian sentiments amongst them of which we have had rather a surprising measure of evidence from internment camps here. This new political step however, may on the other hand tend to incline them more towards Russia, in which case of course we shall be more ready to regard them favourably.[113]

By this time Nolan was perhaps becoming a little exasperated by the complexity of the Ukrainian problem. Ukrainians were proving very different from the Czechs, for example, whose political outlook was much more coherent. The Ukrainian case exemplified in miniature the many difficulties Britain faced in trying to cope with East European aliens during the war. It never succeeded in grasping why Ukrainians were politically so diverse. Czapski, the PEP investigator who was continuing his visits to the internment camps, offered a possible explanation in December 1916:

It is interesting to see that the Ruthenes in Manchester are strongly pro-Russian and that the Feltham group [in a camp in Middlesex] is just as strongly pro-Austrian. It occurs to us [PEP] that this may be accounted for, partly or wholly, by the circumstance that most of the Feltham Ruthenes had been from one to three or more years in Canada or the United States before the War, and were thus exposed to pro-Austrian agitation which may not have reached the Ruthenes living in Manchester. Of course, I only put this forward as my own view of the matter, but perhaps it will help in explaining this state of things.[114]

Confused, no doubt, by the variety of Ukrainian loyalties, the Home Office allowed Ukrainians to remain under the aegis of the Poles. Nolan pointed out, when discussing in 1917 the possible recognition of Poland as an allied nation, that such recognition would tend to confirm interned Ruthenians "in their adherence to Austria,"[115] but in January 1918 the Polish National Committee was still responsible for providing Ruthenians with certificates of exemption from internment.[116] No Ukrainian organization arose to take responsibility from the Poles. As Nolan wrote in 1916: "Apparently there are few, if any, educated Ruthenes in this country."[117] Ukrainians failed to show that they deserved separate treatment. They lacked representatives, and on the few occasions they were noticed by the British authorities their problems seemed even more complicated than those posed by other East European minorities. Britain knew little about Ukraine before, during or after the war,[118] and tended not to take note even of reliable information.[119] At a time when it was becoming much less generous in its treatment of aliens, it looked upon Ukrainians as the least among the princes of Judah.

VI

In arguing that the First World War was a bad time for aliens in Britain, I have considered them almost entirely from the point of view of the government. Even so I have looked only at certain aspects of the subject. The administration of the internment camps, for example, would provide sufficient material for another paper. Administration apart, the standing of aliens in society constitutes a separate dimension of the problem. I have tried merely to illustrate the way in which an already troublesome problem was further complicated by world war. Britain was not well disposed toward aliens before 1914. It was much less well disposed toward them after experiencing the new domestic and imperial difficulties they created between 1914 and 1918.

Notes

1. See D. French, "Spy Fever in Britain, 1900–1915," *Historical Journal* 21 (1978): 355–70.
2. B. Porter, *The Refugee Question in Mid-Victorian Politics* (Cambridge, 1979), 8.
3. C. Jones, *Immigration and Social Policy in Britain* (London, 1980), 161–2.
4. See C. Holmes, *Anti-Semitism in British Society 1876–1939* (London, 1979), 24–6; and G.R. Searle, "Critics of Edwardian Society: The Case of the Radical Right," in *The Edwardian Age: Conflict and Stability 1900–1914*, ed. A. O'Day (London, 1979), 84, 86, 90, 92–3, 95.
5. *Times*, 30 May 1887.
6. *Ibid.* See also J. White, *Rothschild Buildings: Life in an East End Tenement Block 1887–1920* (London, 1980). For personal reminiscences of Jewish life in the East End of London, see S. Brodetsky, *Memoirs: From Ghetto to Israel* (London, 1960), chap. 2, "Whitechapel Ghetto"; and E. Litvinoff, *Journey Through a Small Planet* (London, 1976).
7. *Times*, 30 May 1887.
8. J. A. Garrard, *The English and Immigration 1880–1910* (Oxford, 1971), 25–6; and W. J. Fishman, *East End Jewish Radicals 1875–1914* (London, 1975), 70.
9. R. S. Churchill, *Winston Churchill* 2: Compassion (London, 1969), part 1, 355.

10. 5 Edw. 7, chap. 13. The history of attempted aliens legislation between 1887 and 1905 is provided by B. Gainer in *The Alien Invasion: The Origins of the Aliens Act of 1905* (London, 1972), 166–88.

11. See, for example, Public Records Office, Home Office Papers (hereafter HO), class 45, piece 10342/140204, expulsion orders of July 1906 served on Samuel Berkan and Rubin Kravtchik, both subjects of Russia and both convicted of larceny the previous April.

12. Great Britain, *Parliamentary Debates* (Commons), 4th ser., 163 (1906): 885; cf. HO 45/10341/139774, files 4–11.

13. HO 45/10629/199699/6.

14. *Ibid.*, 4.

15. *Ibid.*, 1.

16. 1 and 2 Geo. 5, chap. 28, clauses 6, 8 and 9.

17. See HO 45/10629/199699/5, circular from Sir Edward Troup, to Chief Constables, [January 1914], thanking them for their "excellent work ... with regard to the registration of aliens."

18. HO 45/10629/199699/6, 1913 Report, 17.

19. 4 and 5 Geo. 5, chap. 12. On 7 August Parliament redefined its concept of British nationality in the British Nationality and Status of Aliens Act, 1914: 4 and 5 Geo. 5, chap. 17.

20. See M. Pugh, "Asquith, Bonar Law and the First Coalition," *Historical Journal* 17 (1974): 831.

21. This occurred after the Germans sank the *Lusitania*. See P. and L. Gillman, *"Collar the Lot!" How Britain Interned and Expelled Its Wartime Refugees* (London, 1980), 16. This book is about internment in 1940 but has a chapter on the treatment of aliens in the First World War. The "stop-go" approach toward internment in the first six months of the war in HO 45/10760/269116.

22. HO 45/10782/278567/35, printed circular to Chief Constables, 12 June 1915, ordering enforcement of the deportation policy "as speedily as circumstances permit."

23. HO 45/10833/327753/16.

24. HO 45/10629/199699/6, 1913 Report, 47.

25. HO 45/10833/327753/18. On the internment camps throughout the war, which were largely in the Isle of Man, see HO 45/10946/266042 and HO 45/10947/266042.

26. HO 45/10881/338498/2, circular of 21 June 1917. In a letter of 10 October 1917 to Member of Parliament J. A. R. Marriott, Home Secretary Sir George Cave explained which classes of aliens were allowed to remain at liberty: HO 45/10756/267450/721. Although harsh, aliens policy was not as severe as it might have been.

27. HO 45/10629/199699/6, 1913 Report, 47.

28. This fraction was by comparing the War Office estimate of 75,000 enemy aliens in 1914 with the 1911 census figure for the total number of aliens.

29. HO 45/10833/327753/32, 18. The figure for adult alien enemies must refer only to those at liberty, for otherwise it conflicts with the contemporary War

Office estimate of 23,000 enemies at large, the remainder having been interned or repatriated. The total number of enemy aliens in the country had not greatly diminished, but since the committee decided simply to repatriate enemy internees, the part played by enemy aliens in long-term plans was considerably smaller than in 1914.

30. HO 45/10833/327753/32, 1.

31. *Ibid.*, 15–16.

32. In the British Nationality and Status of Aliens Act, 1918 (8 and 9 Geo. 5, chap. 38), and the Aliens Restriction (Amendment) Act, 1919 (9 and 10 Geo. 5, chap. 92).

33. HO 45/10833/327753/38, 57, 66, 158. The Home Office, which had had most to do with them, took the most moderate line on aliens at the end of the war. An official writing on the day of the Armistice advocated reducing restrictions, but another official, while agreeing with the memorandum, maintained that "care must be taken not to give a handle for the anti-alien agitators to take hold of and work up a fresh agitation." HO 45/10899/371591/1.

34. A. J. P. Taylor, *English History 1914–1945* (London, 1970), 216–17.

35. See Gillman and Gillman, *"Collar the Lot!"*. Reviewing the Gillmans' book, A. J. P. Taylor (*Observer*, 18 May 1980) and Bernard Wasserstein (*Times Literary Supplement*, 27 June 1980) spoke harshly of Britain's treatment of aliens in 1940. However, a former internee, William Guttmann (*Observer*, 29 June 1980), drew attention to the rapid abandonment rather than the introduction of the severe anti-alien policy.

36. For the way in which the "victims of Yalta" continue to arouse strong feelings, see the acrimonious correspondence in the *Daily Telegraph*, 20 and 23 May 1980, in connection with the projected memorial in London. Nikolai Tolstoy now believes there should be a public inquiry into the behaviour of the British administration in the 1940s; see " 'Victims of Yalta'—an Inquiry?," *Encounter* 54, no. 6 (1980): 89–92.

37. The 1911 census gave the figure of 49,700 resident male Russians and Poles, the vast majority of whom would have been Jews. See HO 45/10629/199699/6, 1913 Report, 47. The next largest group consisted of the 32,400 Germans.

38. Czechs and Yugoslavs in Britain constitute the focus of H. Hanak's *Great Britain and Austria-Hungary During the First World War: A Study in the Formation of Public Opinion* (Oxford, 1962); this book appeared before the relevant public records were made available.

39. HO 45/10761/269578/3a.

40. HO 45/10761/269578/5.

41. HO 45/10818/317810/4.

42. HO 45/10761/269578/59, Eduard Beneš to A.J. Balfour, 11 May 1918.

43. HO 45/10795/303789/1.

44. HO 45/10795/303789/2.

45. *Ibid.*

46. The latter consideration was much more substantial in the case of

Alsace-Lorrainers. See HO 45/10760/269510.

47. HO 45/10795/303789/6, copy of a note from the Serbian Legation to the Foreign Office, 13 March 1916, stating that fit Serbs between the ages of eighteen and forty-five should proceed at once to Corfu or Biserta.

48. See N. Davies, "The Poles in Great Britain 1914–1919," *Slavonic and East European Review* 50, no. 118 (January 1972): 86.

49. HO 45/10881/338498/8; cf. HO 45/10761/269578/62. Recognition took place in February and August 1918 respectively.

50. HO 45/10761/269578/59.

51. The detailed handling of the Poles during the First World War is recorded in HO 45/10740/262173, HO 45/10836/330094 and HO 45/10889/352661.

52. For attitudes toward Jews in the early part of the war see E. D. Levy, "Antisemitism in England at war, 1914–1916," *Patterns of Prejudice* 4, part 5 (1970): 27–30.

53. Great Britain, *Parliamentary Debates* (Commons), 5th ser., 83 (1916): 1084. For a brief account of the attempts to enlist Russians see Holmes, *Anti-Semitism in British Society*, 127–30.

54. HO 45/10818/318095/42.

55. The *Herald*, 15 July 1916, wrote that "conscription, unjust in itself, is giving rise to situations which . . . cannot without great difficulty be justly met." See offcut in HO 45/10818/318095/23.

56. Copy in HO 45/10818/318095/14.

57. *Ibid.*, 28.

58. Great Britain, *Parliamentary Debates* (Commons), 5th ser., 85 (1916): 663,838,2047, 2255.

59. *Ibid.*, 2458–9.

60. Only about 400 had done so by 1 October 1916. *Ibid.*, 86 (1916): 9–10.

61. See HO 45/10822/318095/562, minutes of February 1918 on the consequences of stopping the recruitment of Russians in Great Britain; and Great Britain, *Parliamentary Debates* (Commons), 5th ser., 106 (1918): 1209–11, questions of 3 June on the operation of the Military Service Convention with Russia.

62. Public Record Office, Colonial Office Papers (hereafter CO), class 42, piece 999, folio 282.

63. See CO 42/987/233 (the investigation of a complaint by one Mrs. Thomas of Montreal in 1915), CO 42/992/420a and CO 42/988/528 (the investigation of alarm voiced by Arthur Gilmer of Alberta in 1915).

64. HO 45/10889/352661/3 (January 1918).

65. HO 45/10761/269578/67.

66. HO 45/10795/303789/1.

67. HO 45/10833/327753/31.

68. HO 45/10833/327753/18, 85, 118 (documents from 1917 and 1919 on the disposal of aliens, including correspondence between Britain and the colonies on their respective practices).

69. HO 45/10833/327753/30.

70. HO 45/10818/31780/7, a Home Office minute of 7 February 1917: "Any of us who have been following the dealing of this question by the War Office may feel some doubt whether they ever became aware of its practical importance." The War Office was extremely reluctant to enlist aliens.

71. HO 45/10833/327753/38, minute of 18 October 1918.

72. CO 42/984/405.

73. CO 42/981/25.

74. CO 616/12/481–3.

75. CO 42/987/493.

76. HO 45/10833/327753/60a.

77. *Ibid.*

78. HO 45/10823/318095/693.

79. HO 45/10823/318095/702.

80. CO 42/978/217–18, 246.

81. CO 42/982/24–8; CO 42/984/130–1.

82. CO 42/981/450–1, CO 42/987206–8 and CO 42/988/93–4.

83. CO 42/981/225.

84. HO 45/10833/327753/143, letter from Major General W. D. Otter, 19 December 1918.

85. HO 45/10818/31780/10.

86. HO 45/10629/199699/4.

87. See above, fn. 17.

88. HO 45/10629/199699/4.

89. Great Britain, *Parliamentary Debates* (Commons), 5th ser., 116 (1919): 2188–9.

90. See HO 45/10833/327753/143, 155.

91. King was opposed to the war from the outset, maintaining that the violation of Belgian neutrality was not sufficient reason for taking up arms; see M. Swartz, *The Union of Democratic Control in British Politics During the First World War* (Oxford, 1971), 17. Having moved further to the left, he was even more outspoken in his opposition to military intervention in Russia in 1918–19; see his pamphlets, *Why Does Killing Go On in Russia?* (Glasgow, n.d.) and *Our Policy Towards Russia: What It Has Been and What It Might Be* (London, 1919). In Parliament between 1914 and 1918, King was a perpetual thorn in the government's flesh.

92. Great Britain, *Parliamentary Debates* (Commons), 5th ser., 69 (1915): 267. On the Russian offer to the Poles, see P. S. Wandycz, *The Lands of Partitioned Poland, 1795–1918* (Seattle, 1974), 355.

93. On the foundation and significance of *Svoboda*, see B. P. Procko, "The Rise of Ukrainian Ethnic Consciousness in America During the 1890's," in *The Ukrainian Experience in the United States: A Symposium*, ed. P. R. Magocsi (Cambridge, Mass., 1979), 51–63.

94. See CO 42/992/447–9 for the King-Bonar Law exchange.

95. But see HO 45/10760/269116/15, where the Commissioner of Metropolitan Police, in a memorandum of 30 October 1914, mentions Ruthenians separately in a list of East European minorities.

96. HO 45/10740/262173/34.

97. HO 45/10836/330094/7, letter from Laurence Alma Tadema to the Home Office, 22 July 1916, asking for the continuation of Czapski's secondment from the Canadian Expeditionary Force.

98. HO 45/10836/330094/12.

99. *Ibid.*

100. HO 45/10836/330094/13.

101. HO 45/10836/330094/10.

102. HO 45/10836/330094/13.

103. *Evening Standard*, 20 October 1916. The decision to prosecute King was taken by the Cabinet. See Public Record Office, Cabinet Papers, class 41, piece 37, document 34, H. H. Asquith to the King, 6 October 1916.

104. "Germany's Penny Plotters: Mystery Man of the King Case," *Evening Standard*, 23 October 1916.

105. H. Sevrez, "Mr. King's American Correspondent: George Raffalovich As I Knew Him," *Evening Standard*, 25 October 1916.

106. His most significant publications in this connection were a seventy-two-page pamphlet, *The Ukraine: Reprint of a Lecture Delivered on Ukrainian History and Present-Day Political Problems*, 2d impression (London, 1914), published under the pseudonym Bedwin Sands; and a translation, Michaelo Hrushevsky [*sic*], *The Historical Evolution of the Ukrainian Problem* (London, 1915). See also "Ruthenians and Poles," a correspondence between Raffalovich and V. Stepankowsky in the *Saturday Review* between 27 July and 21 September 1912, and the following articles by Raffalovich: "Marlborough and a Crown," *Commentator*, 12 and 19 February 1913 (recalling Peter the Great's offer of Ukraine to the Duke of Marlborough in 1707): "The Ukraine," *New Age*, 10 April 1913; "The Problem of the Ukraine," *Outlook*, 31 May 1913; "The Future of the Ukraine," *New Age*, 23 October 1913; and "The Future of the Ruthenians," *British Review* 11, no. 1 (July 1915): 26–38 (also published under the Sands pseudonym).

107. See S. Shumeyko, "American Interest in Ukraine During World War I," *Ukrainian Quarterly* 2, no. 1 (Autumn 1945): 69.

108. *Evening Standard*, 25 October 1916.

109. G. Raffalovich, "The Problem of the Ukraine," *Outlook*, 31 May 1913.

110. *Evening Standard*, 25 October 1916.

111. *Ibid.*

112. HO 45/10836/330094/13.

113. *Ibid.*

114. *Ibid.*

115. HO 45/10740/262173/49, minute of 7 June 1917.

116. HO 45/10889/352661/6.

117. HO 45/10836/330094/12, minute of 6 October 1916.

118. The best pre-1914 work on Ukraine appeared in an academic journal: T. Volkov, "The Ukraine Question," *Russian Review* 1, no 4 (1912): 106–19. A. Toynbee took a "Russophile" view of Ukraine in *Nationality and the War* (London and Toronto, 1915), maintaining that "the Little Russians must abandon their particularism, and allow themselves to be reabsorbed in the indivisible body of 'Holy Russia'" (319). In the postwar period, R. H. Ullman found it "amazing that during 1919 the Cabinet never once addressed itself directly to the question of whether British policy should work towards a united or a dismembered Russia" (*Anglo-Soviet Relations, 1917–1921*, 3 vols. [Princeton, 1961–72], 2: 220); ignorance no doubt played a part in this omission.

119. The future Sir Lewis Namier, who worked in the Foreign Office during the First World War, stood up valiantly for the Ukrainians of Eastern Galicia at the time of the peace treaties, but for all his influence, the Poles were allowed to secure the province. See T. Hunczak, "Sir Lewis Namier and the Struggle for Eastern Galicia, 1918–1920," *Harvard Ukrainian Studies* 1, no. 2 (June 1977): 198–210.

Chapter 7

Ukrainian Canadian Response
to the Paris Peace Conference, 1919

Nadia O. M. Kazymyra

On 11 November 1918 the terms of Armistice between the defeated Central
Powers and the Allied Forces took effect. The Great War was over. The
world now awaited the Paris Peace Conference which would determine the
political future of Europe and ensure the return to peace and stability. For
the Allies this meant transforming Germany into a skeleton of its former
self. The fate of the Austro-Hungarian empire, however, had been sealed
before the war ended when its subject nationalities proclaimed their
independence. In principle, the Allies were simply to ratify these successor
states but the outburst of territorial disputes compelled them to intercede,
fearing that national tensions would obstruct any lasting settlement in
eastern Europe and would leave the young republics vulnerable to the
growing Bolshevik threat. As a result, the Allies often proved reluctant to
readjust the boundaries of the Austro-Hungarian empire according to
nationality. Their hesitation was most noticeable in the handling of the
territorial dispute between Poland and the West Ukrainian National
Republic (Zakhidno-Ukrainska Narodna Respublika—ZUNR), referred to
internationally as the "Eastern Galician Problem."

The West Ukrainian People's Republic, comprised of the provinces of
Galicia and Bukovyna and the Transcarpathian region, was formed on
1 November 1918. Its creation provoked an immediate challenge from the
Poles who laid claim to most of this ethnically Ukrainian territory, and the
new republic became embroiled in a protracted war against Poland. On
22 January 1919 the ZUNR united with the Ukrainian National Republic
(Ukrainska Narodna Respublika—UNR), formed earlier on the territory of
the Russian empire, even though the UNR was struggling against the

Bolsheviks, the Russian pro-monarchist forces and the Ukrainian anarchists. Although the union was more declarative than real,[1] the Ukrainians reasoned that the Allies would prefer dealing with one Ukrainian delegation, seeking international assistance to solve the complex problems that hindered the solidification of a united independent Ukrainian state. For this reason, the Ukrainians sent a joint diplomatic delegation to the Paris Peace Conference to present their case for political self-determination.

By 1919 the fate of the Ukrainian state had assumed great importance among Ukrainians in Canada. Alienated by their classification and treatment as enemy aliens during the war, many felt their existence as a people to be threatened in Canada and turned their attention to the struggle for Ukrainian independence overseas.[2] The realization of Ukrainian political aspirations, however circumscribed, also strengthened the immigrants' own sense of Ukrainian national consciousness. As a result, Ukrainians in Canada felt compelled to help their compatriots in Europe to secure the recognition of the united Ukrainian republic.

* * *

In early December 1918 the Winnipeg-based Ukrainian Canadian Citizens' Committee (League) (UCCC),[3] which represented all Ukrainian organizations except the outlawed Ukrainian Social Democratic Party, announced its first significant undertaking. Through the Ukrainian-language press, it appealed to all Ukrainians in Canada to support its effort to send representatives to the Paris Peace Conference to counter the widespread Polish propaganda that was undermining support for Ukrainian independence. The delegates, representatives of Ukrainians in Canada, would be "well acquainted with the languages, institutions and ideals of the English, French, and Ukrainian people," and would serve as "intermediaries between the Allies and the rising Ukrainian nation with the purpose of giving publicity to the Ukrainian cause."[4] The UCCC, in turn, would hold press conferences and brief the Canadian government about Ukrainian independence. As funds were crucial to the undertaking, the UCCC encouraged the formation of local branches throughout Canada, but indicated that the Winnipeg body would direct and administer all fund-raising campaigns.

The UCCC's ambitious project and perception of its role at the Paris Peace Conference originated with several young educated Ukrainians in Winnipeg, under the influence of University of Saskatchewan graduate, Osyp Megas, a former editor of *Kanadyiskyi farmer* (Canadian Farmer) and school inspector, who was then rector of the Petro Mohyla Institute in Saskatoon. The UCCC echoed Megas' view that widespread publicity was needed to realize the Ukrainians' objective—the recognition of Ukraine as a distinct, ethnographically determined political entity, and a member of the proposed League of Nations.[5]

On 15 December 1918 the first of several public meetings was called by the UCCC in Winnipeg to discuss the despatch of two representatives to the Paris Peace Conference. The selection of the delegates, however, was hampered from the outset by the recent split in the Ukrainian Catholic Church.[6] Rivalry quickly developed between the Ukrainian Catholics and the independent-minded members (*samostiinyky*) of the new Ukrainian Orthodox Church, the outspoken dissenters who dominated the UCCC executive. Their uneasy partnership finally dissolved in late February 1919 over a financial disagreement. The administration of the Ukrainian Catholic *Kanadyiskyi rusyn* (Canadian Ruthenian) had consistently refused to transfer funds collected to the UCCC executive on the grounds that the money was destined for the Quarter Million Fund, just launched by Bishop Nykyta Budka to assist the Ukrainian National Council (also known as the Ukrainian Press Bureau for the UNR) in Paris.[7] The bureau, the Catholics maintained, would use the money to counter unsympathetic, pro-Polish publications that were gaining popularity throughout France.[8] Budka's disapproval of the UCCC leadership and his desire to limit the UCCC's sphere of influence—which extended over twenty-five branches across Canada—no doubt lay behind his launching of the Fund and the establishment of the Ukrainian National Council (UNC)[9] at the first convention of Catholic laity in Manitoba and Saskatchewan in January 1919. The activities of the UNC appeared to complement those of the UCCC,[10] and many Ukrainian Canadians, who only wanted to see their donations assist the mother country, did not understand the basis for the conflict between the two organizations. The squabbling bred mistrust and weakened support for both groups.

Nevertheless, the UCCC was determined to send two men to Paris and decided upon Osyp Megas and Ivan Petrushevich, the British-educated former editor of *Kanadyiskyi rusyn* who had fallen out of favour with Budka for associating with the *samostiinyky*. The two Ukrainians obtained passports from the Canadian government after the usual restrictions on the movement of alien enemies had been waived, but they did not receive the accreditation anticipated by the UCCC.[11] The French, adamant supporters of an independent Poland, had at first not permitted the ZUNR-UNR delegation to enter the country and later had pressured the other Allies to deny it official representation and the right to lobby at the deliberations.[12] Nevertheless, Megas and Petrushevich departed for Europe with confidence and high expectations. Members of the UCCC firmly believed that Ukraine's quest for independence would win international sympathy and, ultimately, the endorsement of the Paris Peace Conference. Their confidence rested on the apparent British and American commitment to the principle of self-determination for peoples in the disintegrated Austro-Hungarian empire. However, Ukrainian Canadians were soon disillusioned. Following their union, the two Ukrainian republics pressed for recognition of Ukrainian territory in both Russian and Austro-Hungarian spheres,[13] but the Allies remained intransigent: the affairs of each former empire were to be treated separately.

Ukrainians in Canada were unaware of the Allies' determination—especially that of France and Great Britain—to maintain the territorial integrity of imperial Russia by supporting the anti-Bolshevik White Army. In a secret agreement of 23 December 1917, France and Britain had agreed to two zones of responsibility in the southern part of the empire; the former was to take charge of forces in the Crimea, Ukraine and Bessarabia, and the latter in the area southeast of the Black Sea including the Caucasus. The UNR, in effect, could not and would not be recognized.[14] Eastern Galicia, the base of the ZUNR government, was to be treated as part of the Polish case for independence.

American support of national self-determination for the peoples of the Austro-Hungarian empire did not necessarily extend to the Russian empire. However, Ukrainians in Canada did not see the need to handle the two empires separately and did not think the Americans would do so. In fact, they trusted the Americans because of their past efforts to understand Ukrainian issues. The Americans, for example, had reports from their mission in Kiev and had some knowledge of the UNR before it signed the Treaty of Brest-Litovsk. In September 1917 President Wilson had enlisted over 150 scholars to prepare a series of reports and maps on eastern Europe as the basis for the Americans' peace proposal.[15] Initially these specialists had assumed that Bolshevism would give way to constitutional democratic government, but when it became clear that this was not to be, they decided to accept the independence of non-Russian nationalities and redraw the borders.[16] While Wilson respected his advisors' recommendations, prior commitments, especially to Premier Clemenceau of France, to preserve the territorial integrity of the former Russian empire prevailed. Wilson remained essentially blind to the contradictions inherent in his support of a united Russia and his pledge to assist the self-determination of all nations.[17]

The British, French, and American guarantees of the boundaries of the Russian empire, while granting self-determination to specific nationalities in the old Habsburg domains, prevented the emergence of a united Ukrainian state. Nevertheless, the absence of an effective Russian spokesman in Paris and obstacles that prevented a meeting with the Bolsheviks at Prinkipo on 15 February 1919 hindered the Allies in their first objective.[18] Then, as it became apparent that Allied intervention in Russia had failed, it became equally clear that the fate of the former empire would be decided by the Bolsheviks, and the subject of the UNR was removed from the peace conference agenda.

Ukrainian Canadians gained a more accurate picture of the Allied position on Ukraine once a steady stream of reports from Osyp Megas began to reach the UCCC. His observations, published regularly in *Ukrainskyi holos* (Ukrainian Voice), tended to sway popular opinion among Ukrainian immigrants because there was little coverage of the subject elsewhere. The optimism characteristic of December 1918 and January 1919 began to ebb as a result of Megas' reports. European diplomatic circles were largely ignorant or misinformed about political conditions in Ukraine. The prevailing view in Paris was that a strong Polish state and not a Ukrainian republic would be the most effective barrier against the Bolshevik threat, thus ensuring the stability of eastern Europe. The Ukrainian delegation which had arrived piecemeal in late February 1919, was jarred by the indifference toward Ukraine and realized the urgency of publicizing its claims. The main obstacles facing the Ukrainians were not only their inexperience in international affairs and the Allies' refusal to recognize them but the more mundane question of a language barrier. Thus the arrival of Megas and Petrushevich in mid-March 1919 was welcomed by the chairman of the Ukrainian delegation, Hryhorii Sydorenko. Both Ukrainian Canadians were named associate members of the delegation and employed as English translators.[19] While Sydorenko recognized their invaluable skills as well as the need to retain the support of Ukrainians in Canada, if only for financial reasons, others in the delegation were reluctant to work with the representatives of the Ukrainian emigrants, whom they remembered as politically unsophisticated, poor and illiterate.

Megas was intolerant of such pretentiousness. But what angered him most was the regional partisanship within the Ukrainian delegation which obstructed serious work.[20] Its heterogeneity—separate representatives from the ZUNR and the UNR—created internal tensions. These differences also led to discord between the two Canadians, as Petrushevich supported the narrower interests of the ZUNR delegates and Megas insisted that the political future of Ukraine should be solved without partisanship. He worked toward this end, while Petrushevich remained content to serve strictly as a translator.

Megas advocated a campaign to inundate the various diplomatic missions and their press bureaus with literature about Ukraine to counter the propaganda for Poland and Romania. The French journal *Le Temps* was the most damaging propagandist, circulating stories that Ukrainians were either Bolsheviks or Germanophiles and thus undeserving of Allied consideration and dangerous to Allied interests.[21] Megas himself made an unsuccessful attempt to explain the Ukrainian position to the newspaper's editor.[22]

Ukrainians in Canada were more willing to listen to Megas' appeal. New branches of the UCCC were created and sent telegrams to the British and Canadian delegations, urging recognition of the Ukrainian delegation and arguing that as the Ukrainian independence movement was national in scope,[23] it deserved their attention. The UCCC requested that the Canadian delegation

> give immediate recognition to the Ukrainian Republic...[help] settle the boundaries of the Ukrainian Republic on ethnographic principles... [together with] the Allied governments strengthen the Ukrainian Republic by compelling the Poles to withdraw their forces from Ukrainian territory..., Eastern Galicia and Kholm in particular,... [and] immediately repatriate one hundred thousand...Ukrainian soldiers, war prisoners held by Italy, and facilitate [their] transportation...into [the] ranks of General Petliura.[24]

Because they believed that Canadian foreign policy closely followed the British, Ukrainians in Canada anticipated official Canadian endorsement of their aspirations[25] and expected the Canadian delegation to act on their behalf in Paris. They were unaware that Canada's goal at the conference would be to demonstrate independence of action within the British empire, and a determination not to be drawn into European affairs which did not affect it directly.[26] Consequently, the Canadian delegation's cordiality to the Ukrainians fostered false hopes; the Canadians relayed messages to the British but never became actively involved in Ukrainian matters.

Megas continued to lobby in various diplomatic circles for the recognition of the Ukrainian delegation and the right to present its case before the Peace Conference. His vigorous attempts to convince the Allies to discuss a united Ukrainian republic proved futile when they elected to focus on Eastern Galicia, the territorial base of the ZUNR, also claimed by the Poles. As Eastern Galicia was seen as a buffer against Bolshevik aggression in western Europe, the Allies felt compelled to intercede in the Polish-Ukrainian conflict. Their proposals, which confirmed their predisposition toward Polish interests, formed the subject matter of many of the reports Megas sent to Canada.

There were several instances of Allied intervention in the Eastern Galician question. The Sub-Commission of the Inter-Allied Commission,[27] established on 29 January 1919, was dispatched to Lviv to verify allegations by the Polish prime minister, Ignacy Paderewski, that the aggressor in Eastern Galicia was "the murderous Ukrainian Bolshevik Army,"[28] and to negotiate an armistice between the belligerents. Paderewski's allegations that the ZUNR army—strongly nationalistic and anti-communist—was somehow linked to the Bolshevik forces overrunning the UNR, increased the confusion of the Allied Powers. The sub-commission finally recommended ceding the Boryslav oil fields and approximately one-third of Eastern Galicia[29] to the Poles, including the city of Lviv. The Ukrainians rejected the "Berthélemy proposal" on 1 March after much discussion with the sub-commission, and the Allies then held them responsible for the resumption of Polish-Ukrainian hostilities.

The French, who continued to fear that failure to support the Poles militarily against the Ukrainians would jeopardize the stability of eastern Europe, sought international support for a strong Polish state. They stressed the historical legitimacy of Polish territorial claims and Polish ability to maintain a powerful state while belittling the capabilities and arguments of the ZUNR. Later, however, they conceded that it was the strategical location of Poland that swayed their foreign policy and not Polish strength. Nonetheless, Paderewski's wish for military assistance to protect Lviv and the concern of the French for their own well-being led to a second attempt at Allied intervention in Eastern Galicia.[30]

The American member of the sub-commission, R. Lord, proposed a hearing for both parties in Paris on 19 March on the condition that a truce be called along the existing military line giving the Poles control of Lviv and the Lviv-Peremyshl railway. Several members of the Ukrainian delegation, disturbed by French insistence on transporting General Joseph Haller's army[31] to Galicia before a truce, met Lord to discuss the consequences of his proposal. Lord explained that for the Americans "neither a great Poland, a great Roumania, nor a great Lithuania exists... [because] we are guided only by ethnographical factors [in deciding the future of eastern Europe]."[32] The Ukrainians interpreted this to mean that the Americans supported the claims of the ZUNR. Reporting to the UCCC, Megas confirmed that "we [Ukrainians] are given the greatest assurance among minorities that no harm will come to our cause nor will it be allowed to occur [in the future]."[33] Satisfied, the Ukrainians accepted Lord's proposal, but the Poles pressed for the implementation of the earlier solution and hostilities resumed.

The failure of the second truce and the cautious stance of the Allies toward the ZUNR highlighted the difficulties plaguing the Ukrainian delegation. Without recognition or a hearing before the Peace Conference, the Ukrainians had little hope of arguing their case effectively and thus far their protests had fallen on deaf ears. With few alternatives open to them, the Ukrainians now intensified their lobby among those Europeans and Americans who might intercede on their behalf. They even hoped to use the congenial rapport established between the UCCC and the Canadian government during discussions concerning the dispatch of their two representatives to Paris.

On 27 March, Megas and Sydorenko visited Prime Minister Borden to seek assistance in obtaining recognition for the Ukrainian delegation in Paris and to impress upon him the strong anti-Bolshevism of the Ukrainians.[34] Sydorenko appealed to Borden again in April to pressure the

British delegation to explain why the chairman of the Inter-Allied Commission in Warsaw had promised both General Piłsudski and Prime Minister Paderewski moral and material aid on 28 March. Did this mean that the Allies supported Polish attacks against the Ukrainians, then struggling to contain the Bolshevik offensive?[35] No satisfactory answer was given.

The aborted armistice of 19 March and the continued impasse in the Polish-Ukrainian dispute forced a resumption of negotiations. It became increasingly clear that the frontiers of Poland could not be established without simultaneously settling the status of Eastern Galicia. General Botha, chairman of the newly appointed Inter-Allied Commission for the Negotiations of an Armistice Between Poland and Ukraine, was named mediator of a new armistice until the Peace Conference determined the eastern borders of Poland. In the meantime a truce was called and Polish and Ukrainian claims were slated to be heard by the Inter-Allied Commission and the Commission on Polish Affairs. For the first time, ZUNR representatives were recognized as distinct from their UNR counterparts and summoned for discussion by the Supreme Council of the peace conference.[36]

Polish and ZUNR military experts arrived in Paris to present their cases at a time when Bolshevik advances threatened the lands of both sides. The Polish delegation continued to favour the "Berthélemy proposal" and wanted to link the Polish-Romanian frontiers, arguing that the ZUNR government would be unable to control its army, which would lead to anarchy and eventual Bolshevik victory. The Poles blamed the Ukrainians for the violation of the armistice of 19 March, alleging that the latter had used the interval to improve their military position.[37] The Ukrainians countered by charging that Polish use of the armistice to smuggle arms into Lviv had compelled them to withdraw from the truce. The Ukrainian delegation (Sydorenko, Colonel Dmytro Vitovsky and Dr. Mykhailo Lozynsky) declared a precondition for armistice—the establishment of the border along the Sian River to the Carpathian Mountains. On the basis of both Ukrainian and Polish presentations, however, the commission drafted a new proposal on 12 May advocating the Polish-Ukrainian frontier of 19 March, with Lviv and one-half of the Boryslav oil fields going to the Poles. The Ukrainians agreed to these conditions, but the Poles rejected them.[38]

The Ukrainians' willingness to accept the terms of the armistice was dictated by the extreme plight of the Galician army. Megas, in his dispatches to Canada, described the sickness, hunger and shortages of weapons, ammunition, clothing and medical supplies. Beseeching Ukrainians in Canada to come to the army's assistance immediately, he wrote:

Are you aware of the superhuman sacrifices that Ukraine-Galicia made and continues to make.... The hospitals are full with wounded, the roads are in disrepair, hunger reigns over villages; there is a lack of cheese, butter, meat, clothing.... But in spite of these conditions, there are more volunteers for the army than the commanders can arm and clothe.... Should we be astounded by their failures? No, we should rather be amazed at the superhuman heroism of our ill-fated Galician army.[39]

Megas recommended that the UCCC make contact with the International Red Cross for food, clothing and medicine to alleviate the army's desperate state, and begged the committee to seek the assistance of American philanthropists to found a Ukrainian Red Cross in Canada.[40] As a result, an ad hoc Ukrainian Relief Committee was formed in August 1919 to collect funds while plans were laid to establish the Ukrainian Red Cross. There is no evidence that the UCCC asked the Canadian government for aid.[41]

Indeed, both Polish and Ukrainian forces were war weary and in need of proper nutrition, medicines and clothing. The Ukrainians had hoped that the draft proposal of 12 May might bring an end to the fighting but news of Haller's offensive on the Ukrainian front suspended discussion on the armistice conditions. The Ukrainian delegation objected to the Poles' violation of the truce, their propaganda campaign against the ZUNR and the military intervention of Haller's army in Galicia after Allied assurances to the contrary.[42] The Supreme Council of the Peace Conference, perplexed by the breach in armistice negotiations, hesitated to take firm action in the matter, while the Poles ignored its reprimand and occupied Kalush, Stanyslaviv and Halych at the end of May.[43]

Ukrainians in Canada were outraged by Poland's violation of the truce. The UCCC, appealing to Ukrainian patriotism, wrote:

Every last one of us must protest against Polish tyranny on Ukrainian soil and against the abrogation of the Ukrainian right to independence.... We cannot remain indifferent to Polish fabrications against Ukrainians which deceive the Western Allies and conceal their own crimes and offenses.[44]

Telegrams were sent to world leaders, including Prime Minister Borden, demanding "the withdrawal of the Polish troops from all Ukrainian territories,"[45] but none of the recipients responded. Indecision continued to mark Allied policy. The Supreme Council of the Peace Conference authorized the Council of Foreign Ministers to study the possibility of a plebiscite, but there was little sympathy for the proposal since Polish propaganda had created the impression that the Galicians were largely illiterate and incapable of self-rule. The Ukrainian lobby had made few inroads. Megas' suggestion that the Ukrainian delegation protest aggressively over Eastern Galicia had been ignored.[46] Much to his dismay,

Megas remained on the periphery of the discussions, while the Ukrainian delegation, on the verge of collapsing, offered feeble resistance to the rapid change of events.

Disenchanted, Megas conceded: "I travelled to Paris with great enthusiasm, but I will most likely return a pessimist if I do not meet better persons, . . . [whom] I believe exist among our leaders." He was convinced, however, that "our menagerie here [in Paris] is completely incapable . . . [of] conducting political negotiations and has no finesse in diplomatic manoeuvring, writing, etc."[47] Megas was helpless as the rift widened between the two halves of the Ukrainian delegation, whose interests conflicted. While Megas recognized the damaging effects of Polish, Romanian, Czech and French enmity toward the Ukrainians, he pointed to personal ambition—"the height of foolishness"—and not to differences over issues of principle, as a major factor in the lack of co-operation within the Ukrainian delegation and its weak efforts to retain Eastern Galicia and the territorial sovereignty of the UNR. In Megas' opinion, the demise of the Ukrainian delegation was caused "by idiocy and servile, self-seeking flattery of some of our most prominent delegates and the lack of discipline and subordination of personal interests to the common goal."[48]

Paderewski played upon regional differences within the Ukrainian delegation, exaggerated the Galician liaison with German and Austrian forces (not only were the Ukrainians weak politically but they were also sustained by the enemy), and argued that the precarious Ukrainian government was an easy target for the Bolsheviks. Unable to find an alternative solution, the Allied Supreme Council finally succumbed to Polish pressure and on 25 June authorized the Polish troops to advance to the river Zbruch, thereby occupying Eastern Galicia. The Poles had skilfully created a fait accompli through force and propaganda.[49]

Several weeks passed before Ukrainians in Canada learned of the decision of 25 June. In the meantime, the UCCC continued to believe that the Allies would not be swayed by Polish imperialism and increased its pressure on the Canadian government and on other Allies not to abandon the principle of national self-determination in Eastern Galicia. Ukrainians in Canada maintained that

> the civilized world must reckon with the fact that Ukraine lived and will live. . . . As long as Ukraine will not be recognized as an independent country within her ethnographic borders, so long will peace in Europe be impossible. . . . The Allies must recognize the fact, that Ukraine belongs far more to the Ukrainians than Palestine to the Jews.[50]

The Central Committee of the Ukrainian National Council, the UCCC's rival, sent Roman Kremar to Ottawa from May through July to prompt the Canadian government to demand a British investigation into the Eastern Galician dispute.[51]

Kremar's lobbying, the telegrams flooding the prime minister's office and the efforts of two members of parliament (H. A. Mackie, Edmonton East, and M. R. Blake, Winnipeg North) brought the Eastern Galician question to the floor of the Commons on 7 July (see Appendix III:19). In reply to requests for current information on the status of Ukrainians in eastern Europe, Borden outlined the Allies' position on the UNR, and stated his belief that they would hesitate to recognize its independence because such a move "would involve breaking up the Russian Empire." He then presented the position of both parties on the dispute in Eastern Galicia without revealing his own sympathies, but quoted at length a 27 May peace telegram from the president of the conference admonishing Piłsudski for military attacks against the Ukrainians. The latter, it stated, had committed themselves to an armistice, judging by their acceptance of the truces of 19 March and 12 May. Probably unaware of the 25 June decision, Borden declared his confidence that regardless of how the boundaries of Eastern Galicia were drawn, the rights of Ukrainians would not be violated.

Ukrainians in Canada were at first satisfied by the prime minister's assurances, but shortly thereafter, news of the 25 June decision appeared in the Ukrainian-language press. An obituary for Eastern Galicia, first published in *Ukrainskyi holos*, was reprinted in other Ukrainian newspapers in North America for over a month.

> Ukrainians in Canada mourn...for their brothers and sisters in Galicia, Kholm and Volhynia who at this very moment are being slaughtered by Polish Premier Paderewski's punitive expedition for the only reason that they, in accordance with the principle of self-determination, proclaimed by the Allies, refused to submit to the Polish yoke and insist upon governing themselves on their own soil.[52]

Sorrow was accompanied by anger. As *Kanadyiskyi farmer* commented, the Allies had cheated the Ukrainians:

> A month ago if anyone had stated that the Allies would have placed Eastern Galicia under the imperialist heel of Poland we would have spat in his face. We would have been justified. The Allies had fought a war...to liberate...small nations in Europe and in the end having suppressed the enemy of liberty and freedom declared...that each nationality would obtain its independence.... But today? Today we know [otherwise].[53]

Protest followed as Ukrainian Canadians sent telegrams to the Allied Powers throughout the summer of 1919 denouncing Polish actions in Eastern Galicia.

In contrast, protests from the Ukrainian delegation continued to weaken. By mid-July, as the situation in Eastern Galicia appeared irreversible, co-operation among the Ukrainian delegates was negligible. Several organized the Committee for an Independent Ukraine (Komitet Nezalezhnoi Ukrainy)[54] in an attempt to keep the issue alive by means of a publicity campaign. Frustrated by his inability to work with the Ukrainian delegation, Megas had resigned as translator on 1 May to work independently. Recognizing the hopelessness of the Ukrainian cause in Eastern Galicia, he spent October and November 1919 in Kamianets Podilskyi, the seat of both the ZUNR and the Directory of the UNR, to survey the state of the Ukrainian army and also to collect material for his book, *Tragediia halytskoi Ukrainy* [The Tragedy of Galician Ukraine], published in Winnipeg in 1920.

The fate of Eastern Galicia was sealed by the decision of 25 June, even though the region's legal status remained unsettled. The Supreme Council delayed its decision, unable to find a compromise between Polish claims for outright annexation and British desires for an interim Polish administration prior to a plebiscite. The protracted postponement so annoyed the UCCC that it proposed holding a plebiscite in Canada for Ukrainians there to determine the political status of Eastern Galicia.[55] It is doubtful whether this proposal would have been taken seriously, but it became a dead issue when the Draft Statute for Eastern Galicia, accepted by the Supreme Council on 22 November, authorized Poland to administer the territory to the river Zbruch for twenty-five years.

Ukrainians in Canada responded to news of the accord with rallies and a new flurry of telegrams.[56] Although individual Ukrainian missions protested throughout Europe, the Ukrainian delegation in Paris had ceased to function in August. The factions within it had become irreconcilable after the UNR established a diplomatic mission in Warsaw, a move the Galicians considered a betrayal.

Ukrainian Canadians continued to protest but eventually were forced to face unpleasant reality. They had failed both to gain recognition of the united Ukrainian state and to muster support for the ZUNR, despite their success in collecting funds to publicize Ukrainian aspirations for independence and to sponsor two representatives in Paris.

In spite of generous Ukrainian Canadian monetary support of the cause, however, the financial committee of the Ukrainian delegation reported that it had received no donations from Canada.[57] In fact, when the UCCC issued a financial statement, it was revealed that from December 1918 to 18 August 1919 the executive in Winnipeg had collected $17,292.19, over $15,000 of which had been used for office equipment, the secretary's salary, telegrams, transportation, an honorarium for Petrushevich and support for the families of the two delegates; the largest sum, $7,194.70, was spent on Megas' voyage and expenses, as he received nothing from the Ukrainian delegation. No funds had been sent directly to the Ukrainian delegation.[58]

From August to the end of December 1919 the tiny sum of $1,816.83 was collected, reflecting the Ukrainians' hesitancy to part with their limited resources as the unfavourable reports from Paris increased. Questions were also asked of the Ukrainian National Council. By 25 January 1920 it had collected $13,633.01 for the Quarter Million Fund. This money had supported various projects; for example, $1,365.90 went to the Ukrainian Press Bureau in Paris, $445.78 to the two Canadians in Paris, $2,400.00 to the Ukrainian lobby in Ottawa, $651.88 for English-language press releases and $831.70 for cables.[59]

Ukrainians in Canada were naturally disheartened by the financial reports. Many had not realized that administration costs would be so high and had expected that their donations would go directly to the Ukrainian delegation. The moment was ripe for the Ukrainian socialists to challenge the entire undertaking but their newspaper, *Ukrainski robitnychi visty*, was beset by technical problems and the postwar escalation of police surveillance impeded their political activities.[60] Even without these drawbacks, the socialists admitted, it was difficult to influence the "sizeable percentage of Ukrainian workers and famers... lured by nationalist slogans which they could neither understand nor decipher."[61]

Rumours discrediting the Ukrainian delegation and reports that the policies of the ZUNR and UNR governments worked at cross purposes further undermined the Ukrainian immigrants' confidence in Ukrainian diplomacy. They could not understand why the two governments, in a final effort to gain control of their territory, sought military assistance from dubious friends: the UNR courted the Poles and Romanians while the ZUNR looked to the Russian monarchist forces under Denikin. Ukrainians in Canada eventually blamed both the Ukrainian diplomats and world powers for their insincere attempts to resolve the Ukrainian territorial question.

After the work of the Ukrainian delegation in Paris had ended, the two Ukrainian representatives from Canada remained in Europe. Petrushevich elected to work for the UNR mission in London while Megas went to observe conditions in Ukraine. "The word 'tragedy',," he claimed, "does not even come close to portraying the present situation."[62] His appeal for help led to the formation of the Ukrainian Red Cross in Canada in December 1919, which had received $18,488.75 in donations by April 1920.[63] In spite of such demonstrations of financial commitment to the homeland, Ukrainians in Canada were generally spiritless, little motivated to rejuvenate their own organizational work. But their apathy dissolved with the arrival of two representatives of the ZUNR-in-exile, seeking to mobilize the Ukrainian community on a hitherto unknown scale.[64] For Ukrainian Canadians, Eastern Galicia would remain a live issue.

Notes

1. The ZUNR retained its autonomy for political reasons. It maintained that its military superiority and economic resources would enable it to act both as a buffer against the Bolshevik threat and as the gateway to Europe for the UNR. ZUNR policies and actions were dictated by the hope of receiving a favourable territorial and political settlement at the Paris Peace Conference.

2. Several thousand Ukrainian Canadians contemplated returning to the homeland. Frank Dojacek, a Winnipeg publisher and owner of several ethnic newspapers, had warned the chief press censor in 1918 that 90 per cent of the Ukrainian population would leave Canada at the end of the war if the restrictions against them were not removed. Although this figure was undoubtedly an exaggeration, the idea of returning to one's homeland was common among Slavs by 1918 because of the hostility confronting them in Canada. For example, a resolution passed by Slavs in the Vancouver area called for representatives to visit all nine provinces to induce Slavs to return to the lands of their birth. Dojacek to E. J. Chambers, 26 October 1918, Chief Press Censor Files, file 364–1, vol. 163, Secretary of State Papers, Public Archives of Canada (hereafter PAC), Ottawa, Ontario; and untitled report, 9 February 1919, Chief Press Censor Files, file 229, vol. 74, PAC.

3. The Ukrainian Canadian Citizens' Committee was formed in the summer of 1918, probably reflecting prairie Ukrainians' desire to seek government intervention to ease their lot as enemy aliens. For unknown reasons the UCCC remained dormant until December 1918 when it was jarred into action by the prospect of a peace settlement and the redrafting of European boundaries. Its aims, formulated one year after its establishment, were "(1) to educate the Ukrainians living in Canada in the institutions of their adopted country and to develop in them an interest in the principles of good citizenship, (2) to develop social intercourse and mutual understanding between the Ukrainians and their co-citizens, [and] (3) to interest our co-citizens in the case of Ukrainian democracy" (*Ukrainskyi holos*, 20 August 1919).

4. *Kanadyiskyi rusyn*, 4 December 1918.

5. *Ibid.*, 27 November 1918. For an account of the paucity of printed materials in English about Ukraine before 1919, see V. J. Kaye-Kysilevs'kyj, *Ukraine, Russia and Other Slavic Countries in English Literature*, Slavistica no. 40 (Winnipeg, 1961), 9–16 and 24–32. See S. Dnistrianskyj, *Ukraina and the Peace Conference* (n.p., 1919) for an example of Ukrainian attempts to popularize their case for independence among the British and Americans.

6. *Ranok*, 11 December 1918.

7. The Ukrainian National Council was founded in Paris in December 1918 specifically to publish information about the UNR. Its chairman was Fedir (Theodore) Savchenko. *Ukrainskyi holos*, 1 January 1919.

8. *Kanadyiskyi rusyn*, 8 January 1918.

9. The aim of the Ukrainian National Council was the "procurement of Canadian citizenship, with full rights and obligations as well as the attainment of an independent and united Ukraine overseas" (*ibid.*, 5 February 1919).

10. The Ukrainian National Council collected funds for the Ukrainian Press Bureau in Paris and for the purchase of food and clothing for Ukrainian prisoners of war in Italy and famine-stricken areas in Galicia. Grain depots were to be established throughout Alberta, for example, and the member of parliament for Edmonton East, H.A. Mackie, was to obtain assurances from the Canadian government of safe passage of the grain shipment; it appears, however, that the plan was unsuccessful. *Ibid.*, 19 and 26 February, 5 and 6 March 1919; 1 March 1919, Sir Robert Borden Papers, 19677, vol. 94, PAC; and 19 March 1919, Borden Papers, 13823, vol. 247, PAC.

11. J. H. Calder to Borden, 29 January 1919, Borden Papers, 87402–8, vol. 162, PAC.

12. Hryhorii Sydorenko, chairman of the Ukrainian delegation and former minister of railways for the UNR, arrived in Paris on 26 January 1919; entry into France was finally granted to fourteen other delegates while the rest remained in Berne, Switzerland. *Ukrainskyi holos*, 26 March 1919. See also a letter from Sydorenko to the president of the peace conference, asking admission for the Ukrainian delegation; *ibid.*, 10 February 1919.

13. *Kanadyiskyi rusyn*, 5 February 1919; *Ranok*, 5 March 1919; and *Ukrainskyi holos*, 5 March 1919.

14. See G. A. Brinkley, "Allied Policy and French Intervention in the Ukraine, 1917–1920," in *The Ukraine, 1917–1921: A Study in Revolution*, ed. T. Hunczak (Cambridge, Mass., 1977), 323–51. The Allies hoped that the creation of a united Russian democratic federation would both ensure stability and eradicate German influence in the east. This was foremost in French foreign policy especially after some non-Russian nationalities had turned to the Germans for help against the Bolsheviks, resulting in German occupation of their lands. This had happened to the Ukrainians, who signed a separate peace treaty with the Central Powers at Brest-Litovsk in February 1918, turning to them for military aid to stop the Bolsheviks once it became clear that no effective assistance was forthcoming from the Allies. German intervention resulted in the overthrow of the UNR in April and the establishment of the German-supported Hetmanate under Pavlo Skoropadsky.

15. See C. Warvariv, "America and the Ukrainian National Cause, 1917–1920," in *The Ukraine, 1917–1921: A Study in Revolution*, 362–72.

16. An Outline of Tentative Recommendations of January 21, 1919, Inquiry Archives, U.S. National Archives, Washington, D.C., cited in *ibid.*, 371.

17. Poland, Finland and the Baltic States, all former territories of the Russian empire, were exceptions as Wilson supported their independence.

18. G. A. Brinkley, *The Volunteer Army and Allied Intervention in South Russia, 1917–1921* (Notre Dame, Indiana, 1966), 107–12; and minutes of the 14th session of the Supreme War Council, 14 February 1919, Sir Robert Borden Papers, file 3b, vol. 27, PAC.

19. Sydorenko to UCCC, 19 April 1919, Petro Woycenko Papers, PAC.

20. Megas to Woycenko, 22 March 1919, Woycenko Papers, PAC.

21. *Ukrainskyi holos*, 30 April 1919.

22. *Svoboda*, 5 April 1919.

23. Megas to Woycenko, 3 April 1919, Woycenko Papers, PAC.

24. 24 April 1919, Borden Papers, 87682, vol. 162, PAC.

25. *Kanadyiskyi rusyn*, 4 December 1918.

26. R. C. Brown and R. Cook, *Canada 1896–1921: A Nation Transformed* (Toronto, 1974), 287–90.

27. The members of the Sub-Commission were chairman General Berthélemy (France), Dr. R. Lord (United States), Mr. Stabile (Italy) and General A. Carton de Wiart (Great Britain).

28. L. L. Gerson, *Woodrow Wilson and the Rebirth of Poland, 1914–1920* (New Haven, 1953), 115–17.

29. The area specified extended from the Buh River to Kaminka, 20 kilometres east of Lviv, bordered by the railroad tracks to Stryi.

30. L. J. Haczynski, "The Problem of Eastern Galicia at the Paris Peace Conference: A Re-examination of American Materials in the Archives of the United States" (Ph.D. thesis, Fordham University, 1971), 99–106; and E. Lukasz, "The Ukraine at the Paris Peace Conference, 1919" (M.A. thesis, University of Chicago, 1962), 34–5.

31. Haller's army was composed of Polish nationals in France taken prisoner by German and Austrian forces, as well as volunteers from Canada and the United States.

32. *Ukrainskyi holos*, 9 April 1919.

33. Megas to Taras Ferley, 20 April 1919, Woycenko Papers, PAC.

34. Borden to Lloyd George, 27 March 1919, Borden Papers, 87577, vol. 162, PAC.

35. Sydorenko to the chairman of the peace conference, 4 April 1919, Borden Papers, 87601, vol. 162, PAC.

36. *Ukrainskyi holos*, 2 July 1919.

37. Haczynski, "The Problem of Eastern Galicia," 140–3; and British Delegation Daily Bulletin, no. 88 and 93, Borden Papers, file 4, Vol. 428, PAC.

38. Haczynski, "The Problem of Eastern Galicia," 144–6; and Lukasz, "Ukraine at the Paris Peace Conference," 33.

39. Megas to Woycenko, 17 May 1919, Woycenko Papers, PAC.

40. Megas to the UCCC, 7 and 17 May 1919, Woycenko Papers, PAC.

41. British Delegation Daily Bulletin, no. 89, Borden Papers, file 4, vol. 428, PAC.

42. Megas to Woycenko, 3 April 1919, Woycenko Papers, PAC.

43. Eastern Report, 5 June 1919 (containing the message from the peace conference to General Pilsudski, 27 May 1919, and a note informing of Polish advances into Eastern Galicia, 29 May 1919), Borden Papers, file 42b, vol. 442, PAC.

44. *Ukrainskyi holos*, 2 July 1919, UCCC to Allied Powers and to Sydorenko.

45. *Ibid.*, 2 and 9 July 1919; and *Kanadyiskyi ukrainets*, 8 July 1919.

46. Megas to Woycenko, 4 June 1919, Woycenko Papers, PAC.

47. Megas to Woycenko, 30 May 1919, Woycenko Papers, PAC.

48. *Ranok*, 13 August 1919.
49. H. W. V. Temperley, *A History of the Peace Conference of Paris*, 6 vols. (London; 1920–4), 6: 245; 1: 335–8; 4: 84–5 and 103–5.
50. *Kanadyiskyi farmer*, 11 July 1919.
51. *Kanadyiskyi ukrainets*, 19 August 1919.
52. *Ukrainskyi holos*, 16 July 1919.
53. *Kanadyiskyi farmer*, 18 July 1919.
54. *Ukrainskyi holos*, 23 July 1919. The committee was organized by Mykhailo Hrushevsky, Dmytro Isaievych, Mykhailo Lozynsky and Fedir Savchenko.
55. *Ibid.*, 24 September 1919.
56. *Ibid.*, 30 July to 10 December 1919; the issues between these dates acknowledge seventy-seven Ukrainian centres for sending telegrams to various world leaders.
57. S. Shelukhyn to Woycenko, 28 July 1919, Woycenko Papers, PAC.
58. Treasurer's report file, Woycenko Papers, PAC.
59. *Kanadyiskyi ukrainets*, 1 May 1920.
60. M. Volynets, *Zhovtoblakytna dolarokharna perezva* (Winnipeg, 1932), 54.
61. *Ukrainski robitnychi visty*, 30 July 1919.
62. *Ukrainskyi holos*, 10 December 1919; see also O. Megas, *Tragediia halytskoi Ukrainy* (Winnipeg, 1920) and *Iliustrovani spomyny z heroiskoi Ukrainy 1914–1920* (Winnipeg, 1920).
63. D. Doroshenko and S. Kovbel, eds., *Propamiatna knyha ukrainskoho narodnoho domu y Vynypegu* (Winnipeg, 1949), 315.
64. *Kanadyiskyi ukrainets*, 17 November 1920.

Chapter 8

Ukrainian Diplomatic Representation in Canada, 1920–3

Oleh W. Gerus

Ukrainians in Canada keenly followed the struggle of their homeland for independence from its beginning in 1917. Initial support for Ukraine was reinforced by community action seeking to generate public sympathy (among both Ukrainians and their fellow Canadians) and government support for the Ukrainian position, and to provide material aid to destitute war victims in Ukraine.[1] The formation and work of the Ukrainian Canadian Citizens' Committee, the Ukrainian National Council and the Ukrainian Red Cross Society of Canada were prominent examples of Ukrainian Canadians' involvement in the affairs of their former homeland. However, as Canada did not recognize the newly formed Ukrainian republic, there was no accredited Ukrainian diplomatic representation in this country; neither was there any unofficial representation. Ukrainian officials paid surprisingly little attention to the potential value of the numerous Ukrainian immigrants and settlers abroad.

Only in 1920, after the Ukrainian political leadership found itself in exile, did the governments of both the Ukrainian National Republic (Ukrainska Narodna Respublika—UNR) and the West Ukrainian National Republic (Zakhidno-Ukrainska Narodna Respublika—ZUNR) turn to their countrymen in diaspora. Since most Ukrainian immigrants originated from Galicia, it was natural that the government of the ZUNR, better known as the Galician government, should take the initiative in sending its envoys to them.[2] In 1920 Professor Ivan Bobersky established a Galician representation in Canada by opening a Ukrainian Bureau in Winnipeg. Theoretically, Bobersky was a special delegate to the Ukrainians of Canada rather than to the Canadian government. In 1922 this limited representation was enlarged by the addition of Dr. Osyp Nazaruk and its functions expanded.

I

In November 1918, with the collapse of the Austro-Hungarian empire, the Ukrainian political leadership of Galicia, which had advocated Ukrainian autonomy under the Habsburgs, declared the establishment of the West Ukrainian National Republic headed by politician Evhen Petrushevych.[3] Such a declaration invited immediate Polish reaction. War broke out, but the surprisingly effective Ukrainian Galician Army frustrated the Polish invasion. As the conflict intensified, the Galician issue became an item on the agenda of the Paris Peace Conference.[4] There, Polish diplomacy, which emphasized Poland's historical claims to Galicia and distorted reality by denouncing the Ukrainians as Bolsheviks, German agents or primitive aborigines, was supported by France and the United States.[5] The atmosphere in Paris mitigated against a fair resolution of the problem, but the Galician government had deluded itself into believing that the Wilsonian principle of national self-determination would ultimately favour Galicia.

By July 1919, in the face of the Franco-Polish offensive, the Galician government and the army left Galicia for Eastern Ukraine. The Polish military occupation was approved by the Peace Conference as a temporary measure pending the settlement of the political status of that land in conformity with the wishes of the people. The Treaty of St. Germain of September 1919 legalized the dismemberment of Austria and transferred the Austrian sovereignty of Galicia to the Supreme Council of the Peace Conference. Thus, despite Polish efforts to integrate Ukraine or Eastern Galicia into the new Polish state, the region, in theory, belonged to the Supreme Council and Poland was merely its agent. Thus the diplomacy of ZUNR successfully postponed legalization of the Polish occupation.

Petrushevych had joined forces with the Directory of the UNR under Symon Petliura in July 1919. The two Ukrainian republics had been symbolically united since January of that year but until the summer acted quite separately—Galicia was embroiled with Poland, and the UNR with Russia. It quickly became apparent that cultural and political differences between the Eastern and Western Ukrainians, caused by centuries of separation, were so profound that common action was practically impossible. Petrushevych's obsession with Poland was reciprocated by Petliura's concern with Russia—Red and White. Both leaders were prepared to make approaches to each other's enemy in an effort to attain their primary goals—Kiev for Petliura, Lviv for Petrushevych.

This disagreement on priorities and policies extended to the Ukrainian diplomatic delegation in Paris, as the Galician members began to act independently of the official group.[6] After Petliura made an alliance with Poland at the expense of Galicia (Warsaw Treaty, May 1920), the UNR delegation formally broke into two mutually hostile camps. Because most western diplomats were either ignorant or badly misinformed about the Ukrainian situation, the existence of two Ukrainian delegations harmed not only their respective positions but the Ukrainian cause as a whole.

The Petrushevych government, which established itself in Vienna, believed that the international situation was favourable to Galicia's prospects.[7] American withdrawal from European affairs and British suspicion of French empire-building in eastern Europe encouraged Petrushevych to intensify his anti-Polish campaign. The British prime minister, Lloyd George, was the only international leader to show genuine concern for the Galician problem.[8] Thus, Petrushevych publicized real and alleged Polish persecutions and held the Allied Powers morally responsible for the suffering of the Ukrainian population. At all times he pointedly disassociated himself from the UNR and Petliura, whose reputation, even in emigre circles, before his assassination in 1926 was notorious.

Petrushevych argued that an independent and neutral Ukrainian Galician state was both viable *and* in the interests of the west. ZUNR submissions to the League of Nations stressed that Galicia's size of 70,000 square kilometres and its population of six million (74 per cent of whom were Ukrainian) made it larger than Holland or Belgium. Galicia had a valuable economic resource—oil—and strategically would be a barrier to Bolshevism.[9] The diplomatic campaign and public pressure, especially in Canada, succeeded to the extent that in 1921 the League of Nations, on the motion of Canada's delegate, S. J. Doherty, called upon the Allied Powers to resolve the political status of Galicia promptly. The League's Council of Ambassadors was entrusted with the task, and it was assumed that a decision would be reached in 1922.

As Petrushevych desperately needed money to maintain diplomatic pressure on the Council of Ambassadors, the coalition parties of the ZUNR government resolved to launch a major collection drive among Ukrainian emigrants. Petrushevych had been impressed with the success of Irish nationalists in collecting huge sums of money from Irish Americans for the struggle against the British. He expected a similar response from Ukrainian emigrants and chose a totally unrealistic sum of one million dollars as a target. The Galician envoy to the United States, Lovhin Tsehelsky, opened the North American campaign in June 1921 and in Canada engaged a Montreal trust firm to sell the Galician bonds. However, the campaign floundered and by the time a discredited Tsehelsky was replaced by Luka Myshuha, the future editor of *Svoboda*, only $1,500.00 had been collected in Canada. Petrushevych also enlarged the Canadian representation, established in 1920, from a mere information and propaganda agency to a diplomatic and financial mission.

II

Between 1920 and Osyp Nazaruk's arrival in Canada in 1922, Ivan Bobersky, largely on his own initiative, had effectively publicized the plight of Ukrainians under Polish occupation. A distinguished educator and youth organizer who had always wanted to visit Canada, Bobersky had taught a number of future nationalist leaders, including Evhen Konovalets, as a professor at the Ukrainian Classical Gymnasium in Lviv. The president and moving force behind the Galicia-wide athletic organization, Sokil, he had also been instrumental in developing an extensive para-military base for the *Sichovi Striltsi* (Sich Sharpshooters), the forerunner of the Ukrainian Galician Army. In 1918 he became chief of the Military Press Department of the ZUNR.[10] A mild-mannered and tactful person with a wry sense of humour, Bobersky enjoyed the respect of those who knew him. In Canada he travelled extensively, delivering vividly illustrated lectures about the condition of the Ukrainian people under Poland. Bobersky's activities helped to rekindle Polish-Ukrainian antagonisms in Canada, and relations between the two groups remained tense for many years. Bobersky's travels and his vast correspondence allowed him to compile the first directory of Ukrainians in Canada (over two thousand names), which proved useful to the Ukrainian Red Cross Society in its collection drive and vital to the subsequent financial campaign of the ZUNR.

The fractious nature of the Ukrainian community in Canada, particularly the passionate religious conflict between Catholic and Orthodox, motivated Bobersky to help create a recognizable national co-ordinating body.[11] Initially the central committee of the Ukrainian Red Cross appeared the most likely national spokesman, but the Ukrainian community was not yet ready to lend its allegiance or support to any one organization.[12]

The petitions and telegrams emanating from Ukrainian rallies and sent to Ottawa, London and Geneva helped to keep the Galician issue in public view. Ironically, it was the short-lived Conservative government of Arthur Meighen—the man responsible for the War-time Elections Act which disfranchised many Ukrainians as enemy aliens—that raised the Galician question at the League of Nations in September 1921. Hoping to capitalize on the Ukrainian vote during the December 1921 election, the Conservatives produced a curious, if not cynical, thirty-page pamphlet, *Ukrainska Sprava v Ottavi* (Ukrainian Affairs in Ottawa), which detailed the pro-Ukrainian position of the Unionist government and included a letter of appreciation from Petrushevych. The Ukrainian electoral response was rather disappointing; most of western Canada held Ottawa responsible for current economic difficulties and voted for the Progressives, thus toppling Meighen and cooling his ardour for the Ukrainian cause.

Pro-Galician and anti-Polish rallies in Canada helped to crystallize the national consciousness of many immigrants and even temporarily helped to overcome mutual religious antagonisms. Bobersky was instrumental in organizing such rallies in 1922 in order to bring the Ukrainian factions together in a common front.[13] Large rallies receiving substantial publicity were held in Edmonton, Saskatoon, Brandon, Fort William and Winnipeg. The Winnipeg demonstration of 22 April 1922 was meticulously organized and effectively attracted the attention of the Canadian press. An estimated ten thousand Ukrainians, the largest number to gather publicly in Winnipeg until the unveiling of the Shevchenko monument in 1963, marched from the Ukrainian National Home to the Polish Consulate, which was amply protected by Winnipeg police. Led by Bobersky in his Sokil uniform, the demonstrators displayed placards expressing the sentiments of the organizers:

> Polish atrocities in Ukraine call to heaven for vengeance.
> Save us from our "friends" the Poles.
> Forty million Ukrainians in Europe are determined to die rather than live under slavery.[14]

The demonstration ended with a huge meeting at the Industrial Bureau where Bobersky and others, including such noted non-Ukrainians as Alexander Hunter and Charles W. Gordon, delivered a series of emotional speeches. A telegram was sent to Ottawa denouncing Poland and demanding that the government take affirmative action. Relations with the small Polish community in Winnipeg became quite strained, as the Poles logically supported their homeland, although no outbreaks of violence occurred. *Ukrainskyi holos* (Ukrainian Voice), for example, urged the Ukrainian public to boycott a Winnipeg wrestling match that was to feature Stanislav Zhyshka, who, *Holos* claimed, was a renegade Ukrainian who considered himself a Pole.[15]

The second Ukrainian delegate to Canada was Dr. Osyp Nazaruk, appointed by Petrushevych in the summer of 1922. A lawyer by training (hence "Doctor") and a gifted publicist by profession, Nazaruk was totally immersed in politics and proved to be one of the more colourful and intelligent personalities of the Ukrainian political spectrum.[16] A leading member of the Galician Radical Party, he served briefly as minister of propaganda in Petliura's united Directory and later joined forces with Petrushevych. In the Galician government he engaged in a power struggle with Kost Levytsky, the minister of foreign affairs, and his appointment to the Ukrainians of Canada as an extraordinary ambassador can be interpreted as a form of political exile. Nazaruk had a reputation for abrasiveness and anti-clericalism and his new posting therefore was viewed in some circles as inappropriate.[17]

Their contrasting personalities notwithstanding, Nazaruk and Bobersky, as head and secretary respectively, formed an energetic and effective team. When the Galician National Defence Loan of fifty thousand dollars was announced by the Petrushevych government on 16 August 1922 (bearing 6 per cent for ten years beginning six months after the restoration of the ZUNR to power), Bobersky began preparatory ground work for the campaign before Nazaruk's arrival. As it turned out, for the duration of their activities in Canada, Bobersky filled the function of stage manager while Nazaruk basked in the limelight as star performer.

Officially the two-man delegation had a number of responsibilities: to co-operate with the Galician mission in Washington which was engaged in its own collection of funds; to make the necessary representations to Washington and Ottawa; to keep the Ukrainian community informed of the activities of the ZUNR; and most important, to organize and conduct the national defence loan in Canada.[18] From the money collected, Nazaruk received three hundred dollars a month, with ten dollars going to his wife in Galicia, and Bobersky two hundred dollars a month. These were high salaries for the day, but the work of the two more than justified them.

By the time Nazaruk arrived in Winnipeg on 2 September, the Ukrainian community leaders and press, prepared by Bobersky, gave the distinguished delegate a warm welcome at the railway station and assured him of support.[19] The office of Bobersky's Ukrainian Bureau became the official headquarters of the Galician delegation. In the middle of September, Luka Myshuha, the Galician representative in Washington who had revived the sagging collection campaign in the United States so that it surpassed its goal of one hundred thousand dollars,[20] arrived for strategy talks.

Bobersky's personal directory of Ukrainians in Canada became the key to the entire campaign. Bobersky wrote to every community with over twenty families urging the local teacher, merchant or priest to form a committee and arrange for a public meeting to be attended by either him or Nazaruk. Potential organizers were provided with detailed information about publicizing and holding a meeting on Polish oppression in Galicia. In communities not visited by the delegation, Bobersky urged the local leadership to collect funds on its own; such collections, he suggested, should be made before the meeting while people were still interested. Bobersky was always concerned about the possibility of alienating the local Ukrainian elite from the campaign, and in light of the latter's own organizational financial needs, the danger always existed. However, in 1922 at least, most Ukrainian organizations agreed to give priority to the Galician goal and even made institutional donations.

The national loan campaign was launched officially on 24 September 1922 in Winnipeg. The crowd of over three thousand who attended a mass rally at the Industrial Bureau contributed an initial $3,109.00.[21] From Winnipeg, Nazaruk and Bobersky travelled to all Ukrainian communities across Canada. The hectic pace continued until 116 public meetings had been held, the last one at Kenora, Ontario, on 2 September 1923. Nazaruk spoke in seventy communities, Bobersky in forty-six. According to the final report released by Bobersky, a total of 6,741 Ukrainians and their organizations had made contributions and bought bonds in the amount of $33,290.38. That sum constituted the largest single Ukrainian contribution to date.[22]

In order to appreciate the efforts of Bobersky and Nazaruk and to evaluate the results of the campaign, it is necessary to understand the conditions under which they worked in Canada. The activities of the Galician government and the perception of those activities in Canada also had a major bearing on the campaign. Canadian economic conditions in general and those of Canadian Ukrainians in particular were critical to the success or failure of the defence loan. Bobersky and Nazaruk realized that the prevailing economic recession, especially low grain prices and the indebtedness of many Ukrainian farmers, militated against the attainment of the fifty-thousand-dollar goal. The Ukrainians generally occupied a low rung on the economic ladder, and from these "labourers, peasants, and shopkeepers" Nazaruk had anticipated contributions of no more than twenty-five thousand dollars.

Closely related to the economic situation was the problem of Ukrainian political maturity in Canada. The level of Ukrainian consciousness of the majority of the immigrants was deplorably low. The 1921 census showed that only one quarter of the estimated 250,000 Ukrainians actually regarded themselves as such, while others remained loyal to their old-country regionalism or, even worse, considered themselves Russians or Austrians, a fact loudly condemned by the nationalist *Ukrainskyi holos*.[23] Both Nazaruk and Bobersky recognized this problem but generally kept their criticisms to themselves for the duration of the campaign.[24] Bobersky, for instance, considered the Bukovynians to be nationally retarded and the least generous of all Ukrainians: "Everyone in Canada knows," he wrote to Nazaruk, "that the Bukovynians have no interest whatsoever in national organization, books or newspapers." He cited as an example one Mr. Farion from Sifton, Manitoba, who owned two stores and several sections of land but only gave one dollar for the cause.[25] Bobersky's opinion of the Ukrainians in Alberta was even more uncomplimentary: "Please don't forget," he tried to cheer up Nazaruk, who was having transportation problems in that province, "that Albertans are the most backward segment of Ukrainians in Canada; one needs great patience to survey this Canadian Africa."[26] Nazaruk himself observed that while the Ukrainians were poor and ignorant, they were multiplying so fast that they frightened the Anglo-Saxons. Both Bobersky and Nazaruk attributed Ukrainian national backwardness to the legacy of Polish and Russian socio-economic oppression, however, and were optimistic about the future providing that the Ukrainians could be organized throughout Canada. They were also impressed with the influence of Canadian democracy upon traditional Ukrainian social attitudes.[27]

That minority of the Ukrainian population in Canada which was nationally oriented and active, was itself fragmented along religious and political lines. Years later, reflecting on the nature of Ukrainian Canadian society, Bobersky characterized the two main groups as

> the democrats or Catholics and the independents or Orthodox, who preferred to call themselves "nationalists." The nationalists came mainly from teachers' families and were always undiplomatic and arrogant in their behaviour, wanting to monopolize the situation; they did not fully appreciate the farmers, workers and clergy. The democrats (Catholics) had too many societies in Canada, not one of which knew how to win the respect and leadership of its own group, let alone of the entire immigration.[28]

Catholic-Orthodox friction, which prevented joint economic ventures, was, as Nazaruk astutely observed, between the Catholics and the recent converts to Orthodoxy (the Neo-orthodox as he called them), while relations between the traditional Orthodox, mainly Bukovynians, and the Catholics were good. Both Nazaruk and Bobersky feared that continuing friction would lead to apathy among the majority, which in turn would accelerate the process of assimilation.

In the short term, Ukrainian religious friction in some areas of Canada frustrated the defence loan campaign, as the faithful of one persuasion occasionally refused to meet in the hall belonging to the other group. Neutral halls were often difficult to locate. Bobersky and Nazaruk had to exercise a great deal of tact in such situations, and had to avoid being identified too closely with either protagonist.[29] This was particularly trying for Nazaruk who thrived on polemic challenges. The communist sympathizers were the only group to feel the effect of his pen, however; when *Ukrainski robitnychi visty* (Ukrainian Labour News) questioned the legitimacy of the Petrushevych government and opposed the financial drive, Nazaruk responded to accusations of graft with such stimulating articles as "Why do skunks stink?"[30] On occasion he even engaged in public debate with the communists.

The economic and political condition of the Ukrainians notwithstanding, there was a group within Canadian Ukrainian society that patriotically supported national and religious needs. Prior to the Galician loan, several other major fund-raising campaigns had taken place. The Red Cross Society had already collected over $30,000 and would eventually surpass $50,000 in its drive to provide medicine and food for Galicia and Bukovyna. The Mohyla Institute in Saskatoon was desperately seeking $35,000 to ward off bankruptcy, while St. Joseph's College in Yorkton, Saskatchewan, was looking for $350,000; finally, there was the Sheptytsky Bursa in St. Boniface, Manitoba.[31] In addition to these organized ventures, thousands of immigrants were obliged to support their families in the old country. Thus, not only was the potential source of money limited, but the demands on it were extensive.

The activities of Petrushevych's government-in-exile in Europe also had a major bearing on the financial campaign, influencing both the generosity of the donors and the attitude of its representatives. By 1922 it was apparent that the Petrushevych coalition was not only suffering from internal problems, but that its credibility as the sole legitimate spokesman of Galicia had been severely challenged by dissident Galician emigre politicians. The most serious threat came from the supporters of Colonel Evhen Konovalets. These young nationalists rejected Petrushevych's parochialism and territorial separation in favour of Ukrainian unity (*sobornist*) and Galician independence as a step toward *sobornist*, not as an end in itself. Furthermore, they did not believe that the Ambassadors' Conference had the miraculous power to undo the Polish entrenchment in Galicia. This growing defeatism or scepticism was shared by some members of the Galician government who argued for accommodation with Poland, a policy which Petrushevych rejected. Consequently, Petrushevych found himself in a dilemma. His understandable reluctance to consult the Galician-based Ukrainian National Council, which had vested him with temporary dictatorial powers, left him open to charges of isolationism and undue reliance on family members and political favourites, who were justifiably held responsible for conducting naive diplomacy.[32] The growing criticism of Petrushevych's lack of political accountability was fuelled by allegations of corruption. In addition, there were the continuing innuendos by Petliura's exiled government of the UNR, accusing Petrushevych of Russophilism.

The European scene was closely watched by the Ukrainian press in Canada. *Ukrainskyi holos*, edited by Myroslav Stechishin (who had been secretary of the UNR mission in Washington), strongly favoured Ukrainian *sobornist* while supporting Galician aspirations. Stechishin himself was a follower of Petliura. Regarding *Ukrainskyi holos* as the most influential Ukrainian newspaper in Canada, Bobersky and Nazaruk did not wish to alienate Stechishin. As a result they emphasized the Ukrainian rather than the Galician dimension of their work and did not distinguish between the two as was the case in Europe. In fact, Nazaruk had informed Petrushevych that in Canada the term "Galician" had a derogatory meaning and thus the delegation would officially use the name West Ukrainian National Republic rather than Galician Republic.[33] Even during the fund-raising campaign, Bobersky and Nazaruk played on the Ukrainianism rather than the Galician parochialism of their listeners.

Most Ukrainian fund-raising ventures have been tinged with allegations of irregularities. The national loan drive was no exception, despite the fact that Bobersky took special pains to have the accounts regularly audited by the Manitoba provincial accountant and Ukrainian community leaders. Furthermore, financial details were published in the press. This open approach helped to maintain the credibility of the Galician representatives in Canada, but unfortunately the recipient of the money, "Dictator" Petrushevych, did not see any need for public accountability of his government's expenses. Consequently, rumours abounded about the misuse of funds for personal needs. Bobersky and Nazaruk, aware of the damaging impact of such publicity, repeatedly urged and later demanded that Petrushevych disclose his government's expenditures to reassure the public.[34] Petrushevych's reluctance to do so, combined with the growing political isolation of his government from the Ukrainian political scene in Galicia, turned Nazaruk into a private but harsh critic of the government, especially of his rival Kost Levytsky. "Kostiur'o," as Nazaruk called him contemptuously in letters to his friends, was little more than a flirtatious drunk, a weak person with no grasp of foreign policy, capable of only petty intrigues. Nazaruk found it most frustrating to defend the Galician government against growing public scepticism.[35]

Growing doubt in Canada about the future of the ZUNR was reinforced by developments in Europe in 1922. With the normalization of Polish-Czech relations and the fall of Lloyd George, Galicia's shaky international support evaporated. In addition, the highly-publicized Polish law granting extensive autonomy to the Ukrainian provinces (a law which was never implemented) and the introduction of conscription in Galicia was interpreted by many Ukrainians, including Bobersky and Nazaruk, as the end of independence hopes. "Only a miracle could save us now," noted Bobersky.[36] Thus, when the Council of Ambassadors met in March 1923, few Ukrainian leaders expected a favourable outcome, despite Petrushevych's official optimism. Indeed, the ambassadors were satisfied that Poland was handling the minority question adequately and recognized the incorporation of Ukrainian Galicia into Poland.

Although not unexpected, the decision left a feeling of betrayal among the Ukrainian public on both sides of the Atlantic. The Galician government-in-exile now lost its raison d'être, but Petrushevych was determined to carry on with a reconstructed government in Berlin. His invitation to Nazaruk to join him was declined. Although the Galician diplomatic missions were dissolved, Petrushevych wanted to continue the Canadian financial campaign until September 1923, as he wanted money for political activities in Galicia. However, Bobersky and Nazaruk, after consulting with Myshuha in Washington and the executive of the Ukrainian Radical Party, decided to take matters into their own hands.[37] They would continue the fund-raising until the end of 1923, but devised a new formula so that Petrushevych would receive only one-third of the funds collected, with two-thirds going directly to Galicia.

With the announcement of the Polish amnesty, thousands of Ukrainian political emigres returned to Galicia. It was logical to assume, as Bobersky and Nazaruk did, that the centre of Ukrainian political life would be Lviv and not Berlin. In their eyes Petrushevych no longer represented Galician reality (indeed, Petrushevych eventually assumed a strong pro-Soviet position and became a spokesman for Soviet Ukraine). Initially, Bobersky and Nazaruk shifted their focus from the failure of the Petrushevych government to the immediate and future political needs of Galicia, which required money. Somewhat surprisingly, the Canadian response to the campaign continued to be good. Although the original target of $50,000 was not reached, the collection of $33,000 was an achievement that surprised many people. The response to the campaign suggested that a patriotic (or perhaps gullible) segment of the Ukrainian community in Canada persistently believed in an uncertain cause.

Undoubtedly, the Galician diplomatic representation contributed to the crystallization of Ukrainian national consciousness as well as to the organizational growth of an important proportion of the Ukrainian Canadian population.[38] Bobersky and Nazaruk experienced many personal and political frustrations while dealing with an immigrant community in the process of adjustment to the host society. Despite Bobersky's meticulous planning and Nazaruk's oratorical skills, several of their fund-raising meetings were interrupted by Soviet or Polish sympathizers, or failed to take place because of hostility or indifference. "How can we defeat Poland," lamented Bobersky in January 1923, "when less than 20 people show up?"[39] Both men often found themselves emotionally drained and physically exhausted from the demanding workload of writing, speaking and travelling. Prairie travel and the Ukrainian cooking left Nazaruk with chronic stomach disorders.

III

When the campaign ended and the final report was published and the last bank draft sent to Europe, both Bobersky and Nazaruk anticipated staying in Canada indefinitely. Nazaruk unsuccessfully sought a teaching position at the Mohyla Institute[40] and even tried enrolling in the Manitoba

Law School and articling for Jaroslaw Arsenych, but the nullification of his Galician passport in 1923 forced him to leave Canada. Bobersky then arranged for Nazaruk to become editor of *Sichovi visti* (Sich News), the organ of the Sich Athletic Association in Chicago. But in 1927, frustrated and homesick, Nazaruk returned to Lviv, where he remained a controversial figure, until the outbreak of the Second World War. He died in Cracow in 1940. Nazaruk's short Canadian experience, especially his disenchantment with the ZUNR, seems to have been a turning point in his ideological development. Canada was the beginning of the "road to Damascus" that led him to abandon republicanism and anti-clericalism in favour of Ukrainian monarchism (hetmanism) and "born-again" Catholicism.[41]

Bobersky remained in Canada until the Great Depression, working for a trans-Atlantic shipping company interested in further Ukrainian colonization in Canada. Constantly preaching Ukrainian unity, he retained his prestige in the Ukrainian community largely through his ability to rise above the continuing factionalism. This prestige was reinforced by his honesty in conducting the national loan and his accountability to the public. He showed that most of the money had indeed been sent to Europe and that the collectors' expenses were kept to a minimum. Bobersky left Canada in 1931, survived the war and died in Yugoslavia in 1947.[42]

Notes

1. In Ukraine, where many armies crisscrossed the land, there were millions of casualties. In Galicia alone nearly 400,000 buildings were destroyed or severely damaged. In the spring of 1920 a typhus epidemic swept the region—over 100,000 cases with 10,000 fatalities. Ukrainian Red Cross in Canada, *Zvit za 1921* (Winnipeg), 3.

2. At the time of the First World War an estimated 450,000 Ukrainians lived in the United States, 250,000 in Canada and over 50,000 in Latin America. On the diplomatic level, ZUNR envoys operated in Paris (the seat of the Peace Conference), Vienna, Budapest, Berlin, Prague, Geneva, London and Washington.

3. The following works are useful on Ukrainian political aspirations: K. Levytsky, *Istoriia politychnoi dumky halytskykh ukraintsiv, 1848–1914* (Lviv, 1926); and M. Lozynsky, *Ukrainska Halychyna. Okremyi koronyi krai* (Vienna, 1915).

4. See M. Stachiw and J. Sztendera, *Western Ukraine at the Turning Point of Europe's History, 1918–1923*, 2 vols. (New York, 1969–71); and L. Vasylkivsky, "Prychynky do istorii ukrainskoi dyplomatii v 1917–21 rokakh," *Suchasnist* 6 (June 1970): 109–24, and 7–8 (July-August 1970): 140–52.

5. The most recent evaluation of the American position is by C. Warvariv, "America and the Ukrainian National Cause, 1917–20," in *The Ukraine, 1917–1921: A Study in Revolution*, ed. T. Hunczak (Cambridge, Mass., 1977), 352–81.

6. For example, two Galician members of the Ukrainian delegation, V. Paneiko and S. Tomashivsky, openly flirted with conservative Russian circles in Paris. Vasylkivsky, "Prychynky do istorii ukrainskoi diplomatii," 118.

7. Ivan Bobersky Papers, file 53, Ukrainian Cultural and Educational Centre (hereafter UCEC), Winnipeg, Manitoba.

8. K. Zelenko, "Velykobritaniia i Ukraina," in *Ievhen Konovalets ta ioho doba* (Munich, 1974), 883–906.

9. See, for example, "The Case of East Galicia," Bobersky Papers, file 72, UCEC. It was assumed that the Galician government required a minimum of $1,500 (U.S.) per month to sustain its activities. Bobersky Papers, file 26/372, UCEC.

10. Autobiography, Bobersky Papers, file 1, UCEC.

11. Bobersky Papers, file 114, UCEC; and D. Doroshenko and S. Kovbel, eds., *Propamiatna knyha ukrainskoho narodnoho domu u Vynypegu* (Winnipeg, 1949), 310.

12. On organizational life, see O. Gerus, "Ethnic Politics in Canada: The Formation of the Ukrainian Canadian Committee," in *The Jubilee Collection of the Ukrainian Free Academy of Sciences in Canada*, ed. O. Gerus et al. (Winnipeg, 1976), 467–80.

13. Doroshenko and Kovbel, *Propamiatna knyha*, 317–28.

14. *Ukrainskyi holos*, 26 April 1922.

15. *Ibid.*, 10 November 1922. However, violence occurred outside Winnipeg as several Polish roadside crosses were destroyed at Oakburn, Manitoba; see H. Radecki and B. Heydenkorn, *A Member of a Distinguished Family: The Polish Group in Canada* (Toronto, 1976), 191.

16. For biographical data on Nazaruk, see *Viacheslav Lypynskyi*, ed. I. Lysiak-Rudnytsky (Philadelphia, 1976), 7: vii–xiv.

17. Lev Levytsky, chief of the "External Group of the People's Labour Party," argued that Nazaruk would not only create disunity among the Ukrainians in America but also compromise the cause by pursuing personal material goals. Bobersky Papers, file 52/542, UCEC. However, it should be noted that Levytsky had unsuccessfully lobbied for Nazaruk's job.

18. Directives 17, 18 and 19 of the ZUNR, 3 August 1922, Bobersky Papers, file 39/473, UCEC.

19. *Ukrainskyi holos*, 6 September 1922. The Ukrainian leaders included Father P. Oleskiw from the chancellery of the Ukrainian Greek Catholic Church; Taras Ferley, chairman of the Ukrainian Central Committee; M. Hawryliuk, head of the St. Nicholas Mutual Benefit Association; and the editors of *Kanadyiskyi farmer* (O. Hykawy), *Kanadyiskyi ukrainets* (I. Rudakevych), *Kanadyiskyi ranok* (Z. Bychynsky) and *Ukrainskyi holos* (Myroslav Stechishin).

20. V. Trembitsky, "Amerykanski ukraintsi v dopomozi ukrainskii derzhavi i narodu, 1914–1923," *Almanakh U.N.S.* (Jersey City, 1971), 49–62.

21. *Ukrainskyi holos*, 27 September 1922.

22. Doroshenko and Kovbel, *Propamiatna knyha*, 301.

23. *Ukrainskyi holos*, 11 April 1923.

24. Nazaruk did share some of his less controversial views on Canada with the readers of such Ukrainian newspapers in North America and Europe as *Ukrainskyi prapor* (Vienna) and *Sich* (Chicago).

25. Bobersky Papers, file 52/540, UCEC.

26. Bobersky Papers, file 52/572, UCEC.

27. Bobersky Papers, file 26/369, UCEC.

28. Bobersky Papers, file 66/1, UCEC. Bobersky ignored Protestant "Ukrainianism," as have most observers who emphasize its tendency toward assimilation. However, in welcoming Nazaruk to Winnipeg, Paul Crath (Pavlo Krat), as the representative of Ukrainian Presbyterians in Canada, maintained that "there are three groups of us—Orthodox, Protestant, and Catholic. The Orthodox constitute the strongest group because they are supported by the majority of our intelligentsia, businessmen, and nationally conscious farmers. Protestants—Presbyterians, Methodists, Baptists—stand shoulder to shoulder with the Orthodox in national matters; they also struggle together against the Catholics. In general, the Orthodox-Protestant bloc directs Ukrainian life in Canada." Nevertheless, Crath urged Nazaruk to remain above the internal squabbles and not to side with any group. Bobersky Papers, file 52/69, UCEC.

29. Bobersky Papers, file 52/540, UCEC.

30. On the question of Ukrainian communism, see Nazaruk's interesting fifteen-page booklet, *Bolshevyky a inteligentsiia* (Vancouver, 1923).

31. *Iuvileina knyha 25-littia instytutu im. Petra Mohyly v Saskatuni, 1916–1941* (Winnipeg, 1945), 116, 123, 127.

32. See Bobersky Papers, file 26/369, UCEC; and A. Motyl, *The Turn to the Right: The Ideological Origins and Development of Ukrainian Nationalism, 1919–1929* (New York, 1980), 93–104.

33. Bobersky Papers, file 39/470, UCEC.

34. Bobersky Papers, file 26/381, UCEC.

35. Bobersky Papers, file 52/582, UCEC. For another view of the Petrushevych government, see M. Lozynsky, *Moie spivrobitnytstvo z prezydentom Petrushevychem* (Lviv, 1925).

36. Bobersky Papers, file 53/632, UCEC.

37. Bobersky Papers, file 26/381, UCEC.

38. This letter sent to Bobersky from a participant at a rally in Alvena, Saskatchewan, is typical of a substantial response to the national defence loan: "Our tiny community responded splendidly to aid the native land and its government. There are no more than one hundred families of us and twenty are of the Latin rite.... The meeting was held in 'Svoboda' school at 2 p.m. sharp. Mr. A. Turta [the author] was elected chairman and D. Andrunyk and V. Kolbusa as secretaries. D. Andrunyk spoke first introducing Dr. Nazaruk

who talked for an hour and a half. During his speech our priest, Fr. Fylyma, arrived. He had waited for Dr. Nazaruk at Rosthern, but Dr. Nazaruk was unable to reach Rosthern because the earlier meeting at Winnipeg had lasted too long, and there is no train on Saturday. And so it happened that Rosthern, a bigger community than Alvena did not see the delegate, although so many people had gathered there that there was no room to park the horses. But our little Alvena did host the delegate from the Galician government. Fr. Fylyma spoke after Dr. Nazaruk and was followed by others. Although there were not too many people present, the response to the collection was most generous—$360 cash and $63 pledged. Little Alvena had never had such success before. Dr. Nazaruk also encouraged us to build a community hall and urged every home to have a Ukrainian newspaper. We will remember this and I think that we will have our 'national home' in the near future.... Our fund-raising meeting was a success and we wish the same to other communities in Canada" (Bobersky Papers, file 51/6, UCEC).

39. Bobersky Papers, file 52/567, UCEC.
40. The main stumbling blocks in reaching an agreement with the Mohyla Institute were Nazaruk's objections to its uncompromising Orthodox posture and his high salary demands. Bobersky Papers, file 52/55, UCEC.
41. For Nazaruk's political reorientation, see his correspondence with the chief ideologue of Ukrainian monarchism, *Viacheslav Lypynskyi*, 7: vii–xiv.
42. Both Nazaruk and Bobersky left their incisive and not always flattering impressions of Ukrainians in Canada. Nazaruk published his in newspapers and journals while Bobersky kept a massive personal archive. In addition to his own diaries, hundreds of personal and official letters, relevant organizational material and newspaper clippings, the Bobersky collection at the Ukrainian Cultural and Educational Centre has many of Nazaruk's letters from the 1922–3 period and a spectacular photographic section (nearly 10,000 pictures and negatives). For a history of the Bobersky library, see M.H. Marunchak, *Studii do istorii ukraintsiv Kanady*, 5 vols. (Winnipeg, 1973–80), 5: 233–45.

Appendices

I. A QUESTION OF LOYALTY

1. Pastoral letter issued by Nykyta Budka, Bishop of the Ruthenian Greek Catholic Church in Canada, 27 July 1914

2. Pastoral letter issued by Nykyta Budka, Bishop of the Ruthenian Greek Catholic Church in Canada, 6 August 1914

3. An address to the Canadian people by the Canadian Ukrainian editors, July 1916

4. Address by Osyp Megas to the Second National Convention, Saskatoon, December 1917

II. GOVERNMENT POLICIES

A. Internment

5. Proclamation respecting immigrants of German or Austro-Hungarian nationality, 15 August 1914

6. Public notice to alien enemies, 2 September 1914

7. Order in Council respecting alien enemies, 28 October 1914

8. Order in Council authorizing the apprehension and internment of alien enemies in certain cases, 26 June 1915

B. Possession of Firearms
  9. Order in Council prohibiting the use or possession of firearms or explosives by alien enemies, 3 September 1914

  10. Order in Council authorizing the issue of licenses to alien enemies to have possession of firearms in certain cases, 26 January 1915

C. Military Service
  11. Enlistment of persons of foreign birth

  12. An act respecting military service, assented to 29 August 1917

  13. Official citation, Filip Konowal, Victoria Cross

D. Disfranchisement
  14. The War-time Elections Act, assented to 20 September 1917

E. Censorship and Association
  15. Order in Council respecting enemy publications, 25 September 1918

  16. Regulations respecting unlawful associations, 25 September 1918

  17. Order in Council amending the Order in Council respecting enemy publications, 13 November 1918

F. Immigration
  18. An act to amend the Immigration Act, assented to 6 June 1919

III. UKRAINIAN INDEPENDENCE

  19. Disposition of Eastern Galicia, 1919

  20. West Ukrainian National Republic, 1923

APPENDIX I

A QUESTION OF LOYALTY

1. Pastoral letter issued by Nykyta Budka, Bishop of the Ruthenian Greek Catholic Church in Canada, 27 July 1914*

TO THE REVEREND CLERGY AND ALL THE FAITHFUL OF CANADIAN RUS'-UKRAINE

For a number of years great misfortune have oppressed our old Fatherland. It is not only a matter of that distress which has driven thousands of our brothers into the wide world, and which in the last few years, as the result of flooding, has been transformed into widespread famine, but also moral distress, namely, the demoralization of our brothers in Galicia and in Hungary by a legion of spies, agents, pamphlets and newspapers, paid for by the rubles of our Russian neighbour, either directly from Russia or through Serbia, America and Canada.

Looming over this sad state of affairs for several years now has been the spectre of war, a war, however, which the peace-loving emperor Franz Josef I has ever striven to avert and postpone.

And then an incident occurred which would try the patience of even the most peace-loving of men. On 28 June of this year, in Sarajevo, Franz Ferdinand, heir to the Austrian throne and a man of great hope at this difficult moment for Austria, perished, along with his wife, from the bullet of a Serbian student. The loss of an experienced heir to the throne was very painful to our aged monarch, Franz Josef I, and to all the peoples of Austria, especially to us Ruthenians, who placed great and justified hope in him. The enemies of Austria, especially the enemies of the Ruthenian-Ukrainians, do not disguise their joy at this tragic loss.

Canadian Ruthenian-Ukrainians, sympathizing with the misfortune of our old Fatherland, gave expression to their feelings in church services for the slain and prayers for the fate of their native land.

Now misfortune is at its height, for to all our other misfortunes has been added the greatest of them all, namely, war, at present with Serbia but possibly in a short time also with Russia, a war of inestimable consequences which could change not only the face of Austria but of all Europe, and which could touch us Ruthenians especially closely.

The aged emperor of Austria has not lived to enjoy a peaceful death. His reign began in 1848 with war, and at the end of his long life the Most High has not spared

---

*Translated by John Sokolowski

him that cross and misfortune from which he had long tried to protect his subjects, and he must now wage war.

An official summons has reached Canada, calling all Austrian subjects who are under military obligation to return to Austria, there to be ready to defend the state.

God knows what the outcome will be. Perhaps we shall have to defend Galicia against seizure by Russia with her greedy appetite for Ruthenians; perhaps we shall have to defend our parents, wives, children, brothers and native land before an insatiable enemy. Perhaps after the war we shall remain in Austria, as it is or strengthened by millions of our brothers from abroad. It is also possible, however, that we shall find ourselves under the heavy hand of the Muscovite despot. All is in the hands of God and we cannot foresee what will happen. In any event, all Austrian subjects have to be at home, in position and ready to defend our native home, our dear brothers and sisters, our people. Whoever is called should go to defend the threatened Fatherland. All who have not been called up and are unregistered, but who are subject to military service, and all deserters have been granted amnesty by the emperor—that is, freedom from punishment if only they immediately report to the consulate and depart for the old country to defend the Fatherland.

It is also fitting that those who have decided to remain for the rest of their lives in the new Fatherland, Canada, being bound merely by a part of their lives to the old country, should also participate in this great adventure of Austria and our native brethren—for indeed, the fate of our people too is being decided over there.

Our participation should not be limited to reading the newspapers to find out about the events of the war, but we should help our old Fatherland however we can.

Our God, the Lover of Mankind, is the God of peace and brotherly love and so He loathes the angers, jealousies and injustices which lead to war. He, being just and gracious, in His unfathomable providence bids the deciding agents to propose such plans and expedients as to avert all that which affects the severity and length of war so that the calamity of war will end quickly without unnecessary bloodshed. If it has pleased Divine Providence to decide the fate of our old homeland with bullets, then let us fervently and frequently pray to Almighty God that this settling of accounts, by the grace of God, be done as soon as possible so as to cause minimal distress. Let us send up heartfelt prayers to the Heavenly Ruler of the World for harmony and prudence, for the suffering soldiers and their anxious, tearful families, for the peace of the entire world and for the spreading of the Kingdom of God among men; He will surely heed our entreaties and have mercy upon us.

"O Lord, save the king and hear us on that day when we shall call upon Thee."

In these harsh times let us help, with our sincere prayers, those who are threatened. Let the will of God be done!

In order to sustain the spirit of prayer and sympathy we direct the reverend clergy to encourage the faithful to the Apostleship of Prayer and to good works—especially Holy Communion, harmony among those who have quarreled, and the abandonment of drunkenness, blasphemy and cursing—so that these good works, done with the intention of averting misfortune from our brothers in the old country, should obtain for us the grace and mercy of the Lord God.

During every Divine Liturgy, until the threat of misfortune is averted from Austria, all priests are to add in both litanies the prayers from the service "For Peace," which follows after the service "For General Intentions," and after the Liturgy on Sundays and holy days they are to celebrate Benediction with the Exposition of the Most Holy Sacrament.

Nykyta, Bishop
Winnipeg, Man., 27 July 1914

This letter is to be read in all churches.

SOURCE: *Kanadyiskyi rusyn*, 1 August 1914

2. Pastoral letter issued by Nykyta Budka, Bishop of the Ruthenian Greek Catholic Church in Canada, 6 August 1914*

TO THE REVEREND CLERGY AND THE FAITHFUL CANADIAN RUTHENIAN-UKRAINIANS

Not long ago the news that Austria was at war with Serbia stirred the entire world. All other states adopted a wait-and-see position, and England especially strove with all its might to localize the war and restore peace.

At that moment, when no state except Austria and Serbia was threatened by war, and England was not calling its subjects to defend their state, we published our pastoral letter in which we indicated that Austria through the I[mperial] and R[oyal] Consulate in Canada was calling upon its subjects to join the Austrian colours; and we said that all Ruthenians who had come to Canada for a short time only should obey Austria's call and go to defend their families and property. And now in the course of a few days political relations have changed completely. Today all Europe is enveloped by war; today England and the entire British state are threatened by enemies; today our new fatherland, Canada, calls its faithful subjects to rally around the English flag ready to give up their property and lives for the good of the British state.

Today all peoples who live under the flag of the British state are sending their sons to defend it.

And so at this moment when England is turning to us, its faithful subjects, with a call to join the colours, when the British state needs our help also, now, as its loyal sons, we Canadian Ukrainians have a great and holy obligation to join the colours of our new fatherland, under those of the British state, and, if necessary, to sacrifice our property and blood for it.

Ruthenians, citizens of Canada! It is our great duty to come to the defence of Canada, for this is the country which has taken us to its bosom and given us protection under the banner of liberty of the British Empire, where we have found not only bread but the possibility of spiritual development.

It is our sacred duty to be ready to sacrifice our property and blood for the good of Canada, for this is the new fatherland to which we have sworn loyalty and bound ourselves by oath to sacrifice all our property and lives if ever required of us.

This is our beloved fatherland, for here are our families, our children, our property, our hearts and our entire future.

Therefore, at this most important let us remember that as loyal sons of Canada, faithful to the oath we have sworn to our fatherland and our king, we should unite under the flag of the British state.

Set aside all party strife and misunderstandings, all indifference and lack of concern.

We consciously, out of a feeling of deepest attachment and obligation, want to help and will help our new homeland when it is threatened by an enemy.

---

*Translated by John Sokolowski

Ruthenians, citizens of Canada! You who have already sworn an oath of allegiance to our king, George V, as well as those of you who are not yet citizens but wish to become so, remember that the oath binds you to loyalty. In our country, as in any other in a state of war, anyone guilty of a disloyal act or word can expect the death penalty as a traitor.

Loyalty requires actions and sacrifices; if the state should demand or need such, everyone must be prepared to give even his life. If it were necessary and feasible to form Ruthenian regiments out of Ruthenians who are Canadian citizens, that surely would be a visible sign that Ruthenians in Canada are true citizens ready to give everything, including their lives, for their Fatherland. But we want to indicate once again that we must fulfill this obligation not only out of compliance with the laws, but out of a profound sense of our obligations.

God alone knows how this, the greatest war in history, will end. Let us implore God fervently that He deign, through His almighty power, to bring it to its quickest possible conclusion and that our new Fatherland, Canada, should suffer no harm.

In view of the fact that our earlier letter of 27 July referred to a time when the war was exclusively a war between Austria and Serbia, when few believed that it would spread to other states and England was at peace and not summoning its subjects to the defence of their state, we emphatically declare that in light of the changed political situation our previous letter of 27 July of this year no longer serves any purpose and must not be read publicly in the churches. Instead, we order all priests to read this pastoral letter during Divine Service in their parishes and to instruct the Ruthenians, in accordance with this letter, in their obligations toward the British State.

Given in Winnipeg, 6 August 1914.
Nykyta, Bishop.

SOURCE: *Kanadyiskyi rusyn*, 8 August 1914.

3. An address to the Canadian people by the Canadian Ukrainian editors, July 1916

The Ukrainians of Winnipeg, and of Western Canada in general, have found themselves heavily handicapped since the outbreak of the war by the fact of their Austrian birth, which has led, they claim, the Dominion Government, as well as Canadian employers of labor, to unjustly class them as Austrians, and therefore enemy aliens. Many have been interned, though they are no more in sympathy with the enemy than are the Poles, for they are as distinct a nationality—a small nation with national ideals, national history and a national literature, which hopes to emerge from the war in the enjoyment of a wide measure of national autonomy.

This feeling of unfair treatment found vent at the instance of the Ukrainian Social-Democrats in mass meetings of Winnipeg Ukrainians held in the Grand Opera house on June 4, 11 and 25, when a resolution was adopted asking the editors of the Canadian Ukrainian papers to set before the Canadian people the fact that Ukrainians in their midst are deserving of support and sympathy. Accordingly, the address given below was prepared and, at a mass meeting held on July 2, was adopted unanimously. It bears the signature of six of the Canadian Ukrainian papers, including those published in Edmonton and Toronto, being as follows:

"We, the quarter million Ukrainians in Canada, are part of the Slavic people, numbering thirty-five millions, which inhabit the ancient dominion of the Ukraine. Until the thirteenth century we were independent duchies, joined together under the rule of their grand dukes. During the seventeenth and eighteenth centuries we were in name and fact a democratic republic, with a culture equal to the civilization of the Western Europe of that period. It was due to the unprotected nature of our prairie country that today the Ukrainian people is divided between Russian [*sic*] and Austro-Hungary. In Russia there are over thirty million Ukrainians, and Russia has become great since Ukraine joined her.

"Though we are thus divided between foreign powers, we have a common national ideal and aspiration to be joined together again in one national body, believing that in that case only shall we have the opportunity to develop our nation.

"The present European war brought to many subject nationalities the hope of freedom—Alsace-Lorraine, Poland, Bohemia, the southern Slavs. The same hope is cherished by every Ukrainian.

"But, while in Canada the Bohemians and Slavonians, though Austrians by birth, are treated as welcome settlers; though Jews are given a free hand to collect in Canada for their kinsmen in Russia, Austro-Hungary and Turkey; though Great Britain has gone so far as to promise the Poles independence, and in Winnipeg the head of the Polish committee is Mayor Waugh—yet, for unknown reasons, the Ukrainians in Canada are treated as enemy Austrians. They are persecuted, by thousands they are interned, they are dismissed from their employment, and their applications for work are not entertained. And why? For only one reason, that they were so unhappy as to be born into the Austrian bondage.

"And this injustice, which is done our people in Canada, has impelled the editors of the Ukrainian-Canadian newspapers to explain thus to the Canadian people who we are, what are our claims, what our values.

"First of all we proclaim that after Canada, and the British empire to which as Canadian citizens we owe allegiance, we have love only to Ukraine in Europe, and we want to see there such another democratic government as we enjoy in Canada.

"But we do not rest our national aspirations upon the dynasty of the Hapsburgs, because Austria favors the Poles and our national lands have been given over to the Poles—Eastern Galicia, Kholm and Volinia provinces. We see no good to the Ukraine from the advance of Austria eastward, because their proteges, the Poles, claim the whole Ukraine as part of 'historical Poland.' We understand that every county of the Ukraine conquered by Austria from Russia will be given up to Poland. This Austrian deed marks all Ukrainians as foes of the House of Hapsburg.

"Thus the Canadian people have no right to treat Ukrainians as Austrians; on the contrary, Canada should turn her warm sympathies to this unhappy people, tortured by Polish aristocrats and Austrian officials.

"We realize that all the injury done Canadian Ukrainians in the name of the government of Canada was due in part to the ignorance of the Canadian people concerning the Ukrainian question and, in part, to denunciations—too easily accepted at their face value—by the enemies of our nationality, Poles and others. It was also due to the unfortunate pastoral letter of Bishop Budka on the eve of the war between Germany and Great Britain when he called upon all Austrian-born, including Ukrainians or Ruthenians, to return from Canada to fight for Austria. But a whole nation should not be answerable for the mistake of one man, and during the two years of the war that has over and over again been wiped out by the loyal conduct of Canadian Ukrainians to the land of their adoption and the great empire that guarantees them liberty and justice.

"We believe that these facts have only to be brought before the Canadian people for them to recognize our sincerity and our loyalty, and, actuated by democratic ideals and love of justice, to change their attitude towards us.

"Realizing, too, our bona fides, the Canadian government will proceed to release from the detention camps the unjustly interned Ukrainians, exactly as it has already released the Bohemians—Austrian-born, too—at the request of Mr. Smetanka, president of the Bohemian association. Canada needs workmen, and all these men are available. We believe, too, that Ukrainians will be better treated, and the unhappy fact that accursed Austria is the land of their nativity will no longer serve to close the shops against them.

"Good hearts of the Canadian people are bearing relief to the unfortunate Belgians. But Canadians do not know that during these two years of war in the Ukrainian countries of Galicia and Bukowina, where have been the most sweeping movements of the opposing armies, thousand of women and children have perished of starvation; thousands of innocent little ones have been torn by wolves and wild dogs in the Carpathian mountains. And those of our women and children still living there are facing daily want and hunger. The Galician Ukraine, more than any other country, needs immediate relief, and we believe that the hearts of the Canadian people will go out to the heart-broken fathers and brothers in Canada whose dear ones are dying in Galicia.

"The Canadian post office has cut off communication with Galicia, and caused gloom and pain for Ukrainians in Canada, who thus cannot tell whether their relatives are alive or dead. Thousands of our Ukrainian boys have enlisted with the Canadian overseas force, and many have already lost their lives fighting beside their English brethren on the battlefields of France. And as the price of their blood we have the right to ask the Canadian people for better treatment of the Canadian Ukrainians.

"If Canadian fathers and kinsmen are allowed to send food to the starving Canadian prisoners in Germany, let us too be permitted to release our women and children and bring them to Canada.

"This is what the Canadian Ukrainians want and need at present. But when the war is over and cannon and swords are turned into plows and reaping-hooks, then the quarter million Canadian Ukrainians—the only Slav subjects in the great British empire—would be a link between the Anglo-Saxon and Slavonic worlds, and, first of all, between Great Britain and the Ukraine, the richest country in natural resources of Europe, but waiting national inspiration and industrial support from the British world.

"O. Hykawy, of Kanadyjsky Farmer, the Ukrainian Liberal weekly, Winnipeg, Man.

"A. Jolla, for Robotchyj Narod, the official organ of the Ukrainian Social-Democratic party of Canada, Winnipeg, Man.

"Rev. E.M. Glowa, of Ranok, the Ukrainian Presbyterian weekly, Winnipeg, Man.

"P.C. Crath, of Kadilo, the Ukrainian humoristic gazette, Winnipeg, Man.

"M. Bellegay, of Kanadyjetz, the Ukrainian Methodist weekly, Edmonton, Alta.

"J. Stefanitzky of Robitnyche Slowo, the Ukrainian Social-Democratic weekly, Toronto, Ont."

SOURCE: *Manitoba Free Press*, 17 July 1916.

4. Address by Osyp Megas to the Second National Convention, Saskatoon, December 1917

First of all I want to assure our English-speaking citizens that this is not a Bolshevik gathering and that we do not aim at sectionalism or racial nationalism but we are striving to cooperate among ourselves and with our English-speaking citizens toward the educational uplift of our younger generation. Nor do we ourselves feel that we are an alien gathering. We gather here as Canadians always true to our new land of adoption and loyal to the British empire.

Some of us are able to speak Ruthenian only, others again are able to understand English as well. To be of real benefit to all, this convention will be conducted in both languages.

With the rest of Canada the Ruthenian citizens fully realize the gravity and the seriousness of the present war situation and our responsibility toward Canada and the British empire. This convention, therefore, being representative of the Ruthenian citizens of Western Canada, wants to assure the government in this country that the Ruthenians intend to stay wholeheartedly and resolutely with the rest of Canada during the present gigantic struggle against the despotic militarism of the Central powers and that we are willing to contribute our share to the common sacrifice.

Being only a small minority—some 400,000 in Canada—we are deprived of proper means by which we could express our desires and wishes, and we feel therefore, that a gathering of this sort will constitute in a way a kind of Ruthenian parliament expressive of our thoughts and feelings.

The chief purpose of this convention is to further stimulate the Ruthenians of the province toward the continuation of the educational campaign initiated with such great success by our institute some two years ago....

In carrying out of this educational scheme we expect a friendly co-operation of our English-speaking citizens. It is better for us all, for Canada in general, to have our younger ideals and Canadian spirit. We do not want to be isolated from the rest of Canada by holding tenaciously and exclusively to our old habits and customs.

If the so-called foreigner in Canada has failed to respond to the ways of the land, to the call of duty, the English-speaking elements have themselves largely to blame for it. The non-English have been isolated and estranged by the personal prejudice of the many English-speaking Canadians, they have been looked to for the hewing of the wood and carrying of water, they have been frequently exploited by the professional vote-getter and by the unscrupulous tradesman who would see the nation in perdition so long as nothing interfered with his wealth-getting schemes. Coldness and reserve seems to characterize especially now the attitude of most of our English speaking citizens when they are called upon to deal with the strangers who stand within our gates. Fortunately enough there are many English-speaking citizens who have always taken a friendly attitude toward the Ruthenians....

Were it not for the fact that there is still some misconception, shall I say ignorance, in official circles, and even among our educated English-speaking people about the true national status of the Ruthenians or the Ukrainians as a distinct nationality I would not make any special mention on this matter. The government not only here in Canada but also in Great Britain and the United States seem to cling to the old idea that the Ruthenians are Austrians and the Ukrainians from

Russia are Russians pure and simple. Such is not the case, however. The Ruthenians from Austria and the Ukrainians from Russia are one and the same homogeneous race, with the same one language and common traditions. The best proof of this well known fact is the recent uprising in South Russia and Austria, which culminated in the formation of the Republic of Ukraine, by the newly formed government in Kieff.

The Ukrainian Central Rada has issued a manifesto to Ukrainians proclaiming a Ukrainian democratic republic to form part of the all-Russian federal republic, pending the meeting of the Ukrainian constituent assembly in January.

Ukrainian troops numbering 500,000 have occupied the headquarters of all staffs on Rumanian and Austrian fronts, seizing wireless and telegraph systems on the two fronts which have been united under the command of Lieut.-General Stcherbatcheff.

Ukarainian [sic] troops have moved to the borders of Ukrainia, where they have taken up positions. Orders have been issued to mobilize all Cossacks in Ukrainia.

Ukrainian currency appeared in the city of Kieff, bearing a pledge of payment reading "Ukraine National Republic." In this connection I may state that the Ruthenians all over the world are taking steps to organize protests against the Bolshevik proposal of peace without annexations. It is also a fact that there are over 5,000,000 Ukrainians inhabiting the provinces of Galicia and Bukowina, and they are still suffering under the Austrian yoke. They are exceedingly anxious to be united with the Ukraine proper. They want to see Galicia and Bukowina annexed by Ukraine and these will later form a part of a federated Republic of Russia.

All the above facts prove that the Ruthenians are not Austrians by any means and it is highly desirable that the governments of the allied powers and of Canada, recognize this fact at once, giving thus their official recognition of the independence of the Ukrainian people.

The new Franchise Act in Canada was a very unpleasant blow to the naturalized Ruthenian citizens who were always proud of being British subjects with all the privileges granted us in connection with our naturalization papers. We always looked upon our naturalization papers as a form of contract between us and the government and we suddenly, to our great surprise, found that the contract was only a 'scrap of paper.' Would [it] not have been better for us and for Canada to retain the full privileges of our citizenship and also make us live up to its full responsiblity on a par with other English-speaking Canadians. We certainly have never had any desire to change our citizenship and are satisfied to live and work here as British subjects.

SOURCE: *Regina Morning Leader*, 29 December 1917.

APPENDIX II

GOVERNMENT POLICIES

A. INTERNMENT

5. Proclamation respecting immigrants of German or Austro-Hungarian nationality, 15 August 1914

Whereas a state of war exists between the United Kingdom of Great Britain and Ireland and the German Empire, and the Austro-Hungarian Monarchy;

And whereas certain instructions have been received from His Majesty's Government in connection with the arrest and detention of subjects in Canada of the German Empire and of the Austro-Hungarian Monarchy and particularly of those who attempt to leave Canada;

And whereas there are many persons of German and Austro-Hungarian nationality quietly pursuing their usual avocations in various parts of Canada, and it is desirable that such persons should be allowed to continue in such avocations without interruption,—

Now Know Ye that by and with the advice of Our Privy Council for Canada, We do by these presents proclaim and direct as follows:

1. That all persons in Canada of German or Austro-Hungarian nationality so long as they quietly pursue their ordinary avocations be allowed to continue to enjoy the protection of the law and be accorded the respect and consideration due to peaceful and law-abiding citizens; and that they be not arrested, detained or interfered with, unless there is reasonable ground to believe that they are engaged in espionage, or engaging or attempting to engage in acts of a hostile nature, or are giving or attempting to give information to the enemy, or unless they otherwise contravene any law, order in council or proclamation.

2. THAT

(a) All German or Austrian or Austro-Hungarian officers, soldiers or reservists who attempt to leave Canada;

(b) All subjects of the German Empire or of the Austro-Hungarian Monarchy in Canada engaged or attempting to engage in espionage or acts of a hostile nature, or giving or attempting to give information to the enemy, or assisting or attempting to assist the enemy, or who are on reasonable grounds suspected of doing or attempting to do any of the said acts;

be arrested and detained.

3. That in addition to and without affecting the power already vested in the Militia in that behalf power to effect the arrest and detention of all or any person or

persons coming within any of the classes mentioned in paragraph (2) hereof be vested in the Chief Commissioner and the commissioners and constables of the Dominion Police Force; the Commissioner, officers and constables of the Royal North West Mounted Police; and such other persons as may be authorized so to do by the Chief Commissioner of Dominion Police.

4. That such authorities and officers mentioned in paragraph (3) hereof, or the militia be authorized to release any such person so arrested or detained as aforesaid of whose reliability they may be satisfied on his signing an undertaking in the form following:—

Undertaking.

I...at present of .... in the Province of .... in the Dominion of Canada, do hereby declare that I am a German (an Austro-Hungarian) subject; I now in consideration of my exemption from detention as a subject of Germany, (Austria-Hungary), do hereby undertake and promise that I will report to such official and upon such terms as the Canadian authorities may from time to time prescribe; that I will carefully observe the laws of the United Kingdom of Great Britain and Ireland and of Canada and such rules as may be especially laid down for my conduct; that I will strictly abstain from taking up arms and from doing any act of hostility towards the Government of this Country, and that, except with the permission of the officer under whose surveillance I may be placed, I will strictly abstain from communicating to anyone whomsoever any information respecting the existing war or the movement of troops, or the military preparations which the Authorities of Canada or Great Britain may make, or as respects the resources of Canada, and that I will do no act that might be of injury to the Dominion of Canada or the United Kingdom of Great Britain and Ireland and the Dominions and possessions thereof.

Dated this.........................day of .... 1914.

WITNESS,

....

5. That any such person so arrested and detained as aforesaid, of whose reliability the officer or authority making the arrest is not satisfied, or who refuses to sign such undertaking or having signed same fails to abide by its terms, be interned by such authorities and officers or militia according to the usages and laws of war in such places as may be provided by the militia, and that if it be deemed necessary that guards be placed on persons so interned, such guards be furnished by the active militia of Canada on the request of such authorities or officers to officers commanding divisional areas and districts.

6. That all such authorities and officers or militia who may exercise any of the powers above mentioned be directed to report in each case to the Chief Commissioner of Dominion Police stating the name, address and occupation of the

person detained or paroled, the date and place of detention and generally the circumstances of the arrest and detention and all such information as may be necessary or useful for the purpose of record and identification.

Of all which our loving subjects and all others whom these presents may concern, are hereby required to take notice and to govern themselves accordingly.

SOURCE: Canada. Department of the Secretary of State, *Copies of Proclamations, Orders in Council and Documents Relating to the European War* (Ottawa, 1915), 49-52.

6. Public notice to alien enemies, 2 September 1914

It has come to the attention of the Government that many persons of German and Austro-Hungarian nationality who are residents of Canada are apprehensive for their safety at the present time. In particular the suggestion seems to be that they fear some action on the part of the Government which might deprive them of their freedom to hold property or to carry on business. These apprehensions, if they exist, are quite unfounded.

The policy of the Government is embodied in a Proclamation published in *The Canada Gazette* on 15th August. In accordance with this Proclamation restrictive measures will be taken only in cases where officers, soldiers or reservists of the German Empire or of the Austro-Hungarian Monarchy attempt to leave Canada or where subjects of such nationalities engage or attempt to engage in espionage or acts of a hostile nature or to give information to or otherwise assist the King's enemies. Even where persons are arrested or detained on the grounds indicated they may be released on signing an undertaking to abstain from acts injurious to the Dominion or the Empire.

The Proclamation after stating that "there are many persons of German and Austro-Hungarian nationality quietly pursuing their usual avocations in various parts of Canada and that it is desirable that such persons should be allowed to continue in such avocations without interruption," directs as follows:—

> "That all persons in Canada of German or Austro-Hungarian nationality, so long as they quietly pursue their ordinary avocations be allowed to continue to enjoy the protection of the law and be accorded the respect and consideration due to peaceful and law-abiding citizens; and that they not be arrested, detained or interfered with, unless there is reasonable ground to believe that they are engaged in espionage, or engaging or attempting to engage in acts of a hostile nature, or are giving or attempting to give information to the enemy, or unless they otherwise contravene any law, order in council or proclamation."

Thus all such persons so long as they respect the law are entitled to its protection and have nothing to fear.

SOURCE: *Extra Canada Gazette*, 2 September 1914.

7. Order in Council respecting alien enemies, 28 October 1914

The Committee of the Privy Council have had before them a report, dated 28th October, 1914, from the Minister of Justice, stating that it is expedient and necessary to take measures to prevent espionage and also to prevent alien enemies in Canada who are likely to render effective military assistance to the enemy from returning to the enemy's service, and to provide for the proper supervision and control of such aliens as may be so prevented from leaving Canada, and the detention under proper conditions and maintenance where required of such of said aliens as it may be found necessary to intern as prisoners of war, and that it is likewise desirable considering the lack of opportunity for employment that aliens of enemy nationality who are not likely to add to the strength of the enemy's forces and who desire and have the means to leave the country be permitted to do so.

The Minister observes that it is considered probable that aliens of both classes will be found grouped in particular localities, principally within or in the immediate neighbourhood of the large cities and towns,— The Minister, therefore, recommends that it be enacted by the Governor in Council under the authority of the War Measures Act as follows:—

(1) One or more offices of registration shall be established in such cities, towns and other places as may be from time to time designated by the Minister of Justice, and an officer shall be appointed by the Governor in Council for each of the offices so established who shall be called "Registrars of Alien Enemies."

(2) The Registrars shall be under the immediate direction of the Chief Commissioner of Dominion Police who shall exercise general supervision over them in the performance of their duties and to whom they shall report as may be required. The Minister shall appoint such assistants to such registrars, clerks and other officers as may be necessary for the proper carrying out of the provisions of the present order.

(3) It shall be the duty of a registrar to examine each alien of enemy nationality attending before him, and to register in a book to be provided for the purpose the name, age, nationality, place of residence in Canada and in the country of nationality, occupation, desire or intention to leave Canada and the names of the wife and children (if any) in Canada of every such alien and such other particulars necessary for identification of such alien of enemy nationality or otherwise as may seem advisable.

(4) Every alien of enemy nationality residing or being within any of the cities, towns or places so designated as aforesaid or within twenty miles thereof, shall as soon as possible after the publication in the *Canada Gazette* of a proclamation designating such city, town or place as one wherein a registry office is to be established under this ordinance, attend before the registrar or one of the registrars, for the city, town or place within or near which he is or resides and truly answer such questions with regard to his nationality, age, residence, occupation, family, intention or desire to leave Canada, destination, liability and intention as to military service, and otherwise, as may be lawfully put to him by the registrar.

(5) No alien of enemy nationality shall be permitted to leave Canada without an exeat from a registrar; provided that the Chief Commissioner of Dominion Police

may in any case, grant or cancel an exeat to an alien of enemy nationality who is registered.

(6) The registrar may issue an exeat to an alien of enemy nationality if satisfied upon the examination and registry that such alien of enemy nationality will not materially assist, by active service, information or otherwise, the forces of the enemy.

(7) If it appears to the registrar that any alien of enemy nationality who is not permitted to leave Canada may consistently with the public safety be suffered to remain at large, such alien of enemy nationality shall be required to declare whether or not he desires and has the means to remain in Canada conformably to the laws and customs of the country, subject to obligation to report monthly to the Chief of Police of the city where or in the neighbourhood of which he is registered. If yes, such alien of enemy nationality may be permitted his liberty, subject to the conditions aforesaid and the provisions of this ordinance. If nay, he shall be interned as a prisoner of war. The registrar shall report to the Chief of Police the names and addresses of those who elect to remain at liberty. Any alien of enemy nationality who in the judgment of the registrar cannot consistently with the public safety be allowed at large shall be interned as a prisoner of war.

(8) If any alien of enemy nationality who is by the terms of this ordinance required to register, fails to do so within one month after publication of the proclamation referred to in section 4 of this ordinance or within seven days after the date when he shall by reason of his residence come within the description of those required to register, whichever date shall be last, or if he refuse or fail to answer truly any of the questions put by the registrar, or if, being registered he fail to report as hereinbefore required or to observe any of the conditions on which he is permitted to be at liberty, he shall in addition to any other penalty to which he may be therefor by law liable be subject to internment as a prisoner of war.

(9) Where any alien of enemy nationality interned under the provisions of this order has wife or children living with and dependent on him, such wife and children shall be permitted to accompany him.

(10) Such provision as may be necessary for the maintenance of aliens of enemy nationality interned as prisoners of war shall be made by the military authorities who may require such prisoners to do and perform such work as may be by them prescribed.

(11) No alien of enemy nationality who is required to register shall be naturalized unless in addition to other requirements he produces and files with his application a duly certified certificate of a registrar that he is registered pursuant to the provisions of this ordinance and that his application for naturalization is approved by the registrar.

The Committee submit the same for approval.

SOURCE: *Extra Canada Gazette*, 28 October 1914.
[Over the next several weeks, subsequent orders in council established the following centres as places of registration: Montreal, Sydney, Regina, Edmonton, Calgary, Fort William, Winnipeg, Toronto, Ottawa, Victoria and Brandon—Ed.]

8. Order in Council authorizing the apprehension and internment of alien enemies in certain cases, 26 June 1915

The Committee of the Privy Council have had before them a report, dated 24th June, 1915, from the Minister of Justice, submitting that conditions have arisen owing to the presence in the country of a great number of foreigners, many of whom are of enemy nationality, and others of the nationalities of His Majesty's allies, in which it is, in the opinion of the Minister, advisable that further provision should be made for the preservation of the peace, for the safety of works and property of public utility, and for the protection of the inhabitants and of the foreigners themselves who are residing in the country.

The Minister further submits that at the beginning of the war it was announced by the Proclamation of Your Royal Highness of 15th August, 1914, that all persons in Canada of German or Austro-Hungarian nationality, so long as they quietly pursue their ordinary avocations should be allowed to continue to enjoy the protection of the law and be accorded the respect and consideration due to peaceful and law-abiding citizens; and that they should not be arrested, detained or interfered with, unless upon reasonable ground to believe that they are engaged in espionage, or engaging or attempting to engage in acts of a hostile nature, or are giving or attempting to give information to the enemy, or unless they otherwise contravene any law, order-in-council or proclamation. It happens that many aliens of enemy nationality residing temporarily in Canada have retained or found employment in connection with various works, industries, trades or pursuits which are being carried on, and they are, and of course ought to be protected in such employment according to the policy of the said proclamation, so far as may be compatible with the public interest.

The Minister has ascertained, however, that owing to the fact that in some cases these aliens of enemy nationality are in common employment with others, many of whom belong to the nationalities of the allied powers, or because of competition for their places by such friendly aliens, and in view of the hostility or animosity which has been aroused and excited by the war and the operations of the enemy, there is serious danger of rioting, destruction of valuable works and property and breaches of the peace involving the loss of life or personal injuries; and, while in the view of the Minister the dangers thus apprehended should, so far as may be practicable or expedient, be prevented by strict administration of existing legal means, he considers nevertheless that cases have arisen, or may arise, where in the general public interest, as well as in the interest of those concerned who are of enemy nationality, provision should be made, as a measure for expediency, for separating and detaining at public charge those aliens of enemy nationality whose presence in any works, employment or community is a cause of such apprehended peril.

The Minister, therefore, recommends that he be authorized, whenever the advisability of such a course shall be established to his satisfaction, to direct the apprehension and internment of aliens of enemy nationalities who may be found employed or seeking employment or competing for employment in any community, such aliens of enemy nationality when so interned to be kept and maintained in all respects as prisoners of war, but subject to be released at any time as may be directed by the Minister, whenever it appears that they may be permitted to be discharged with due regard to the public safety.

The Committee concur in the foregoing and submit the same for approval.

SOURCE: Canada. Department of the Secretary of State. *Copies of Proclamations, Orders in Council and Documents Relating to the European War*, Second Supplement, (Ottawa, 1916), 623-5.

B. POSSESSION OF FIREARMS

9. Order in Council prohibiting the use or possession of firearms or explosives by alien enemies, 3 September 1914

His Royal Highness the Governor General in Council, under and in virtue of the provisions of section 6 of The War Measures Act, 1914, is pleased to make and doth hereby make the following Orders and Regulations for prevention of the use or possession of fire-arms, ammunition, dynamite, gunpowder or other dangerous explosive, within Canada, by alien enemies:—

1. The possession of fire-arms, or any ammunition therefor, or of any dynamite, gunpowder or other dangerous explosive, within Canada by any alien enemy, is prohibited.

2. It shall be the duty of every such person within Canada having in his possession or upon his premises any fire-arms or any ammunition therefor, or any dynamite, gunpowder or other dangerous explosive, within ten days from the publication of this ordinance in the *Canada Gazette*, to cause such fire-arms, ammunition, dynamite, gunpowder or other dangerous explosive, to be delivered to a justice of the peace residing in or near the locality where such fire-arms, ammunition, dynamite, gunpowder or other dangerous explosive are so had in possession or to an officer or constable of the Royal North West Mounted Police.

3. Any justice of the peace or any such officer or constable receiving any such fire-arms, ammunition, dynamite, gunpowder or other dangerous explosive, shall give to the person delivering the same a receipt therefor, and shall report the fact to the Chief Commissioner of Dominion Police or to the Commissioner of the Royal North West Mounted Police, under whose direction the property so delivered shall be retained or otherwise disposed of.

4. If any alien enemy within Canada is reasonably suspected to have in his possession or upon his premises any fire-arms, or ammunition therefor, dynamite, gunpowder, or other dangerous explosive, he may be searched, or his premises, or any place occupied or believed to be occupied by him, may be searched by any peace officer or by any officer or constable of the Royal North West Mounted Police without warrant, and if any fire-arms, ammunition, dynamite, gunpowder or other dangerous explosive be found upon the person or premises of any such alien enemy, or in any such place as aforesaid, the same shall be seized, and if such search and seizure shall have taken place after the expiration of the period of ten days hereinfore mentioned, the property so seized may be forfeited to the Crown, and the person upon whom or upon whose premises or in whose possession any such fire-arms, ammunition, dynamite, gunpowder or other dangerous explosive are found shall further be liable to a penalty not exceeding five hundred dollars, or to imprisonment for any term not exceeding three months.

5. It shall be an offence for any person to give, sell, hire, lease or transfer possession of any fire-arms, ammunition, dynamite, gunpowder or other dangerous explosive to any alien enemy, and any person guilty of any such offence shall be liable to a penalty not exceeding one hundred dollars or to imprisonment for any term not exceeding one month.

6. Any offence declared and any penalty or forfeiture imposed or authorized by this ordinance may be prosecuted, recovered or enforced by summary proceedings and conviction under the provisions of Part XV of the Criminal Code.

7. If any question arises under this ordinance, or in any proceedings instituted thereunder, or with reference to anything done or proposed to be done under the authority thereof, as to whether any person is an alien enemy the onus of proving that any person so suspected or charged is not an alien enemy shall lie upon the accused in such proceeding.

SOURCE: *Canada Gazette*, 5 September 1914.

10. Order in Council authorizing the issue of licenses to alien enemies to have possession of firearms in certain cases, 26 January 1915

The Committee of the Privy Council, have had before them a Report, dated 18th January, 1915, from the Minister of Justice, stating that it is represented that farmers and homesteaders living in remote parts of the country or upon the frontiers are frequently in need of fire-arms for protection against coyotes, or other wild animals, or for use in obtaining game upon which they depend to a considerable extent for food. Some of these people are of enemy nationality, and by the Order in Council of 3rd September, 1914, no exception is made authorizing them to have possession of arms or ammunition for any purpose. This appears to be a hardship, and the Minister considers that consistently with the general purposes of the said order, provisions may be made for the granting of licenses in proper cases to law-abiding settlers of enemy nationality to purchase, have in possession and use fire-arms and ammunition for protection and for procuring game.

The Minister recommends, accordingly, that the Chief Commissioner of Dominion Police and the officers of the Royal North West Mounted Police be authorized to grant such licenses in cases which upon investigation appear deserving of this exceptional treatment.

The Committee concur in the foregoing and submit the same for approval.

SOURCE: Canada. Department of the Secretary of State. *Copies of Proclamations, Orders in Council and Documents Relating to the European War*, Second Supplement (Ottawa, 1916), 592.

C. MILITARY SERVICE

11. Enlistment of persons of foreign birth

(1) [21 July 1917]

Mr. MACNUTT: . . . I wish to ask a question of the Minister of Militia as to the enlistment of naturalized enemy country aliens, with especial reference to Ruthenians who formerly resided in the eastern provinces of Austria. My information is that recruits have not been accepted for the overseas forces for enlistment from among these people, who, if they wished to enlist, had to claim they were Russians. Is it the intention of the Government to accept persons of enemy country birth as recruits in the future, and is it the intention of the Government, under the Military Service Act, to conscript those classes of people of alien birth whom it refused to accept as volunteers?

Sir ROBERT BORDEN: . . . My hon. friend the Minister of Militia and Defence unfortunately is not here today. . . . I am not personally familiar with the facts as to whether persons of foreign birth have been refused by the recruiting officer. It is, of course, perfectly true that the British Government have been very strict as to the enlistment of persons who were born in an enemy country. On the other hand, I believe that there have been a great many people of foreign birth, possibly some of enemy nationality, who have enlisted and gone to the front. I am disposed to think that, although I am not sure. But we will have inquiries made on the subject and will give my hon. friend an answer on Monday or Tuesday.

(2) [25 July 1917]

Sir ROBERT BORDEN: Some time ago the member for Saltcoats (Mr. MacNutt) asked a question with regard to the enlistment of aliens under the voluntary system and under the Military Service Act. The matter of the enlistment of such persons under the voluntary system has been under consideration by the military authorities not only of this country but of the United Kingdom as well, and there has been consultation between the two Governments with regard to it. Upon that consultation the general policy under the voluntary system of recruiting has been not to enlist men of alien enemy birth for combatant service. With regard to the policy under the Military Service Act, it would not be considered desirable to enlist for combatant service any man who, under the policy that has been carried out in respect of voluntary enlistment, would not be accepted. The same principle, we think, should be applied to both: that is, such a man should not be enlisted for combatant service.

SOURCE: Canada. *Parliamentary Debates* (Commons), 129, 4 (1917): 3656-7, 3759.

12. An act respecting military service, assented to 29 August 1917

Whereas by section ten of the *Militia Act*, chapter forty-one of the Revised Statutes of Canada, 1906, it is enacted as follows:—

"All the male inhabitants of Canada, of the age of eighteen years and upwards, and under sixty, not exempt or disqualified by law, and being British subjects, shall be liable to service in the Militia: Provided that the Governor General may require all the male inhabitants of Canada, capable of bearing arms, to serve in the case of a *levée en masse*;"

And whereas by section sixty-nine of the said Act it is further enacted as follows:—

"The Governor in Council may place the Militias, or any part thereof, on active service anywhere in Canada, and also beyond Canada, for the defence thereof, at any time when it appears advisable so to do by reason of emergency;"

And whereas by the said Act it is further enacted that, if at any time enough men do not volunteer to complete the quota required, the men so liable to serve shall be drafted by ballot;

And whereas to maintain and support the Canadian Expeditionary Force now engaged in active service overseas for the defence and security of Canada, the preservation of the Empire and of human liberty, it is necessary to provide reinforcements for such Expeditionary Force;

And whereas enough men do not volunteer to provide such reinforcements;

And whereas by reason of the large number of men who have already left agricultural and industrial pursuits in Canada to join such Expeditionary Force as volunteers, and of the necessity of sustaining under such conditions the productivity of the Dominion, it is expedient to secure the men still required, not by ballot as provided in the *Militia Act*, but by selective draft: Therefore His Majesty by and with the advice and consent of the Senate and House of Commons of Canada, enacts as follows:—

. . .

2. (1) Every male British subject who comes within one of the classes described in section three of this Act, and who,—

(a) is ordinarily resident in Canada; or,

(b) has been at any time since the fourth day of August, 1914, resident in Canada,

shall be liable to be called out as hereinafter provided on active service in the Canadian Expeditionary Force for the defence of Canada, either in or beyond Canada, unless he

(a) comes within the exceptions set out in the Schedule; or,

(b) reaches the age of forty-five before the class or subclass to which he belongs, as described in section three, is called out.

Such service shall be for the duration of the present war and of demobilization after the conclusion of the war.

(2) Nothing in this Act shall prevent any man from voluntarily enlisting in the Canadian Expeditionary Force, so long as voluntary enlistment in such Force is authorized.

3. (1) The men who are liable to be called out shall consist of six classes described as follows:—

Class 1.—Those who have attained the age of twenty years and were born not earlier than the year 1883 and are unmarried, or are widowers but have no child.

Class 2.—Those who have attained the age of twenty years and were born not earlier than the year 1883 and are married, or are widowers who have a child or children.

Class 3.—Those who were born in the years 1876 to 1882, both inclusive, and are unmarried, or are widowers who have no child.

Class 4.—Those who were born in the years 1876 to 1882, both inclusive, and are married, or are widowers who have a child or children.

Class 5.—Those who were born in the years 1872 to 1875, both inclusive, and are unmarried, or are widowers who have no child.

Class 6.—Those who were born in the years 1872 to 1875, both inclusive, and are married, or are widowers who have a child or children.

(2) For the purposes of this section, any man married after the sixth day of July, 1917, shall be deemed to be unmarried.

(3) Any class, except Class 1, shall include men who are transferred thereto from another class as hereinafter provided, and men who have come within Class 1 since the previous class was called out.

(4) The order in which the classes are described in this section shall be the order in which they may be called out on active service, provided the Governor in Council may divide any class into subclasses, in which case the subclasses shall be called out in order of age beginning with the youngest.

4. (1) The Governor in Council may from time to time by proclamation call out on active service as aforesaid for the defence of Canada, either in Canada or beyond Canada, any class or subclass of men described in section three, and all men within the class or subclass so called out shall, from the date of such proclamation, be deemed to be soldiers enlisted in the Military Forces of Canada and subject to military law for the duration of the present war, and of demobilization thereafter, save as hereinafter provided.

(2) Men so called out shall report, and shall be placed on active service in the Canadian Expeditionary Force as may be set out in such proclamation or in regulations, but until so placed on active service, shall be deemed to be on leave of absence without pay.

(3) Any man by or in respect of whom an application for exemption is made as hereinafter provided, shall, so long as such application or any appeal in connection therewith is pending and during the currency of any exemption granted him, be deemed to be on leave of absence without pay.

(4) Any man who is called out and who, without reasonable excuse, fails to report as aforesaid, shall be guilty of an offence, and shall be liable on summary conviction to imprisonment for any term not exceeding five years, with hard labour.

. . .

11. (1) At any time before a date to be fixed in the proclamation mentioned in section four, an application may be made, by or in respect of any man in the class or subclass called out by such proclamation, to a local tribunal established in the province in which such man ordinarily resides, for a certificate of exemption on any of the following grounds:—

> (a) That it is expedient in the national interest that the man should, instead of being employed in military service, be engaged in other work in which he is habitually engaged;
>
> (b) That it is expedient in the national interest that the man should, instead of being employed in military service, be engaged in other work in which he wishes to be engaged and for which he has special qualifications;
>
> (c) That is expedient in the national interest that, instead of being employed in military service, he should continue to be educated or trained for any work for which he is then being educated or trained;
>
> (d) That serious hardship would ensue, if the man were placed on active service, owing to his exceptional financial or business obligations or domestic position;
>
> (e) Ill health or infirmity;
>
> (f) That he conscientiously objects to the undertaking of combatant service and is prohibited from so doing by the tenets and articles of faith, in effect on the sixth day of July, 1917, of any organized religious denomination existing and well recognized in Canada at such date, and to which he in good faith belongs;

and if any of the grounds of such application be established, a certificate of exemption shall be granted to such man.

SOURCE: Canada. *Statutes*, 7-8 Geo. 5, chap. 19.

13. Official citation, Filip Konowal, Victoria Cross

His Majesty the King has been graciously pleased to approve the award of the Victoria Cross to the undermentioned Non-commissioned officer:

No. 144039A./Cpl. Filip Konowal, Canadian Infantry.

For most conspicuous bravery and leadership when in charge of a section in attack [August 1917]. His section had the difficult task of mopping up cellars, craters and machine-gun emplacements. Under his able direction all resistance was overcome successfully, and heavy casualties inflicted on the enemy. In one cellar he himself bayonetted three enemy and attacked single-handed seven others in a crater, killing them all.

On reaching the objective, a machine-gun was holding up the right flank, causing many casualties. Cpl. Konowal rushed forward and entered the emplacement, killed the crew, and brought the gun back to our lines.

The next day he again attacked single-handed another machine-gun emplacement, killed three of the crew, and destroyed the gun emplacement with explosive.

This non-commissioned officer alone killed at least sixteen of the enemy, and during the two days' actual fighting carried on continuously his good work until severely wounded.

SOURCE: *Canada Gazette*, 22 December 1917.

D. DISFRANCHISEMENT

14. The War-time Elections Act, assented to 20 September 1917

. . .

2. During the present war and until demobilization after the conclusion of peace, Part III of the *Dominion Elections Act* shall operate and apply as if amended and shall be deemed to be amended in the following respects:—

. . .

(d) By adding as paragraphs (e), (f), (g), (h) and (i) to subsection (1) of secton 67 [*voter disqualification*—Ed.] the following:—

"(e) Any person who shall have applied pursuant to section 11, subsection (1), clause (f) of the *Act respecting Military Service* for a certificate of exemption from combatant military service on conscientious grounds, whether or not a certificate of exemption from such service shall have been granted, and unless and until it has been refused."

"(f) All persons who on the sixth day of July, 1917, were members of the religious denomination or sect called "Mennonites" (the members of which denomination or sect were exempted from military service by Order in Council of August 13, 1873), and all persons who on said sixth day of July, 1917, were members of the religious denomination or sect called "Doukabors" (members of which denomination or sect were exempted from military service by Order in Council of December 6, 1898): Provided that this paragraph shall not apply to such Mennonites or Doukabors as shall have volunteered for and been placed on active service in the military or naval forces of Canada or of His Majesty in the present war."

"(g) Except as in this paragraph provided, every naturalized British subject who was born in an enemy country and naturalized subsequent to the 31st day of March, 1902. A person shall be deemed to have been born in an enemy country, within the meaning of this paragraph, if he was born in a country with which His Majesty is at war: Provided that a person claiming to vote who was a natural born citizen or subject of France, Italy, or Denmark, and who arrived in Canada before the date upon which the territory in which he was born became part of Germany or Austria (as the case may be) shall not be deemed to have been born in an enemy country if he produces to the deputy returning officer an unrevoked certificate in the form W-3 in the Schedule. Such certificate may be issued by the enumerator of the polling division whereof the person, were it not for his nationality would be an elector, not later than three days before polling day upon satisfactory proof furnished by deposition under oath to the enumerator as to the facts. If at any time before such person has voted the returning officer of the electoral district has reason to believe that the facts did not justify the issue of any such certificate he may revoke the same."

"(h) Every naturalized British subject who was born in any European country (whether or not the sovereign or government thereof is in alliance with His Majesty in the present war) whose natural language, otherwise described as "mother tongue," is a language of an enemy country, and who was naturalized subsequent to the 31st day of March, 1902.

Provided that nothing contained in this section shall be construed as preventing any naturalized British subject (if otherwise qualified) from having his or her name on a list of voters or from voting who—(i) is serving or has served without Canada as one of the military or within or without Canada as one of the naval forces of Canada or of His Majesty or of any of his allies in the present war, or, (ii) produces a certificate signed by the Commanding Officer of a Military District, or an officer thereto authorized by him, that the person is or has been a member of any of such forces and has been engaged in active service within or without Canada during the present war, or is a person who has applied for enlistment as a member of such forces to so serve and has been rejected only because medically unfit, or is a grandparent, parent, son or brother of a person who is or has been a member of any of such forces and has been engaged in active service, or of a person who has so applied and been so rejected; or, (iii) is or has been at any time during the present war a member of the Parliament of Canada or of a province; or, (iv) is a Christian and either a Syrian or an Armenian; or, (v) is a female voter entitled to vote under section 33A of this Act."

"(i) every person who has been convicted of any offence against the Act *respecting Military Service,* passed in the year 1917.;"

(e) By adding as section 67A, between sections 67 and 68, the following:—

"**67A**. Notwithstanding anything appearing in the *Act respecting Military Service*, passed in the year 1917, or in any other Act or Order in Council,—

(1) All persons who are by the terms of paragraphs (g) and (h) of section 67 of this Act disqualified from voting, with such of their sons as on polling day are not of legal age, shall be, and shall be held, exempt from combatant military and naval service; and,

(2) All persons who shall have voted at a Dominion election held subsequent to the 7th day of October, 1917, during the present war shall be held ineligible and incompetent,—(a) to apply for, or to be granted on the application of another, exemption from combatant military or naval service on conscientious grounds, or, (b) to be excepted as a Mennonite or as a Doukabor from the provisions of said *Act respecting Military Service* or exempted as such from combatant military or naval service on conscientious grounds;"

(f) By adding as section 67B immediately following section 67A., the following:—

"**67B**. (1) Any deputy returning officer, either of his own motion or at the request of any agent or scrutineer, after carefully explaining the meaning of paragraphs (g) and (h) of section 67 of this Act, may put to any person claiming to vote at an election the following questions:—

"Are you a naturalized British subject who was born in an enemy country within the meaning of paragraph (g) of section 67 of the *Dominion Elections Act*; or who was born in Europe and whose natural language or mother tongue is a language of an enemy country, and, if you are either, when and where were you naturalized?

"(2) If such a person refuses to answer fully such questions, or by his answer shows that he was born in an enemy country within the meaning of said paragraph of said section, or that his natural language or mother tongue is a language of an enemy country, his claim to vote shall be rejected unless he satisfies the deputy returning officer that he was naturalized as a British subject prior to the 1st day of April, 1902, or is one of the persons excepted in and by said section 67 from the disqualifying operation thereof, or that he is a person who is, while within Canada, entitled by statute to the privileges of a natural born British subject.

"(3) Any person who, being disqualified from voting by paragraphs (e), (f), (g) (h) or (i) of section 67 votes at an election, shall be guilty of an offence and liable upon indictment or summary conviction to a fine not exceeding five hundred dollars and costs, or to imprisonment for a term not exceeding two years; or to both such fine and such imprisonment.

"(4) In the preparation of lists for any polling divisions the enumerator shall not include the names of any persons who are for any reason disqualified from voting, and he shall require of every person other than a British subject by birth, as a condition precedent to the placing of his name on any list of voters, production of a duly authenticated certificate of his naturalization as a British subject or of his having taken the oath or oaths required of a person who is entitled by statute, while within Canada, to the privileges of a natural born British subject. The provisions of section 62 of this Act shall apply to such persons as an enumerator shall omit from or refuse to register on the list of voters because of disqualification or non-production of a certificate of naturalization, or of having taken such oaths or oaths, and, on recount proceedings, upon satisfactory proof by any such persons of absence of disqualification, and in the case of a naturalized British subject upon further proof that he has lost or is unable to find such certificate of naturalization, or having taken such oath or oaths, the recounting judge shall count the ballot of such person pursuant to said section 62 and as therein provided;"

. . .

SOURCE: Canada. *Statutes*, 7-8 Geo. 5, chap. 39.
[*The War-time Elections Act was repealed by An Act Respecting the Election of Members of the House of Commons and the Electoral Franchise, assented to on 1 July 1920.—Ed.*]

E. CENSORSHIP AND ASSOCIATION

15. Order in Council respecting enemy publications, 25 September 1918

His Excellency the Governor General in Council is pleased, under and in virtue of the powers conferred by the *War Measures Act, 1914,* or otherwise vested in the Governor General in Council, to make the following regulations and the same are hereby made and enacted accordingly:—

1. These regulations may be cited as the Order respecting Enemy publications.

2. In and for the purposes of this order:—

(a) "publication" means any book, newspaper, magazine, periodical, pamphlet, tract, circular, leaflet, handbill, poster or other printed matter;

(b) "enemy language" means the language of any country or people for the time being at war with Great Britain or any of her Allies or the langauge of any country (not belonging to Great Britain or any of her Allies) in whole or in part in occupation or under the control of the armed forces of any State or Sovereign for the time being at war with Great Britain or any of her Allies, and without restricting the generality of the foregoing terms, includes specifically the following languages: German, Austrian, Hungarian, Bulgarian, Turkish, Roumanian, Russian, Ukrainian, Finnish, Esthonian, Syrian, Croatian, Ruthenian and Livonian;

For the purpose of the foregoing definition, the certificate of the Secretary of State of Canada that the territory of any country (not belonging to Great Britain or any of her Allies) is in whole or in part in occupation or under the control of the armed forces of a State or Sovereign for the time being at war with Great Britain or any of her Allies shall be deemed to be conclusive evidence of the fact.

(c) "objectionable matter" shall be construed to extend and include the same matters and things as the expression extends to and includes under Order II, clause 1, exclusive of paragraph (m) thereof, of the Consolidated Orders respecting Censorship, dated May 21, 1918, which shall extend, apply, be construed and have effect with reference to this order as if it had been enacted as part thereof.

(d) "person" shall extend to and include any body of persons, corporate or unincorporate.

3. (1) Any person who, unless thereunto duly licensed by the Secretary of State, imports or brings into Canada, or after the 1st October, 1918, prints, publishes, posts, delivers, receives or has in his possession or on premises in his occupation or under his control within Canada, any publication in an enemy language shall be guilty of an offence and liable to a fine not exceeding $5,000 or to imprisonment not exceeding five years, or to both such fine and imprisonment, recoverable or enforceable either by indictment or by summary proceedings and conviction under the provisions of Part XV of the *Criminal Code:* Provided, however, that it shall be no offence under this section for any person to import or bring into Canada, or to print, publish, post, deliver, receive or have in his possession or on premises in his occupation under his control within Canada any publication in an enemy language

which is merely of a literary, scientific, religious or artistic character and does not contain any objectionable matter, or which under the authority of the law of any province, is prescribed in the curriculum of, or forms part of a course of instruction in any university, college, seminary, academy, school or other institution for education or for training in any vocation, but any such publication shall nevertheless be subject to the powers of the Secretary of State of Canada under this order.

(2) If in any prosecution for an offence under this section the person charged claims the benefit of the foregoing proviso the certificate of the Secretary of State of Canada that any publication in any enemy language is not of a literary, scientific, religious or artistic character, or that it contains objectionable matter shall be deemed to be conclusive evidence of the fact.

4. In any prosecution or proceedings brought, had or taken, under this order by or on behalf, or by direction or under the authority of the Attorney General of Canada or of the Attorney General of a province, all matters alleged in the information, charge or indictment shall be without proof rebuttably presumed to be true.

5. (1) The Postmaster General, or any one authorized by him, may, for the purpose of preventing the importation of the circulation or distribution of any publication in an enemy language in contravention of this order, open, examine and ascertain the contents of any newspaper, periodical, letter, circular, pamphlet, parcel or package which may be passing through the post or dealt with in any manner in the mails of Canada; and the like power is hereby conferred upon the Minister of Customs in relation to goods passing through the Customs of Canada.

(2) Any publication in any enemy language found in the mails or Customs of Canada in contravention of this order, shall be seized and held subject to the direction of the Secretary of State of Canada who many order the publication so seized to be destroyed or otherwise disposed of.

6. (1) The Secretary of State may, if he has reason to suspect that any land, building, or place, vehicle, receptacle, or other thing or anything therein or connected therewith has been or is being or is about to be used, constructed, or kept for the purpose of importing into Canada or printing, publishing, storing, delivering or distributing within Canada, any publication in an enemy language, in contravention of this order, or that there is in, on or about the same any publication in an enemy language imported or printed, published, issued, posted, delivered, received or possessed in contravention of this order, issue his warrant to any peace officer or constable directing him to enter, if need be by force, such land, building, or place, vehicle, receptacle, or other thing, at any time of the day or night, and examine and search and inspect the same or any part thereof, and to seize anything found therein or in or about the same or therewith connected, which he has reason to suspect has been or is being used or is intended to be used for any of the purposes aforesaid, including any type or other plant used or capable of being used for the printing or production of any such publication, and all copies of any such publication, or the printer's written copy thereof, and to close the premises used for any of the purposes aforesaid; and the Secretary of State may order anything so seized to be restored or otherwise disposed of, and the premises so closed to remain closed for such period as he may direct.

[2.] Any peace officer, police or constable, so authorized as in this or the next following section provided, may require the assistance of such persons and make use of such force as he may deem necessary for the execution of such warrant.

7. (1) Any judge of a Superior or County Court, or any police or stipendiary magistrate who is satisfied by information in writing upon oath that there is reasonable ground for believing that any land, building, or place, vehicle, receptacle or other thing, has been or is being or is about to be used, constructed or kept for the purpose of importing into Canada or printing, publishing, storing, delivering or distributing within Canada, any publication in an enemy language in contravention of this order, or that there is in, on or about the same any publication in an enemy language imported or printed, published, issued, posted, delivered, received or possessed in contravention of this order, may at any time issue a warrant under his hand, authorizing any constable or other person named therein to enter, if need be by force, such land, building, or place, vehicle, receptacle or other thing; at any time of the day or night, and to examine, search and inspect the same or any part thereof, and to seize and carry before the judge or magistrate issuing the warrant or a justice of the peace for the same territorial division, anything found therein which he has reason to suspect has been or is being used or is intended to be used for any of the purposes aforesaid, including any type or other plant used or capable of being used for printing or production of such publication, and all copies of any such publication.

(2) The judge, magistrate or justice before whom any publication in an enemy language, article or thing so seized is brought, may issue a summons requiring the owner to show cause why such publication, article or thing should not be destroyed, and if the owner does not appear in obedience to the summons, or if upon appearance, he does not satisfy the judge, magistrate or justice that such article or thing had not been used or was not being or intended to be used for any of the purposes in this section hereinbefore mentioned, or that such publication was not imported into Canada, or printed, published, issued, posted, delivered, received or possessed in contravention of this order, the judge, magistrate or justice may order them to be destroyed or otherwise disposed of, and in any other case shall order them to be restored on the expiration of seven clear days to the owner.

(3) For the purposes of this section a summons shall be deemed to be duly served if addressed to the owner of the property seized without further name or description and left at or sent by registered post to the premises on which the property was seized.

(4) If the prosecutor or complainant or any person who has appeared to show cause upon any such summons as aforesaid feels aggrieved by an order made in pursuance of this section, he may have the same remedy by way of appeal as he would if the proceedings under this section were brought or taken under Part XV of the *Criminal Code*.

SOURCE: *Canada Gazette*, 5 October 1918.

16. Regulations respecting unlawful associations, 25 September 1918

His Excellency the Governor General in Council, on recommendation of the Minister of Justice, and under the powers conferred by the *War Measures Act, 1914,* or otherwise existing in that behalf, is pleased to sanction and doth hereby sanction the following regulations:—

1. In and for the purposes of these regulations, or of any amending or further regulations relating to the matters herein provided for, unless there be something repugnant in the subject matter or context.

(a) "Minister" means the Minister of Justice, and includes the Deputy Minister of Justice.

(b) Where it is provided that any offence shall be punishable by fine and imprisonment it shall be competent to the court adjudging the punishment to impose either fine and imprisonment or both fine and imprisonment within the limits specified according to the discretion of the convicting magistrate.

(c) The provisions of *The Interpretation Act,* Revised Statutes of Canada, 1906, chapter 1, shall apply.

2. The following associations, organizations, societies or groups are hereby declared to be and shall while Canada is engaged in war be deemed to be unlawful, associations, viz:—

(a)The Industrial Workers of the World;
The Russian Social Democratic Party;
The Russian Revolutionary Group;
The Russian Social Revolutionists;
The Russian Workers Union;
The Ukrainian Social Democratic Party;
The Social Democratic Party;
The Social Labour Party;
Group of Social Democrats of Bolsheviki;
Group of Social Democrats of Anarchists;
The Workers International Industrial Union;
Chinese Nationalist League;
Chinese Labour Association;

(b) Any association, organization, society or corporation, one of whose purposes or professed purposes is to bring about any governmental, political, social, industrial, or economic change within Canada by the use of force, violence or physical injury to person or property, or by threats of such injury, or which teaches, advocates, advises or defends the use of force, violence, or physical injury to person or property or threats of such injury in order to accomplish such change or for any other purpose, or which shall by any means prosecute or pursue such purpose or professed purpose, or shall so teach, advocate, advise or defend while Canada is engaged in war;

(c) Any association which the Governor in Council by notice published in the *Canada Gazette* declares to be an unlawful association or within the description of the last preceding paragraph.

3. Any person who, while Canada is engaged in war, shall act, or profess to act as an officer of any such unlawful association, or who shall sell, speak, write or publish anything, as the representative or professed representative of any such unlawful

association or become or continue to be a member thereof, or wear, carry or cause to be displayed upon or about his person or elsewhere, any badge, insignia, emblem, banner, motto, pennant, card, or other device whatsoever, indicating or intended to show or suggest that he is a member of or in anywise associated with any such unlawful association, or who shall contribute anything as dues, or otherwise to it or to any one for it, or who shall solicit subscriptions or contributions therefor, shall be guilty of an offence against these regulations, punishable by imprisonment for not less than one year and not more than five years.

4. In any prosecution under this Act, if it be proved that the person charged has at any time since the beginning of the present war been a member of an unlawful association, it shall be presumed in the absence of proof to the contrary that he was and continued to be a member thereof at all times material to the case; and if it be proved that the person charged since the beginning of the war repeatedly:

(a) attended meetings of an unlawful association; or

(b) spoke publicly in advocacy of an unlawful association; or

(c) distributed literature of an unlawful association it shall be presumed in the absence of proof to the contrary that he is a member of such unlawful association.

5. Where in any prosecution any question of unlawful intent or purpose is in issue the fact that the accused is a member of an unlawful association which practises, advocates, or incites with that intent or purpose shall be relevant to the issue.

6. Any owner, lessee, agent, or superintendent or any building, room, premises or place, who while Canada is engaged in war, knowingly permits therein any meeting of an unlawful association, or of any subsidiary association or branch or committee thereof, or any assemblage of persons who teach, advocate, advise or defend the use without authority of law, of force, violence, or physical injury to person or property, or threats of such injury, shall be guilty of an offence against these regulations, punishable by fine of not more than $5,000 and imprisonment for not more than five years.

7. (1) Any property, real or personal, belonging or suspected to belong to an unlawful association, or held or suspected to be held by any person for, or on behalf thereof may, without warrant, be seized or taken possession of by any person thereunto authorized by the Minister or by the Chief Commissioner of Dominion Police, and may thereupon be forfeited to His Majesty.

(2) Any books, newspapers, periodicals, pamphlets, pictures, papers, circulars, cards, letters, writings, prints, handbills, posters, publications or documents of any kind issued by or on behalf of an unlawful association or advocating its propaganda may, without warrant, be seized or taken possession of by any peace officer, police officer or constable, or by any person thereunto authorized by the Minister, and may thereupon be forfeited to His Majesty.

(3) Any person thereunto authorized may without warrant at any hour of the day or night with such assistance as he may require, break into and enter any premises or place owned or suspected to be owned or occupied by an unlawful association, or in which any member of an unlawful association is or is believed to be, and seize any articles, books, documents or papers found therein which belong or are suspected to belong to, or to be used or intended to be used for the purpose of

any unlawful association or for any prohibited or unlawful purpose, and the same may thereupon be forfeited to His Majesty.

(4) A person shall be deemed to be thereunto authorized, within the meaning of this section, if he is authorized in writing by the Minister, or by the Chief Commissioner of Dominion Police, or by any judge of a superior or county court, or by any police or stipendiary magistrate.

8. Any person who, while Canada is engaged in war, knowingly prints, publishes, edits, issues, circulates, sells, offers for sale, or distributes any book, newspaper, periodical, pamphlet, picture, paper, circular, card, letter, writing, print, publication or document of any kind in which is taught, advocated, advised or defended or who shall in any manner teach, advocate, advise or defend the use, without authority of law, of force, violence, or physical injury of person or property, or threats of such injury as a means of accomplishing any governmental, political, social, industrial or economic change or otherwise, shall be guilty of an offence against these regulations punishable by imprisonment for not more than five years and not less than one year.

9. No meeting or assemblage of any kind except church meetings or meetings for religious services only, shall be held in Canada during the present war at which the proceedings or any part thereof are conducted in the language or any of the languages of any country or portion of any country with which Canada is at war, or in the language or any of the languages, of Russia, Ukraine or Finland, and any persons wilfully attending or taking part in any meeting prohibited as aforesaid by this section shall be guilty of an offence against these regulations punishable by a fine of not more than $5,000 and imprisonment for not more than five years, and if found committing such offence may be apprehended without warrant by any peace officer, police officer or constable and taken before any magistrate having jurisdiction to be dealt with according to law.

10. Any person who during the present war wilfully attends or takes part in any meeting or assemblage of persons

(a) At which the doctrines or propaganda of an unlawful association are advocated or defended; or

(b) At which false reports or statements are made which may interfere, or tend to interfere with the operation or success of the military or naval forces of Canada or the Empire or its Allies, or which may cause, or incite or tend to cause or incite sedition, disloyalty, insubordination, mutiny or refusal of duty in the military or naval forces of Canada, or obstruct or interfere with the recruiting or enlistment services of Canada or whereby injury or mischief is likely to be occasioned to any public interest; or

(c) At which any seditious, disloyal, profane, scurrilous or abusive language is uttered as to the established form of government of Canada or as to the military or naval forces or flags of Canada or of the Empire or its Allies or the uniform of the military or naval forces of Canada or of the Empire or its Allies; or

(d) At which any language is uttered tending to bring the established form of government of Canada or her military or naval forces or the flags of Canada or of the Empire or its Allies into contempt, scorn, contumely or disrepute; or

(e) At which any language is uttered which may tend to incite, provoke or encourage resistance to Canada or the Empire or its Allies, or to promote the cause of its or their enemies, or which may tend to urge, incite or encourage any curtailment of production in Canada of any things or products necessary or essential to the prosecution of the war; or

(f) At which any language is uttered which may tend to cause disaffection to His Majesty or to prejudice the relations of His Majesty with any foreign state, or to assist or encourage His Majesty's enemies or otherwise prevent, embarrass or hinder the successful prosecution of any war in which Canada is engaged; or

(g) Who by any act supports or favours the cause of any country with which Canada is at war or opposes the cause for which Canada is at war; shall be guilty of an offence against these regulations punishable by imprisonment for not more than five years and not less than one year.

11. (1) If any judge of any superior or county court, police or stipendiary magistrate is satisfied by information on oath that there is reasonable ground for suspecting that any contravention of these regulations has been, or is about to be committed, he may issue a search warrant under his hand authorizing any peace officer, police officer or constable, with such assistance as he may require, to enter at any time any premises or place mentioned in the warrant, if necessary, by force, and to search such premises or place and every persons found therein, and to seize and carry away any books, periodicals, pamphlets, pictures, papers, circulars, cards, letters, writings, prints, handbills, posters, publications or documents which are found on or in such premises or place, or in the possession of any person therein in contravention of these regulations and the same when so seized and carried away may be forfeited to His Majesty.

12. The punishments and penalties provided by these regulations may be enforced or recovered by indictment, or upon summary conviction in the manner prescribed by Part XV of the *Criminal Code*, before any judge of a superior or county court, or any police or stipendiary magistrate, or before two justices of the peace, or any magistrate having the authority of two justices of the peace.

13. Where by these regulations it is provided that any property may be forfeited to His Majesty, the forfeiture may be adjudged or declared by any judge of a superior or county court, or by any police or stipendiary magistrate, or by any magistrate having the authority of two justices of the peace, in a summary manner; and by the procedure provided by Part XV of the *Criminal Code* in so far as applicable or subject to such adaptations as may be necessary to meet the circumstances of the case.

14. Nothing in these regulations contained shall be deemed to affect the liability of any person offending against these regulations for or to any penalty, punishment, or liability which he would have incurred or been subject to for or in respect of any offence committed, or anything done, published or said, if these regulations had not been passed; and the fines, penalties or punishments herein provided shall be deemed to be cumulative or additional to, and not in any wise to displace or relieve from, any fine, penalty, punishment or liability heretofore provided by law for the same or the like offence.

SOURCE: *Canada Gazette*, 5 October 1918.

17. Order in Council amending the Order in Council respecting enemy publications, 13 November 1918

His Excellency the Governor General in Council, on the recommendation of the Minister of Justice and under the powers conferred by The War Measures Act, 1914, or otherwise vested in the Governor in Council, is pleased to order and it is hereby ordered as follows:—

1. Section 3 of the Order Respecting Enemy Publications, of the 25th of September, 1918, is hereby amended by the addition thereto of the following subsection:—

3. Any license issued by the Secretary of State of Canada under subsection 1 of this section authorizing the printing or publishing of any publication, other than a book, in an enemy language within Canada shall, whether the license is so expressed or not, be deemed to be and is hereby made subject to the conditions that all matter in an enemy language printed in such publication and a true and correct translation of the same, in either the English or French language, shall be printed and appear therein in parallel columns the subject matter whereof shall identically correspond and agree, and that there shall, moreover, be printed or stamped in or on such publication in a conspicuous place the words or inscription in English or French and the enemy language: "This publication is licensed by the Secretary of State under the Order respecting Enemy Publications," and it shall be no offence for any person within Canada to post, deliver, receive or have in his possession or on premises in his occupation or under his control any such publication in an enemy language so licensed and so published; Provided, however, that the license issued by the Secretary of State shall endure only so long as the condition mentioned in this subsection is faithfully observed; and if any person to whom a license is issued violates the terms of the condition aforementioned either by failure to publish the translation or by failure to publish the same in the manner subject to the terms hereinbefore required in respect of the whole or of any part of the matter in an enemy language printed in the publication so licensed or by printing or publishing a translation which is considered by the Secretary of State to be incorrect and misleading in an important particular, or by omitting to print or stamp in or on such publication the words or inscription hereinbefore referred to, the license issued to such person shall forthwith, *ipso facto*, be cancelled, and such person shall moreover be deemed to be guilty of an offence and liable to a fine not exceeding five thousand dollars, or to imprisonment not exceeding five years or to both such fine and imprisonment in respect of each breach of the terms of the condition aforesaid, recoverable or enforceable by indictment or by summary conviction under Party XV of the Criminal Code.

2. The Said Order in Council, as amended by the present order, shall not apply to the Polish or the Arabic language, or to the language of the Czecho-Slovak Nation.

SOURCE: *Canada Gazette*, 30 November 1918.

F. IMMIGRATION

18. An act to amend the Immigration Act, assented to 6 June 1919

[*Subsection six of section three barred the following classes of immigrants from entering Canada—Ed.*]

. . .

(6) Section three of the said Act is further amended by adding the following paragraphs thereto:—

"(j) Persons who in the opinion of the Board of Inquiry or the officer in charge at any port of entry are likely to become a public charge;

"(k) Persons of constitutional psychopathic inferiority;

"(l) Persons with chronic alcoholism;

"(m) Persons not included within any of the foregoing prohibited classes, who upon examination by a medical officer are certified as being mentally or physically defective to such a degree as to affect their ability to earn a living;

"(n) Persons who believe in or advocate the overthrow by force or violence of the Government of Canada or of constituted law and authority, or who disbelieve in or are oppposed to organized government, or who advocate the assassination of public officials, or who advocate or teach the unlawful destruction of property;

"(o) Persons who are members of or affiliated with any organization entertaining or teaching disbelief in or opposition to organized governemnt, or advocating or teaching the duty, necessity, or propriety of the unlawful assaulting or killing of any officer or officers, either of specific individuals or of officers generally, of the Government of Canada or of any other organized government, because of his or their official character, or advocating or teaching the unlawful destruction of property;

"(p) Enemy aliens or persons who have been alien enemies and who were or may be interned on or after the eleventh day of November, one thousand nine hundred and eighteen, in any part of His Majesty's dominions or by any of His Majesty's allies;

"(q) Persons guilty of espionage with respect to His Majesty or any of His Majesty's allies;

"(r) Persons who have been found guilty of high treason or treason for an offence in connection with the war, or of conspiring against His Majesty, or of assisting His Majesty's enemies during the war, or of any similar offence against any of His Majesty's allies;

"(s) Persons who at any time within a period of ten years from the first day of August, one thousand nine hundred and fourteen, were or may be deported from any part of His Majesty's dominions or from any allied country on account of treason or of conspiring against His Majesty, or of any similar offence in connection with the war against any of the allies of His Majesty, or because such persons were or may be regarded as hostile or dangerous to the allied cause during the war;

"(t) On and after the first day of July, one thousand nine hundred and nineteen, in addition to the foregoing 'prohibited classes,' the following persons shall also be prohibited from entering or landing in Canada:—Persons over fifteen years of age, physically capable of reading, who cannot read the English or the French language or some other language or dialect: Provided that any admissible person or any person heretofore or hereafter legally admitted, or any citizen of Canada, may bring in or send for his father or grandfather, over fifty-five years of age, his wife, his mother, his grandmother or his unmarried or widowed daughter, if otherwise admissible, whether such relative can read or not and such relative shall be permitted to enter. For the purpose of ascertaining whether aliens can read, the immigration officer shall use slips of uniform size prepared by direction of the Minister, each containing not less than thirty and not more than forty words in ordinary use printed in plainly legible type in the language or dialect the person may designate as the one in which he desires the examination to be made, and he shall be required to read the words printed on the slip in such language or dialect. The provisions of this paragraph shall not apply to Canadian citizens and persons who have Canadian domicile, to persons in transit through Canada, or to such persons or classes of persons as may from time to time be approved by the Minister."

SOURCE: Canada. *Statutes*, 9-10 Geo. 5, chap. 25.
[*The enemy alien clause in the 1919 Act was repealed by An Act to Amend the Immigration Act, assented to on 30 June 1923—Ed.*]

APPENDIX III

UKRAINIAN INDEPENDENCE

19. Disposition of Eastern Galicia

Sir SAM HUGHES: I have received a cablegram sent by Roman Kramer [*sic*], of Winnipeg, on behalf of the Galicians, of whom there are upwards of four millions in Eastern Galicia, intimating that the fact was to be made public yesterday aby President Wilson and Mr. Lloyd George that that territory, three-quarters of the population of which is made up of Ukrainian people, contrary to the general under-standing, was being handed over to Poland instead of to Ukrania. This is a matter which the Government has had before it on several occasions and I desire to ask what are the facts of the case and if there is any satisfactory and sufficient reason why seventy-five per cent of the population, numbering four or five millions of people, should be handed over to be governed by the Poles?

Sir GEORGE FOSTER: I am afraid one ear was listening to something else while this question was being asked, but if I apprehend the nature of the interrogation, it is this—

Sir SAM HUGHES: I did not catch the minister's first remark.

Sir GEORGE FOSTER: It is not very vital so it is not necessary to repeat it.

Sir SAM HUGHES: The members of the Government are here to answer the questions of the people's representatives.

Mr. SPEAKER: Order. On the Orders of the Day it is for the Government to answer or not, as they choose.

Sir GEORGE FOSTER: To make it perfectly clear I said that at the time the question was being put by my hon. friend in rather indistinct tones, that one of my ears was trying to catch something else, and I did not succeed in gathering the full purport of his question. However, if I understand it aright, the hon. gentleman wants to know whether the Government has any reasons to give why a certain number of people are allocated by the executive of the Peace Conference, or by the Peace Conference, to one country rather than to another. My hon. friend will realize that that is a pretty difficult question for the Canadian Government or myself to answer—

Sir SAM HUGHES: It is a matter that has been before the Government for a long time.

Sir GEORGE FOSTER: —but if he will entrust the telegram to me I will have an answer ready for to-morrow. Whether it will be satisfactory or not, I do not know.

Sir SAM HUGHES: If I may be permitted to make myself clear—this is a matter which has been before the Government for a long time, and before the hon. gentleman returned from Europe Mr. Lloyd George intimated in a cablegram to your humble servant as well as to the Prime Minister of Canada that the matter was being looked after and that these people would in all probability be allocated to Ukrania instead of Poland.

Sir GEORGE FOSTER: Then I suppose we will have to ask Mr. Lloyd George why this has not been done—

Sir SAM HUGHES: It is a matter for the Canadian Government to look after—

Sir GEORGE FOSTER: —and the reasons why it was not done. I am afraid the Government of Canada could not give an affirmative or negative answer.

Sir SAM HUGHES: Then we will have to get after the Government with a sharp stick.

SOURCE: Canada. *Parliamentary Debates* (Commons), 139, 1(1919): 902-3.

20. West Ukrainian National Republic

[26 February 1923]

Mr. M.N. CAMPBELL (Mackenzie) moved:

Whereas Eastern Galicia and Northern Bukowina were constituted on November 9, 1918, as an independent state under the name of West Ukrainian Republic;

And whereas the integrity of this state is guaranteed by the League of Nations of which League Canada is a member; therefore be it resolved that this House urge upon the government the desirability of making representations through its accredited representatives, to the Councils of the League of Nations, the necessity of early, complete and final settlement of the Ukrainian·question.

He said: Mr. Speaker, in presenting the case in support of the resolution before the House, perhaps it is essential that should give a brief resume of the history of the Ukraine and of the Ukrainian people in order that we may arrive at a better understanding of the question. From the dawn of history, there has been a distinct Ukrainian race with a language of its own and possessing a literature that is a thousand years old. The early history of the Ukraine is one series of bloody wars with the Poles and Lithuanians on the west, the Muscovites on the north, and the Turks and Tartars on the east. These wars gave rise to the organization of the renowned Cossacks or free warriors to defend the Ukraine against these invaders. Their early institutions appear to have been very democratic and their Hetman or President was elected by popular vote of the fighting men, and all authority lay in the hands of a general assembly whose decisions were enforced by elective officers.

In 1854 [*sic*], for mutual protection against the Poles on the one side and the Turks on the other, the independent Ukrainian state signed a Treaty of Union with Russia. This union gradually developed into subjugation of the state to Russia. The Cossacks were given many privileges, and became part of Russia's best fighting force. By a treaty with Poland, Russia conceded Galicia, the western part of the Ukraine, to Poland. On the dismemberment of the latter country in 1772 Galicia or west Ukraine became Austrian territory, and remained so until 1918. On the breaking up of that Empire, the members of the Austrian diet representing the eastern part of Galicia met and formed a national government and proclaimed the independent state of West Ukraine. This country has a population of about 6,000,000, seventy-four per cent of which is Ukrainian, about twelve per cent Poles, the balance German and Jews. It is a rich country with oil wells, forests and productive land.

Poland, remembering that this had been a part of her ancient kingdom, invaded the infant state in November 1918, and a bloody war ensued with varying success for several months. The Poles made insistent demands on the Allies for assistance in repelling the supposed Bolsheviks from East Galicia. Fearing the spread of the Bolshevik movement west, the Supreme Council of the Peace Conference consented to military occupation of the country by the Poles with the understanding that the right of self-determination was eventually to prevail. Later, the army commanded by

General Haller was placed at the disposal of Poland. General Haller was a former Austrian officer and his army was composed of Poles recruited from the Allied armies, principally from the army of the United States. This army was well trained, equipped and provisioned and against it the poorly armed fighting force of the Ukrainian state made desperate but ineffectual resistance. Attacked by the Bolsheviki on the one side and by the Poles on the other, the greater part of the army was destroyed, the remnant taking refuge in Czecho-Slovakia. Since then Poland has been in control of the state and is using her military power to stamp out the national and intellectual life of the Ukrainian people. She has taken measures toward incorporating East Galicia into the Polish state. This action the people are fiercely resisting, and are daily coming into bloody conflict with the Polish officers. These conflicts are resulting in a destruction of life and property almost as bad as actual warfare. It is estimated that during the past season over $100,000,000 worth of grain and other farm produce has been destroyed by the peasants rather than have it confiscated by their oppressors. Some idea of the suffering endured by the people of this little state may be understood from the fact that it is estimated that upwards of 100,000 of its soldiers and civilians have died in Polish prisons and detention camps. I have here a mass of evidence dealing with this, but it is too lengthy to give here. I will confine myself to a quotation, not from a Ukrainian but from a Polish paper. The "Robotnik" published in Warsaw in its issue of October 16, 1919, has this to say of the conditions accorded the Ukrainian prisoners in Polish prisons and detention camps:

> The conditions prevailing in the camps for war prisoners in Modlin and Brest are horrible. That at Brest is disgusting and a disgrace to the Polish State.

Then follows a long description of the living quarters and the conditions under which these men are obliged to live.

> Two months ago from 50 to 100 dead were daily taken out of this camp in which about 6,000 prisoners of war were confined. When the interned come out of the camp and stand in line to receive their rations—a veritable procession of death presents itself. All are famished and half frozen. They scramble and fight for the sparce food and the bits left over by the soldiers in the kitchen. They eat wild berries, and even grass.

Then follows a description of the rather brutal treatment meted out to the prisoners by the soldiers.

> In the night they shiver with cold, since they are covered only with rags. Once they tried to light a fire in the camp, but they were chased away by the soldiers with musket butts and the fire extinguished "for fear many might be suffocated by the smoke". They are so enfeebled that they are scarcely able to walk, and give this in excuse when commanded to a more rapid gait. For this they are treated with blows from the butts of muskets, the soldiers deal these out generously, because the "men will die anyhow".

Some of them beg "make an end of it soldier, I have starved enough". In consequence of these blows many really died, they were too weak to stand them. A soldier from Posen goes about constantly with a stick, strikes at random, hitting a head here, a face there and so on; some have even had their eyes knocked out. In despair many have jumped into the river and were drowned, others cut their throats with their knives. Terrible!

Some committees were sent there by the Polish Diet, matters were to be improved. Some of the evil-doers were arrested, and when for a second time enquiries were instituted, order was quickly established. Nevertheless these awful conditions continue and will grow still worse in the coming winter.

It is high time that the guilty be held responsible, it is time to expose this terrible state of affairs to the public.

By the Treaty of St. Germain September 10, 1919, Austria surrendered all interest in East Galicia in favour of the allied governments, who by thus accepting this territory from Austria have become responsible for its final disposal, and morally liable for the protection and welfare of its people. The Supreme Council on December 8th, 1919, drew up Poland's frontier known to-day as the Curzon line between Poland and East Galicia, confirming the fact that East Galicia is outside Polish territory. This is an indication that the action of Poland is illegal, unwarranted and immoral. In the Treaty of Sevres, June 10, 1920, East Galicia appears as a distinct contracting party, recognized as such by the representatives of the allied governments. Again in the Treaty of Spa, July 10, 1920, between Poland and the Allies, Poland stated implicitly that East Galicia was the property of the Allies and promised to evacuate the state on the demand of the allied governments. United States Secretary of State Colby, in a note of August 10, 1920, to the Italian Ambassador and in a statement to the press on October 10, 1920, stated emphatically that Poland must be an ethnographic state and that she must accept the Curzon line as her extreme eastern boundary. He also declared that the government of the United States advised Poland to withdraw her forces from all territory lying to the east of the Curzon line. On this occasion Mr. Colby made mention of East Galicia. He expressed his regret over the fact that Poland led by Imperialism, occupied Vilna, the capital of Lithuania, in the same arbitrary and lawless manner in which she previously had occupied East Galicia. On December 15, 1920 the Executive Committee of the League of Nations Society of London passed a resolution calling upon the British government to take action with a view to establishing the national independence of East Galicia. Similarly on March 20, 1922 the Council of the French League of Nations Society called upon the French government to take action. The Council of the League of Nations at its meeting February 23rd, 1921, reported to the Council of Ambassadors at Paris impressing upon them the necessity of settling the political status of East Galicia. At a meeting of the League of Nations at Geneva on September 23rd, 1921, the Hon. Mr. Doherty, one of the Canadian representatives, moved the following resolution:

That the Assembly of the League of Nations draw the attention of the Supreme Council to the desirability of determining at an early date the legal status of East Galicia.

This resolution was passed unanimously by the league. I have here the report of the Canadian delegate to the third assembly of the League of Nations whose conferences were held between the 3rd and the 30th of September, 1922. On page 4 I find the following:

At the second assembly, on the motion of a Canadian delegate, a resolution was adopted expressing hope of an early setlement [*sic*] of the question of the status of Eastern Galicia. That matter being still unsettled, Mr. Fielding moved a renewal of the expression of last year in the following terms:

"The Assembly of the League of Nations renews its wish, expressed in the resolution adopted by the second assembly on September 27, 1921, that the council of the league draw the attention of the principal allied and associated powers to the desirability of determining at an early date the status of Eastern Galicia."

I beg leave to place upon Hansard a resolution passed at a public meeting held in the city of Winnipeg in May last and which resolution deals fully with this matter. This is signed by the chairman, Rev. Dr. Gordon, the mover, Mr. J.W. Arsenych; and the seconder, Mr. W.R. Wood.

Resolution re: Ukraine

Whereas, Eastern Galicia and Northern Bukowina were constituted on November 9th, 1918, as an independent state under the name of Eastern [*sic.*] Ukrainian Republic;

Whereas, a government of this state was formed by the duly elected representatives of the population of the state and the government under presidency of Dr. Eugene Perushevich still exists—in exile:

Whereas, Poland made an aggressive war upon the Western Ukrainian Republic in order to gain possession of her rich oil-fields, forests and lands;

Whereas, on June 25th, 1919, upon Polish representations, Poland was authorized by the Supreme Council of the Peace Conference to occupy Eastern Galicia by military force, the future of the territory to be decided by the Peace Conference, Rumania in the meantime occupying Northern Bukowina:

Whereas, the territory of Western Ukrainian Republic was described as an entirely separate entity by the Treaty of St. Germain (September 10th, 1919), by the settlement of Spa (July 10, 1920), by the Treaty of Sevres (August 10, 1920) and by the declaration of British government (by Mr. Harmsworth, Under-Secretary to the Minister of Foreign Affairs), in the British House of Commons (July 6th, 1921):

Whereas the Assembly of the League of Nations September 23rd, 1921, upon Motion of the Canadian Representative, Hon. Charles D. Doherty, unanimously passed the following resolution:—

"That the Assembly of the League of Nations draw the attention of the Supreme Council to the desirability of determining at an early date the legal status of Eastern Galicia."

Whereas, up to the present date the legal status of the territory of Western Ukrainian Republic has not been determined:

Whereas, since occupation of the Western Ukrainian territory until present moment, Poland assumes right of sovereignty over this territory and exercises same:

Whereas, this undetermined legal status of the Western Ukrainian Republic and Polish pretensions created abnormal conditions there; and

Whereas, according to press reports, private letters and testimony of eye-witnesses arriving in Canada, the following state of affairs obtains in Galicia: Poland forces Ukrainians to accept Polish allegiance and change of religion: Poland suppresses Ukrainian language on Ukrainian territory; Polish authorities have suppressed Ukrainian public schools, high schools and higher educational institutions and do not allow to establish private schools; thousands of Ukrainian youth are deprived of educational facilities: Ukrainian lectures at the University of Lemberg are abolished; when a private Ukrainian University was established in Lemberg, its president, some professors and many students were imprisoned; practically all Ukrainian cultural, social and benevolent institutions were crippled, hampered and ultimately suppressed and prohibited, and Ukrainian Citizens' Relief Committee at Lemberg, which was handling the Ukrainian Red Cross moneys collected in Canada for the relief of Ukrainians, was deliberately disorganized and prevented from working by the Polish government: Ukrainian economic organizations are prevented to engage in reconstruction of the country: Ukrainian public men are being persecuted, imprisoned, slain or starved without reasonable cause: Ukrainian press is hampered, confiscated and suppressed; with the aid of military forces, a census of population was instituted by Polish authorities, and Ukrainians under pain of imprisonment and maltreatment and heavy fines were forced to declare allegiance to Poland; Eastern Galicia is being colonized by Polish immigrants while the Ukrainians are not allowed to buy land; Polish authorities make requisitions of grain and cattle without payments; the Polish Diet in Warsaw imposed upon Eastern Galicia an extraordinary levy of 20,000,000,000 Polish marks for the upkeep of the large Polish army of occupation; the population of Eastern Galicia, impoverished by the continuous war of eight years' duration will be brought to utter ruin by this levy:

Now therefore be it resolved that we the Canadian citizens in mass meeting assembled in the Convention Hall, City of Winnipeg, this 22nd day of April, 1922, hereby urge the Dominion government and Imperial British government:—

1. To cause a searching investigation of the conditions existing in Eastern Galicia, and to see that justice is done.

2. To see that the claims of the Ukrainian people to an independent state within their ethnographical boundaries and the political status of Eastern Galicia be finally determined.

And that copies of this resolution be forwarded to the Imperial government and to the Delegation of the British Empire at the Economic Conference at Genoa.

Chairman, Dr. C.W. Gordon;
Mover, J.W. Arsenych,
Seconder, W.R. Wood.

I also wish to quote briefly from an address delivered at this meeting by the Rev. Dr. Hunter:

The Ukrainians are the third largest national group in Canada. They number in this country at the lowest estimate 350,000 people. It is time the English-speaking people were getting better acquainted with them.... People of the British races have always believed in fair play and in justice. When nearly half a million of our Canadian population are kept in distress and agitation by reports of hideous cruelty to their friends and relatives in Europe, it is a matter that concerns Canada.

And further, from the Rev. J.M. Shaver's address on the same occasion:

I am here, in the second place, because I believe that your helping your people at home does not make you less valuable Canadians but on the other hand makes you more valuable. The man who can easily forget the land which gave him his mother, his basic moral principles, his early loves and hates and hopes and fears, is a dangerous man. I am always expecting such a man to be a "crook" of some sort. It is the strongest characters who do not change so easily.

Further on Mr. Shaver states:

This brings me the expression of some reasons why you have a right to ask for our sympathy. First of all, because we know what freedom is and we know that the only way to keep our freedom is to help others to get it.

Second, because your sacrifice to save Europe from the invading Tartar and Turk was a sacrifice for us, for which we have never been able to pay.

Third, because you are largest non-English speaking group of fellow-citizens in western Canada to-day.

The occupation of East Galicia by the military forces of Poland remains in force to the present day. But this occupation is provisional and will cease just as soon as the Supreme Council determines the political relationship of this country. In other words the ultimate international status of East Galicia remains as yet to be defined, and the duty of determining this status devolves upon the allied and associated powers or their representative body, the Supreme Council of the Peace Conference, because by article 91 of the Treaty of Saint Germain, the allied and associated powers are the sovereigns of East Galicia.

Until recently, settlers in this country from East Galicia were described on their naturalization certificates as "Citizens of Poland." During the past session, I had frequent interviews with the Under Secretary of State about this matter; and in my letter to him of June 22nd, I dealt with the legal status of these people and pointed out that in reality they were wards of the allied governments. The department, I understand, referred the subject of my letter to the British authorities, and I have here a letter from the department, which in part reads as follows:

Adverting to Mr. Mulvey's letter to you of June 22, 1922, with respect to applicants for naturalization of Ukrainian origin, I beg to inform you that this department is now describing such persons as "subjects of allied powers" and any applicants who received certificates describing them as "Poles" may have their certificates changed by returning them to this department.

The action of the under-secretary of State in this matter of naturalization is greatly appreciated by my constituents as well as by all the people of Ukrainian origin in Canada. If anything further were necessary to prove to this House that Poland has no legal status in East Galicia, it is the fact that our own Department of Secretary of State now legally describes people from that country as "subjects of the allied powers." To-day, 350,000 Canadians of Ukrainian origin beseech the Canadian parliament to hearken to the agonized appeal of 4,000,000 of their suffering and oppressed countrymen in Central Europe. Do not fail them in this the hour of their need. Show them that the great heart of the Canadian people goes out to them in this, their country's darkest hour. Tell them that the country that laid 60,000 of her best and bravest sons on the altar of sacrifice that one small country might be free, has a sympathy as deep as her mighty lakes, as wide as her noble prairies, as vast as her natural heritage; and that this appeal in the interest of justice and right shall not go unheeded by the representatives of the people of Canada.

Mr. L.P. BANCROFT (Selkirk): I desire to say a few words in reference to this important resolution brought forward by the hon. member for Mackenzie (Mr. Campbell), who stated that it might be well for the people of Canada to cultivate the acquaintance of our Ukrainian settlers. We have in Canada to-day about 350,000 of these people who have been settled in the western part of the country for about twenty years. In that time they have developed perhaps more rapidly than any other non-English speaking class of immigrants who have come to this country. So great has been their development that to-day there are hundreds of their young men and women teaching English in our public schools in Manitoba. Quite a number of their women are graduate nurses, while there are several lawyers among them. You will find these people in the high schools and universities of western Canada. There are a large number of successful merchants among them carrying on business according to the standards that are recognized and pursued in this country. They also include a large body of farmers, and they are a people that lean naturally towards mixed farming. Possibly one reason for this is the fact that they produce large families and in this way provide that free labour without which mixed farming cannot be carried on in Canada. Recently they elected four of their nationality as members of the local legislature of Manitoba and these men hold their own with our own people very well. The young Ukrainian men and women who have grown up in this country in the last twenty years and who have been educated in our schools speak English as fluently and as correctly as our own people. In fact their whole record in Canada is one of which any people might be proud. Now, it may be suggested that these people, now that they have made their homes in this country, should forget their troubles in the old land and settle down to business here. But we must remember that they have relatives back in their native country who are being persecuted and if they neglected to look after the welfare of their relatives in any part of the world, they would, I think, be neglecting one of the first duties of citizenship.

In presenting this resolution we are not asking that Canada should interfere in European questions. We are merely asking that Canada take an interest in these new Canadians and so help to make them better citizens, because I believe, Sir, that the best way to make an immigrant take an interest in his country is for the country to take an interest in him. In a word, we are merely asking the government to request the League of Nations to look fully into this question and see that justice is done in Eastern Galicia.

Mr. A.L. BEAUBIEN (Provencher): I do not intend to speak at length on this resolution, Mr. Speaker, because the mover (Mr. Campbell) presented the case in a manner so complete and convincing that it was apparent he had made a study of it. I had the pleasure last year in this House to defend these people when they were being ridiculed by some hon. members for wearing sheepskin coats. Now I am here to urge on the government the desirability of making representations to the League of Nations so that these Ukrainians will be freed from further oppression at the hands of the Poles. I know very well these Ukrainians who have made their homes in western Canada, and I can endorse everything that my hon. friend from Selkirk (Mr. Bancroft) has said about their good qualities as Canadian citizens. As he stated, they generally have large families, and if we had more of these people in the prairies there would be no need for the hon. Minister of the Interior (Mr. Stewart) to encourage child immigration from the British Isles. These people are working hard and making a success of their farms, although their land is more or less inferior in quality, but they are dogged and persevering and will stand the bumps and succeed where we would fail.

We are very proud of that British fair play which we hear so much about. Well, this is a good time to exercise it. When the friends and relatives of these citizens of Canada are being oppressed in Europe, it is the duty of the government to prove to them that we actually practise British fair play, that it is not a mere expression, but means something that can be invoked for the succour of the oppressed. Therefore I think this resolution should receive the unanimous support of this House and that the government should thereupon make representations to the League of Nations urging upon it the desirability and necessity of an early and final settlement of the Ukrainian boundaries, and so relieve the friends and relatives of our Ukrainian fellow ctizens from the sufferings they are now enduring at the hands of Poland.

Mr. H.E. SPENCER (Battle River): I wish to speak very briefly in suport [*sic.*] of the resolution, Mr. Speaker. I happen to have a great many of these people in my constituency, and I can vouch for their good qualities—given a fair chance they are among the best immigrants we have and develop into very good Canadian citizens. I think we cannot do better than ask the government to bring the request of these people before the League of Nations, so that they may realize the value of their Canadian citizenship and its effectiveness in relieving the distress of their friends and relatives in the west Ukrainian Republic.

Mr. ROBERT FORKE (Brandon): Mr. Speaker, it is a far cry from Canada to the Ukraine. However, I happen to have a certain number of Ukrainians in my constituency, and I feel a great deal of interest in them for I find them to be admirable settlers who invariably develop into good Canadians.

But I am not exactly clear about the situation that is involved in this resolution. When we contemplate the troubled state of Europe and the chaotic conditions brought about by the warring and hatred that prevail there, we may be pardoned for wondering just exactly what can be done in the present situation. I have no doubt that the arrangement referred to was made by the League of Nations, and that it was agreed that the boundary line separating the new state from Poland should be definitely ascertained. But while the hon. gentlemen were discussing the resolution I had been thinking that perhaps some member of the government who understands the situation might explain it to us so that we could act intelligently. I repeat, I am not at all clear on the situation. Naturally we would all wish to see peace restored in Europe, and personally I desire to show every sympathy for the friends and relatives of our fellow citizens from the Ukraine, but until we know the situation it is difficult to act effectively. Perhaps we may get the required information from the government.

Hon. W.S. FIELDING (Minister of Finance): If there was any question as to the character of these Ukrainian fellow citizens of ours in the West, I am sure we would all appreciate the information we have received from hon. members who have spoken in praise of them. I do not understand, however, that there is any such question.

I am inclined to think that the preamble of this resolution is based upon a misapprehension of one or two important points. It states that the integrity of the West Ukrainian Republic has been guaranteed by the League of Nations. I think that is a mistake. To the best of my knowledge and belief the Western Ukrainian Republic was never recognized by the League of Nations. I am afraid some of us will have to confess that our knowledge of eastern European politics is not sufficient to warrant us going very deeply into this question, but so far as we would appear to be justified in attempting to deal with it I would call my hon. friend's attention to the fact that that which he is asking to be done by this resolution has already been done. In the session of the second Assembly of 1921 the representative of Canada, the Hon. Mr. Doherty, introduced a resolution on the subject. Wisely, he did not attempt to decide the merits of the dispute. The Poles have always claimed that Eastern Galicia has been Polish for ages, and it is in their hands now under mandate. Of course, it is desirable that the condition should not remain, that the doubt should be removed and the status of Eastern Galicia determined. Mr. Doherty wisely did not attempt to say how the question should be determined, but he did say, in the name of Canada, that it should be settled. The League of Nations has no power to settle it. All the League can do is to express its opinion as to the desirability of settling this long-standing difficult question. The resolution proposed by Mr. Doherty was accepted.

At the recent sitting of the League of Nations, the third Assembly, attention was drawn to the fact that practically speaking the situation remained unchanged, Poland was still in command and the status of Eastern Galicia had not been determined. Thereupon the Canadian delegates again asked the League of Nations to re-affirm the resolution of the previous year. Mark you, Mr. Speaker, they did not undertake to settle the dispute between the Poles and the Ukrainians. They did, however, recognize that the delay was objectionable and the matter should be settled, and thereupon a resolution was moved to renew that expression of opinion. I think my hon. friend read the resolution to which I refer, and therefore I need not read it again. Let me say that the resolution was referred to the committee for consideration, and my hon. friend the Minister of Marine and Fisheries (Mr.

Lapointe) had the honour of being the reporter to report to the League Assembly the conclusion reached. The resolution adopted under the circumstances I have describe is as follows:

> The Assembly of the League of Nations renews its wish, expressed in the resolution adopted by the second Assembly on September 27th, 1921, that the council of the league draw the attention of the Principal Allied and Associated Power to the desirability of determining at an early date the status of Eastern Galicia.

That is exactly what my hon. friend is now asking us to do. The thing which he says we should represent to the League of Nations has already been brought before that body by Canada's delegates, who moved a resolution urging that the status of Eastern Galicia should be determined, and that resolution was adopted unanimously by the League Assembly. So everything that my hon. friend is asking has been done. I think that is a clear and simple statement of the case.

Hon. Sir HENRY DRAYTON (West York): Mr. Speaker, I cannot claim that there are any Ukrainians in my constituency; I do not know whether there are Ukrainians in any of the constituencies represented by this group. But the late government did not have to have the question of the wrongs of the Ukrainians brought to its notice, or the wrongs of any other nations of Europe that required assistance; these things were looked after. As the Hon. Minister of Finance (Mr. Fielding) points out, attention was given to them at the earliest possible moment—in 1921. I want to congratulate the hon. Minister of Finance and his colleague in following the good example that was set by his predecessors; for the present administration did what had been done before—they submitted exactly the same resolutions. I only hope that in some way or other we shall be able to get order out of the turmoil that prevails over there now. I do not know whether the present motion will do anything to assist in that respect; as the Minister of Finance says, what is now asked has already been done. But I am quite sure that the appeals of not only the Ukrainians, but any of the other nations that found themselves in a similar position—yes, the Armenians and many others—received a ready response from the former administration.

Mr. DEPUTY SPEAKER: If any hon. gentleman desires to speak on this subject he should do so now, because when the mover of the resolution speaks his reply will close the debate.

Mr. M.N. CAMPBELL (Mackenzie): Mr. Speaker, I appreciate the information that the Finance Minister (Mr. Fielding) has given us. I may say, however, that I was already aware of a good deal of it; in fact, most of it I have given here in speaking on the resolution. It is possible that the resolution is not quite correctly worded in its reference to the guaranteeing of the integrity of the state of West Ukraine. I understood, however, from the nature of its own constitution that the League of Nations practically guaranteed to stand for the self-determination of peoples, and that was really what I based my resolution on. I quite understand that action has been taken by the league in the matter, but I would remind hon. members about the scriptural proverb respecting the unjust judge and the poor widow. Nothing has resulted from these representations, and I would like to see some expression of opinion from this House on the matter. I appreciate and my constituents appreciate the action that has been taken by both the present and the late government in this connection. I say that I would like to have an expression of opinion from this House, but if the resolution is not in the proper form of course I shall have to withdraw it. But possibly the Finance Minister could say just how it should be worded or whether I should withdraw it or not. I am quite willing to accede to his request in the matter.

Hon. ERNEST LAPOINTE (Minister of Marine and Fisheries): I would ask the hon. member for Mackenzie (Mr. Campbell) to withdraw his resolution, in view of what my hon. friend the Minister of Finance (Mr. Fielding) has said, and especially in view of the suggestion in the resolution that the independence of the so-called state of West Ukraine is guaranteed by the League of Nations. That state has never been recognized in fact. The Ukrainians are asking that it should be so recognized. On the other hand, Poland asks that the Supreme Council of the Allied Powers should define what is the real status of Eastern Galicia. Both parties to the issue are asking for a settlement. Then, the final part of the resolution seems to be based on the assumption that it is for the Council of the League of Nations to settle the question. The council cannot settle it. The Supreme Council of the Allied Powers have reserved to themselves by the Treaty of Saint Germain the right to determine and define the status of Eastern Galicia, either in the formation of an independent state or in its becoming part of Poland. The matter has not yet been determined. The result is that chaotic conditions prevail there, and it is certainly desirable that a decision be arrived at and a settlement effected. That is what the representatives of Canada asked in 1921, as the ex-Minister of Finance (Sir Henry Drayton) has said, and that is what they asked last fall. So that Canada has already declared in favour of an early settlement by the only channel through which it can be done. I think, therefore, that the resolution should be withdrawn.

Mr. CAMPBELL: I beg leave, then, Mr. Speaker, to withdraw the resolution.

Motion withdrawn.

SOURCE: Canada. *Parliamentary Debates* (Commons), 155, 1 (1923): 651–8.

Contributors

Donald H. Avery

Associate professor of history, University of Western Ontario, London. Author of *"Dangerous Foreigners": European Immigrant Workers and Labour Radicalism in Canada, 1896–1932* (Toronto, 1979).

Oleh W. Gerus

Associate professor, St. Paul's and St. Andrew's Colleges, University of Manitoba, Winnipeg.

Nadia O. M. Kazymyra

Archivist, National Map Collection, Public Archives of Canada, Ottawa.

Andrij Makuch

Contract researcher, Ukrainian Cultural Heritage Village, Historic Sites Service, Alberta Culture, Edmonton.

Peter Melnycky

Contract researcher, Ukrainian Cultural Heritage Village, Historic Sites Service, Alberta Culture, Edmonton.

David Saunders

Lecturer in history, University of Newcastle upon Tyne, England.

Frances Swyripa

Research associate, Canadian Institute of Ukrainian Studies, University of Alberta, Edmonton. Author of *Ukrainian Canadians: A Survey of Their Portrayal in English-Language Works* (Edmonton, 1978).

John Herd Thompson

Associate professor of history, McGill University, Montreal. Author of *Harvests of War: The Prairie West 1914–18* (Toronto, 1978) and *Canada 1922–1939: Decades of Discord* (forthcoming, McClelland and Stewart).